Politics, Culture, and Class in the French Revolution

LYNN HUNT

METHUEN & CO. LTD

First published in 1984 by
University of California Press

First published as a University Paperback in 1986 by
Methuen & Co. Ltd
11 New Fetter Lane, London EC4P 4EE

Printed in Great Britain by St Edmundsbury Press,
Bury St Edmunds, Suffolk

British Library Cataloguing in Publication Data
Hunt, Lynn
Politics, culture, and class in the French Revolution.
1. France—History—Revolution, 1789–1815
I. Title
944.04   DC148

ISBN 0-416-42540-2

Chapter 1 is reprinted in expanded form from "The Rhetoric
of Revolution in France," *History Workshop Journal* 15 (1983):
78–94, by permission of the *History Workshop Journal*.

Chapter 3 is reprinted with changes from "Hercules and the
Radical Image in the French Revolution," *Representations* 1
(1983): 95–117, by permission of The Regents of The University of California. © by the Regents of the University of
California.

Tables 1, 2, 3, and the correlation matrix in Appendix A are
reprinted from "The Political Geography of Revolutionary
France," *The Journal of Interdisciplinary History* 14 (1984): 535–
59, by permission of *The Journal of Interdisciplinary History* and
The MIT Press, Cambridge, Massachusetts. The statistical
analysis from which chapter 4 is drawn also appeared in this
article. © 1984 by the Massachusetts Institute of Technology
and the editors of *The Journal of Interdisciplinary History*.

To
J., S., and P.

Contents

Tables

Acknowledgments

WHEN I began the research for this book in 1976, I had a different project in mind. At the time, I intended to write about the local structures of political power in four cities during the French Revolution. As I worked on the four cities, however, I found that my interests began to change in focus, in part because of the impact of my friends and colleagues at Berkeley, and in part because of the influence of new work in French history by François Furet, Mona Ozouf, and Maurice Agulhon. As a consequence, my original social history of Revolutionary politics turned increasingly into a cultural analysis, in which the political structures of the four cities became but one part of the story. Nevertheless, power has remained my central concern in this book, because I believe that power was the central concern of the revolutionaries of France, whether they worked in Paris, in the provincial capitals, or in villages far removed from the political mainstream.

Over the years, I have benefited from the help of many institutions and individuals. My research was funded by fellowships from the University of Michigan Society of Fellows, the American Council of Learned Societies, and, most recently, the Guggenheim Foundation. The research assistance of talented graduate students was funded by the Committee on Research of the University of California, Berkeley, and by the Institute of International Studies at Berkeley. During several trips to France, I enjoyed the hospitality of many libraries and archives. I thank the staffs of the Archives nationales; the Archives départementales of the Gironde, Haute-Garonne, Meurthe, and Somme departments; the Archives municipales of Amiens, Bordeaux, Nancy, and Toulouse; the Bibliothèque nationale of Paris; the Musée Carnavalet of Paris; the Municipal Library of Bordeaux; and the university libraries in Amiens and Toulouse. In London, I worked at the Public Record Office.

Many friends, colleagues, and students have helped me in various ways. The graduate students who have worked with me often provided suggestions that proved fruitful. In France, I was fortunate to have help from two friends: Leslie Martin worked in local archives in 1976 when I was first studying marriage contracts and tax records, and Lizabeth Cohen provided data from Toulouse in 1980. Both maps were drawn by Adrienne Morgan. Colleagues at Berkeley and elsewhere read versions of chapters of the manuscript, and I am grateful to them for their comments. I want to thank in particular Randolph Starn, Reginald Zelnik, Thomas Laqueur, Jack Censer, and Victoria Bonnell for reading through the entire manuscript and offering precise suggestions for its improvement. Joyce McCann graciously read closely every portion of the book and offered ways of making it more readable. More than I perhaps can recognize, my friends have pushed me to think more broadly and more clearly, and this book shows many signs of their impact. Finally, I wish to recognize the less specific but no less real contribution of the University of California at Berkeley. In addition to money and time, the University has provided an invaluable setting of constantly stimulating colleagues and students.

Brief Chronology of the French Revolution 1789–1799

1788	*August 8*	King agrees to convoke the Estates General, which has not met since 1614.
	September 21	The Parlement of Paris recommends that the Estates General follow the same procedures as in 1614.
1789	*May 5*	The Estates General opens at Versailles.
	June 17	The Third Estate decides to call itself the National Assembly.
	July 11	The king dismisses his popular minister, Necker.
	July 14	Fall of the Bastille.
	October 5–6	The "October Days," during which a large crowd marches from Paris to Versailles to bring the royal family back to the capital.
1790	*July 12*	Civil Constitution of the Clergy.
	July 14	Festival of Federation celebrating Bastille Day.
	November 27	Decree requiring oath of loyalty from clergy.
1791	*June 20*	King attempts to flee in disguise and is captured at Varennes.
	October 1	Newly elected Legislative Assembly opens.
1792	*April 20*	Declaration of war on Austria.
	June 20	Invasion of the Tuileries palace by mob.
	August 10	Insurrection in Paris and attack on Tuileries leads to suspension of the king.
	September 2	Verdun lost to Prussian army.
	September 2–6	Murder of prisoners in "September Massacres."

	September 21	Newly elected National Convention meets for first time and abolishes the monarchy.
1793	January 14–17	Voting in trial of the king.
	January 21	Execution of Louis XVI.
	February 1	Declaration of war on United Kingdom and the Dutch Republic.
	March 10	Revolutionary Tribunal established.
	March 11	Beginning of uprising in the Vendée.
	May 4	First "Maximum" on grain prices.
	May 31–June 2	Insurrection leading to arrest of the "Girondins" in the Convention.
	July 27	Robespierre elected to the Committee of Public Safety.
	September 5	Demonstration in the Convention leads to adoption of "terror" as the order of the day.
	October 5	Adoption of revolutionary calendar.
	October 16	Execution of Marie Antoinette.
1794	February 4	Slavery abolished in French colonies.
	March 13–24	Arrest, trial, and executions of "Hébertists."
	March 30–April 5	Arrest, trial, and executions of "Dantonists."
	June 8	Festival of the Supreme Being.
	July 27	"The Ninth of Thermidor"—arrest of Robespierre, Saint-Just, and their supporters (executed July 28–29).
	November 12	Closing of Paris Jacobin Club.
	December 24	Abolition of the "Maximum."
1795	April 1–2	Popular uprising in Paris.
	May 20–23	Second popular uprising, which also fails.
	May–June	"White Terror" in south against former terrorists.
	August 22	Convention approves the Constitution of the Year III.
	October 5	Right-wing insurrection in Paris against new constitution defeated.
	October 26	Directory government begins, after elections of Year IV (October 1795).
1796	April–October 1797	Succession of Italian victories by Bonaparte.
1797	March–April	Elections of Year V register royalist gains.
	May 27	Execution of Babeuf.

	September 4	"Coup of 18 Fructidor, Year V," in which legislature is purged of supposed royalists.
1798	*March–April*	Elections of Year VI mark Jacobin resurgence.
	May 11	"Coup of 22 Floréal, Year VI" against the Jacobins in the councils.
	May–October 1799	Bonaparte in Egypt and Middle East.
1799	*November 9–10*	Bonaparte's coup of 18–19 Brumaire.

Abbreviations

Archives and Libraries

A.N. Archives nationales
A.D. Archives départementales
A.M. Archives municipales
B.N. Bibliothèque nationale
B.M. Bibliothèque municipale
PRO Public Record Office (London)

Journals

AESC *Annales: Economies. Sociétés. Civilisations.*
AHRF *Annales historiques de la Révolution française*
RHMC *Revue d'histoire moderne et contemporaine*

Introduction:
Interpreting
the French Revolution

J'avais vu que tout tenoit radicalement à la politique, et que, de quel-
que façon qu'on s'y prit, aucun peuple ne seroit jamais que ce que la
nature de son Gouvernement le feroit être; ainsi cette grande question du meilleur Gouvernement possible me paroissoit se reduire à
celle-ci. Quelle est la nature de Gouvernement propre à former un
Peuple le plus vertueux, le plus éclairé, le plus sage, le meilleur enfin
à prendre ce mot dans son plus grand sens.

JEAN-JACQUES ROUSSEAU, *Les Confessions*[1]

I saw that everything depended fundamentally on politics, and that,
no matter how one looked at it, no people could ever be anything
but what the nature of its government made it; thus this great question of the best possible government seemed to me to reduce itself to
this. What is the nature of government suitable for forming a people
that is the most virtuous, the most enlightened, the wisest, in short
the best, taking this word in its broadest sense.

WHEN Rousseau proclaimed that "everything depended fundamentally on politics," he was making a provocative and
ambiguous statement. In his view, politics, rather than custom,
morals, or religion, was the root of social life. The character of a
people depended on the nature of its government. By posing "the
great question of the best possible government," Rousseau indicated that government might well be different from what it was; it
might be better. But where was this government to come from?
How could any mortal determine what made a people "the most
virtuous, the most enlightened, the wisest, the best"? How could a
government be more enlightened than the people it was meant to
mold? French revolutionaries had to confront just these issues.

---

[1] *Oeuvres complètes* 1 (Dijon, 1959): 404–5. Unless otherwise noted, all translations are mine.

They took Rousseau as their spiritual guide, but Rousseau was vaguest precisely where they faced the most momentous decisions. Given the unique opportunity to renegotiate the social contract, what form should it take? What was the general will in France in the 1790s? What was the best government possible, taking government, as Rousseau did, "in its broadest sense"?

The Revolution showed how much everything depended on politics, but it did so in ways that would have surprised Rousseau had he lived fifteen years longer. Revolutionaries did not just debate the classical questions of government, such as the virtues of monarchy versus republic or aristocracy versus democracy. They also acted on them in new and surprising ways. In the heat of debate and political conflict, the very notion of "the political" expanded and changed shape. The structure of the polity changed under the impact of increasing political participation and popular mobilization; political language, political ritual, and political organization all took on new forms and meanings. In ways that Rousseau prophesied but could himself only dimly imagine, government became an instrument for fashioning a people. As the deputy Grégoire proclaimed in January 1794: "The French people have gone beyond all other peoples; however, the detestable regime whose remnants we are shaking off keeps us still a great distance from nature; there is still an enormous gap between what we are and what we could be. Let us hurry to fill this gap; let us reconstitute human nature by giving it a new stamp."[2]

Out of the remarkable experience shaped by this goal of reconstitution and regeneration came most of our ideas and practices of politics. By the end of the decade of revolution, French people (and Westerners more generally) had learned a new political repertoire: ideology appeared as a concept, and competing ideologies challenged the traditional European cosmology of order and harmony; propaganda became associated with political purposes; the Jacobin clubs demonstrated the potential of mass political parties; and Napoleon established the first secular police state with his claim to stand above parties.

Neither politics nor the concept of the political was invented by the French, but, for reasons that are still not well understood, the

---

[2] *Rapport sur l'ouverture d'un concours pour les livres élémentaires de la première éducation, par Grégoire* (Séance du 3 pluviôse an II).

French managed to invest them with extraordinary emotional and symbolic significance. Step by step, sometimes with only a vague awareness of what was taking place, the French founded a revolutionary tradition that has endured down to our time. Paradoxically, while multiplying the forms and meanings of politics, the most revolutionary of the French acted out of a profound distrust of anything explicitly political. Leading political figures never called themselves politicians; they served "the public good" (*la chose publique*), not a narrow "partisan spirit" (*esprit de parti*). Politics and politicking were consistently identified with narrowness, meanness, divisiveness, factionalism, opportunism, egotism, and selfishness. While denouncing all these perversions of the ancient ideal of *homo politicus*, the revolutionaries crossed into the modern age: they opened up a new, internal political frontier and reaped the unforeseen fruits of democracy and authoritarianism, socialism and terror, revolutionary dictatorship and the guillotine. The unexpected invention of revolutionary politics is the subject of this book.

We have little sense now of how surprising revolutionary politics were in the 1790s. Almost every history textbook cites 1789 as the watershed of the modern era, and the French Revolution is one of the most written about events in Western history. Yet, as it has become commonplace, it has lost its freshness and novelty. In retrospect the turning point seems so obvious; what would our world be like without parties, ideologies, dictators, mass movements, and even antipolitical, political rhetoric? Recent scholarly debates about the Revolution also seem to take the event for granted. At issue in the controversies is not the character of the experience itself, but rather its long-term origins and outcomes. The Revolution merely serves as the vehicle of transportation between long-term causes and effects; as a result, the emergence of a revolutionary politics has become a foregone conclusion. The three major interpretive positions all share this preoccupation with origins and outcomes.

The Marxist interpretation of the Revolution has come under heavy fire in recent years, in part because it is the most theoretically developed account.[3] Marx himself was passionately interested

---

[3]Useful reviews of the literature can be found in William Doyle, *Origins of the French Revolution* (Oxford, 1980) and Geoffrey Ellis, "Review Article: The 'Marxist Interpretation' of the French Revolution," *English Historical Review* 93 (1978): 353–76.

in the history of the French Revolution. In the mid-1840s, he gathered documentation and read widely in preparation for writing a history of the National Convention.[4] Immediate political interests and then his more general study of capitalism kept him from pursuing this project to completion. Nevertheless, in all of Marx's historical writings, the Revolution served as a touchstone; it fostered the development of capitalism by breaking the feudal stranglehold on production, and it brought the bourgeoisie as a class to power. These two, inseparable elements—the establishment of a suitable legal framework for capitalist development and the class struggle won by the bourgeoisie—have characterized Marxist historical accounts of the Revolution ever since. As the most recent defender of "the classic historiography of the French Revolution," Albert Soboul maintained that the Revolution marked "the appearance, the growth, and the final triumph of the bourgeoisie."[5]

In the Marxist account, the Revolution was bourgeois in nature because its origins and outcomes were bourgeois. Marxist historians trace the origins of the Revolution to the aggressive self-assertion of the bourgeoisie in the face of aristocratic reaction in the 1780s, and they consider the outcome to be the distinctly bourgeois triumph of the capitalist mode of production.[6] The intervening variable—the revolutionary experience—is read in terms of its contribution to this scenario. The bourgeoisie had to ally with the popular classes in order to break the back of the feudal aristocracy; it had to break with the popular classes when the system of the Terror threatened to get out of hand; and it had to ally with Napoleon in order to ensure the consolidation of bourgeois gains in property and legal reform. The outcome (bourgeois economic and social hegemony) followed from the origins (class conflict between bourgeoisie and aristocracy) in seemingly inexorable fashion.

The "revisionist" position challenges the Marxist account on virtually every front, but for the most part revisionists implicitly ac-

[4]Jean Bruhat, "La Révolution française et la formation de la pensée de Marx," *AHRF* 38 (1966): 125–70.

[5]"L'Historiographie classique de la Révolution française: Sur des controverses récentes," *Historical Reflections: Réflexions historiques* 1 (1974): 141–68, quote from p. 142. Reprinted in *Comprendre la Révolution: Problèmes politiques de la Révolution française (1789–1797)* (Paris, 1981).

[6]See, e.g., Albert Soboul, *The French Revolution, 1787–1799: From the Storming of the Bastille to Napoleon*, trans. by Alan Forrest and Colin Jones (New York, 1974).

cept the central premise of the Marxist argument, that is, that an interpretation of the Revolution consists of an account of social origins and outcomes. In the first, wide-ranging attack on Marxist orthodoxy, Alfred Cobban insisted that the Revolution was not made by the bourgeoisie in the interests of capitalist development but rather by venal officeholders and professionals whose fortunes were declining. In the end, their actions benefited landowners in general; the experience of revolution actually retarded the development of capitalism in France.[7] The Marxist account, or what Cobban called "the social interpretation," was mistaken both about the origins and the outcomes of the decade of revolution.

In the same vein, other critics have argued that there was no conscious class conflict between bourgeoisie and aristocracy before the Revolution. Aristocrats did not stand in the way of the bourgeoisie; indeed, they shared many economic, social, and political interests.[8] It was the liberal aristocracy, not a frustrated bourgeoisie, that initiated the revolution against monarchical despotism.[9] When they come to offering an alternative version, the revisionists, following Cobban, still base their analysis on social origins and outcomes. The revisionist position has been most cogently summarized in articles by François Furet and Colin Lucas.[10] Both argue that the origins of the Revolution are to be found in a crisis of social mobility and status anxiety within an amalgamated elite made up of nobles and bourgeois. The growth of population and prosperity in the eighteenth century had not been matched by a widening of the channels of social promotion; as a consequence,

[7] *The Social Interpretation of the French Revolution* (Cambridge, 1964).

[8] For the most recent overview of an enormous literature, see Doyle, *Origins*. The most important specific studies are George V. Taylor, "Non-Capitalist Wealth and the Origins of the French Revolution," *American Historical Review* 72 (1967): 469–96; David D. Bien, "La Réaction aristocratique avant 1789: L'Exemple de l'armée," *AESC* 29 (1974): 23–48 and 505–34; and Guy Chaussinand-Nogaret, *La Noblesse au XVIIIe siècle: De la féodalité aux lumières* (Paris, 1976).

[9] Denis Richet, "Autour des origines idéologiques lointaines de la Révolution française: Elites et despotisme," *AESC* 24 (1969): 1–23; and, more specifically on 1788–89, Elizabeth L. Eisenstein, "Who Intervened in 1788? A Commentary on *The Coming of the French Revolution,*" *American Historical Review* 71 (1965): 77–103.

[10] Furet, "Le Catéchisme de la Révolution française," *AESC* 26 (1971): 255–89, reprinted in his *Penser la Révolution française* (Paris, 1978), English version, *Interpreting the French Revolution,* trans. by Elborg Forster (Cambridge, 1981); and Lucas, "Nobles, Bourgeois and the Origins of the French Revolution," *Past and Present,* no. 60 (1973): 84–126.

friction increased in the various social "stress zones" within the elite. This tension erupted into revolution when the Parlement of Paris obstinately insisted that the newly convoked Estates General follow the procedures established in 1614. This fateful decision precipitated an understandable but unnecessary break between the noble and commoner sections of the elite.[11]

Implicit in this argument about origins is the view that the main outcome of the Revolution was not capitalism but the creation of a more unified elite of notables, whose primary self-definition rested on landowning.[12] Once nobles and commoners alike had learned the price of their misunderstandings and misperceptions, they were able to reunite on the basis of their essential common interests in a status society open to wealth and service. In the revisionist account, the Revolution loses its predetermined quality, because it appears as something of a mistake. However, its meaning is still read in terms of its contribution to long-term social and political outcomes; the revolutionary experience simply serves as a corrective to previous social and political misconceptions and as a learning process of trial and (mostly) error; for example, the bourgeoisie learned that reliance on popular support would jeopardize its cherished legal reforms and even its ability to maintain law and order.[13] In this view, the Revolution was a dramatic, but ephemeral, deviation from the trend toward liberal, elite rule.

On the margins of the debate over the social interpretation stands Alexis de Tocqueville and the modernization account. Tocqueville did not deny the importance of social tensions, but he placed social conflict in an essentially political framework; for him, the Revolution represented the aggrandizement of state power and centralization rather than the triumph of capitalism. No one class won this contest. Frenchmen simply became more equal in their unwitting slavishness to an authoritarian government. Tocqueville traced the origins of the Revolution (and of eighteenth-century social ten-

[11] Lucas, "Nobles, Bourgeois," 120–21.

[12] The successful amalgamation may not have been achieved until ca. 1848. See, e.g., Guy Chaussinand-Nogaret, Louis Bergeron, and Robert Forster, "Les Notables du 'Grand Empire' en 1810," *AESC* 26 (1971): 1052–75.

[13] I am exaggerating the coherence and unity of the revisionist argument here for the sake of schematic presentation. The most comprehensive statement of this view can be found in François Furet and Denis Richet, *La Révolution française*, 2 vols. (Paris, 1965), English version (London, 1970). Other revisionists may well disagree with some particulars of this account.

sions) to the practices of the absolute monarchy. In order to increase state power, the monarchy destroyed the political rights of nobles and thereby made aristocratic social pretensions intolerable to other social groups.[14] Although revolutionaries thought they were contesting monarchical government, they ended up creating an even more powerful state modeled on that same absolute monarchy. Thus, for Tocqueville too, the Revolution was but a link in the chain between origins and outcomes; the revolutionary experience facilitated willy-nilly the transition from Louis XIV to Napoleon.

In a recent comparative study, Theda Skocpol revives the Tocquevillian theme of growing state power.[15] Although she agrees with Tocqueville that the most important outcome of the Revolution was a more centralized and bureaucratic state, she analyzes the origins of the Revolution somewhat differently. Like the Russian and Chinese states later, the French state crumbled because it could not meet the military exigencies of modern international competition. The structural weaknesses of the "agrarian monarchical regimes" also made them susceptible to peasant revolts, which in the context of revolution destroyed former agrarian class relations. War (international competition again) then fostered the emergence of centralizing and bureaucratizing revolutionary elites, who created a "modern state edifice." Despite her emphasis on social structural preconditions and the role of peasant uprisings, Skocpol resembles Tocqueville in the way she sandwiches the revolutionary experience between its long-term origins and outcomes; the actual event of revolution appears only in the interstices of the schema. Here, as in Tocqueville's classic analysis, the Revolution appears as the vehicle of state modernization.[16]

Because current interpretive debates focus on the analysis of ori-

---

[14] Tocqueville, *The Old Regime and the French Revolution*, trans. by Stuart Gilbert (New York, 1955). A useful essay on Tocqueville can be found in Furet, *Penser la Révolution française*, though in his introduction, Furet overemphasizes the differences between Tocqueville and "narrative" historians.

[15] *States and Social Revolutions: A Comparative Analysis of France, Russia, and China* (Cambridge, 1979).

[16] I have not considered Barrington Moore, Jr. in this context, though his account shares many similarities with Skocpol's. The important point is that his interpretation also emphasizes origins and outcomes, especially the outcome of modernization (*Social Origins of Dictatorship and Democracy: Lord and Peasant in the Making of the Modern World* [Boston, 1966], esp. pp. 106–7).

gins and outcomes, it is not surprising that research efforts have
been increasingly devoted to the periods preceding and following
the revolutionary decade.[17] Most research has been undertaken to
test the Marxist account. Army officers, magistrates, and elite cultural institutions of the Old Regime have all been examined in
order to determine the reality of prerevolutionary class cleavages.[18]
Napoleonic and post-Napoleonic elites have also been studied, because their social character is relevant to the analysis of outcomes
of the Revolution.[19] Even though such studies have contributed to
the elaboration of a revisionist position, they have not forced Marxist historians to abandon their ground. Marxists simply argue in reply that the reality of class and capitalism has to be sought in another place or in another manner.[20]

   Although Marxist and revisionist historians have studied revolutionaries and their activities, these studies have had little impact
on their overall origins-outcomes schema. Revisionists maintain either that revolutionary conflicts had no particular social significance or had only very broad and ambiguous social meaning (rich
vs. poor, town vs. country, Paris vs. the provinces).[21] As the par-

[17] Research on the revolutionary decade itself has continued, but it cannot be denied that the theoretical and empirical center of interest has shifted away from the
decade of revolution to the periods preceding and following it. Moreover, most research on the revolutionary decade has failed to make much of an impact on the
contours of historiographical debate about the Revolution. The most important
recent areas of research on the revolutionary decade have been histories of the
press, analyses of various forms of cultural revolution (education, festivals, de-
Christianization), and local studies.
[18] The most significant results are contained in Bien, "La Réaction aristocratique."
On the cultural side, see Daniel Roche, *Le Siècle des lumières en province: Académies et
académiciens provinciaux, 1680–1789*, 2 vols. (Paris, 1978); and Jean Quéniart, *Culture
et société urbaines dans la France de l'Ouest au XVIIIe siècle* (Paris, 1978). Somewhat to
the side of investigations of social milieus stand recent studies of the intellectual
origins of the Revolution. For an overview, see Keith Michael Baker, "On the Problem of the Ideological Origins of the French Revolution," in Dominick LaCapra and
Steven L. Kaplan, eds., *Modern European Intellectual History: Reappraisals and New Perspectives* (Ithaca, N.Y., 1982), pp. 197–219.
[19] Chaussinand-Nogaret, Bergeron, and Forster, "Les Notables du 'Grand Empire'"; Louis Bergeron and Guy Chaussinand-Nogaret, *Les "Masses de granit": Cent
mille notables du Premier Empire* (Paris, 1979); and Thomas D. Beck, *French Legislators,
1800–1834: A Study in Quantitative History* (Berkeley, 1974).
[20] Claude Mazauric, "Quelques voies nouvelles pour l'histoire politique de la
Révolution française," *AHRF* 47 (1975): 134–73.
[21] Cobban led the way in emphasizing the importance of these other kinds of social division in *The Social Interpretation*.

ticulars of the Marxist account have come under increasing attack, Marxist historians have withdrawn to more structural positions: what difference does it make who initiated the Revolution or who held power at any particular time as long as its origins and outcomes can be traced far enough back or far enough forward to substantiate the import of class struggle and the development of capitalism?[22]

The Tocquevillian interpretation, by contrast, has provoked almost no empirical research. Although it resembles the Marxist and revisionist accounts in its emphasis on origins and outcomes, these are conceived in such long and broad terms that it has proved difficult to test empirically. Tocqueville himself, for example, did not tie the development of state power to any particular social group; "democracy" and "equality" were pervasive structural trends, and, though they may have acted as "gigantic brooms," no one seemed to have a handle on their action. As a consequence, the identity and intentions of revolutionary actors have little relevance in the Tocquevillian account: "they had no inkling of this," "nothing was further from their intentions"; the "destined course" of the Revolution had nothing to do with what the revolutionaries thought they were accomplishing.[23]

All three interpretive positions share this programmatic disregard for revolutionary intentions. Tocqueville and those inspired by his analysis deny the significance of who the revolutionaries were or what they thought on the grounds that the revolutionaries were unconsciously caught up in dreams of absolute power, which ultimately shaped the course of the Revolution. Marxists and revisionists alike appear to grant the importance of social identity, yet despite their different analyses, they end up espousing the same Tocquevillian distrust of revolutionary intentions and aims. Because the identity of the revolutionaries fits into neither the Marxist nor the revisionist account (the revolutionaries were neither capitalists nor—after 1791—liberal nobles and elite commoners), both end up denying the importance of who the revolutionaries were or what they thought they were doing. In the Marxist interpretation the revolutionaries facilitated the triumph of capitalism,

---

[22]Mazauric, "Quelques voies nouvelles."
[23]*The Old Regime and the French Revolution*, quotes from pp. vii, 3.

even while expressing hostility to capital, and in the revisionist interpretation revolutionaries mistakenly dragged the process off its course of liberal, notable rule. What the revolutionaries intended is not what came out of the Revolution, hence what the revolutionaries intended matters little. Thus, the focus on origins and outcomes has made the revolutionary experience itself seem irrelevant.

As a consequence, revolutionary innovations in the forms and meanings of politics often seem either predetermined or entirely accidental. In the Marxist account, liberal constitutionalism, democracy, terror, and authoritarian rule all appear as the handmaidens of the consolidation of bourgeois hegemony. In the Tocquevillian analysis, they all serve the progress of centralized power. Revisionist accounts are less consistent in this regard, because revisionists do not refer to a common original text, such as the works of Marx or Tocqueville. In the writings of Richard Cobb, for instance, revolutionary politics express the resentments and frustrations of a militant minority; there is no compelling historical logic behind their actions. People became "terrorists," for example, because they held grudges against their neighbors.[24] Whereas in the Marxist and Tocquevillian interpretations, the politics of revolution are determined by the necessary course from origins to outcomes, in revisionist versions, politics seem haphazard because they do not fit into the origins-outcomes schema. The end result, however, is the same; politics lose significance as an object of study.

This book aims to rehabilitate the politics of revolution. Yet it is not at all a political history. Rather than recounting the narrative of revolutionary events, I have tried to uncover the rules of political behavior. Historians cannot simply add up all the professed intentions of individual actors in the Revolution to get a sense of what they thought about what they were doing. If there was any unity or coherence in the revolutionary experience, it came from common values and shared expectations of behavior. These values and expectations are the primary focus of my account. The values, expectations, and implicit rules that expressed and shaped collective intentions and actions are what I call the political culture of the

[24] R. C. Cobb, *The Police and the People: French Popular Protest, 1789–1820* (Oxford, 1970). For example, "The *sans-culotte* then is not a social or economic being; he is a political accident" (p. 120).

Revolution; that political culture provided the logic of revolutionary political action.

Most scholars who now emphasize "politics" in the French Revolution do so from an anti-Marxist point of view. In an influential article on "Non-Capitalist Wealth and the Origins of the French Revolution," George V. Taylor concluded that "it was essentially a political revolution with social consequences and not a social revolution with political consequences."[25] François Furet took the distinction between the social and the political and blew it up into an explanation for the Terror, which in his view was predicated on "the liberty of the social in relation to the political."[26] The Terror was the logical consequence of the revolutionary distortion of the normal relationship between society and politics; politics was no longer the arena for the representation of competing social interests, but rather a terrorizing instrument for the reshaping of society. Both of these critics have questioned Marxist assumptions about the relationship between politics and society. They argue that revolutionary politics did not follow from social structural preconditions; instead, politics shaped society, at least at certain moments.

Furet's recent book, *Penser la Révolution française*, has the great merit of drawing attention to the importance of "the political." In his efforts to undermine the Marxist "catechism," he has insisted on the necessity of viewing the political in broad terms, not just as policies, decisions, and organizations, but as the fount of new kinds of actions in the world. However, his own discussion of revolutionary politics is entirely abstract. He argues that the political innovations of the decade were revolutionary because they were used to reshape society, but he devotes little attention to showing either how this happened or who participated in such endeavors. As a result, though he succeeds admirably in contesting a mechanistic deduction of politics from social structure, he makes revolutionary politics seem detached from any context. The new political culture is driven only by its own internal logic of democracy.[27]

Much of the difficulty in analyzing the relationship between politics and society comes from our now commonplace language of social analysis. When discussing "the political," metaphors of struc-

---

[25] P. 491.
[26] *Penser la Révolution française*, p. 41.
[27] See my review in *History and Theory* 20 (1981): 313–23.

ture and especially the metaphors of a hierarchy of relationships in space come most readily to mind: levels, tiers, bases, foundations. Politics seem naturally to rest on a social base or substructure, whether one subscribes to a specifically Marxist theory or not. Social networks, groups, classes, or structures are thought to give politics their enduring patterns as well as their potential for change. As a consequence, most debate, whether in general or over the French Revolution in particular, has concerned the relationship between a previously existing social base and the specific political arrangement that is taken as following from it. The character of politics is explained by reference to society, and changes in the political arrangement are traced to prior changes in social relations. Almost all discussion proceeds from the assumption that the essential characteristics of politics can only be explained by their relation to a social ground. Even those who try to escape from this mode of thinking often end up confirming it in spite of themselves. Thus, Furet characterizes revolutionary government as in some sense pathological precisely because its politics do not represent social interests in the normal or expected fashion. When politics come first, the situation is by definition abnormal.

In the analysis presented here, I have endeavored to avoid the metaphor of levels. Revolutionary political culture cannot be deduced from social structures, social conflicts, or the social identity of revolutionaries. Political practices were not simply the expression of "underlying" economic and social interests. Through their language, images, and daily political activities, revolutionaries worked to reconstitute society and social relations. They consciously sought to break with the French past and to establish the basis for a new national community. In the process, they created new social and political relations and new kinds of social and political divisions. Their experience of political and social struggle forced them to see the world in new ways.

One of the most fateful consequences of the revolutionary attempt to break with the past was the invention of ideology. Hesitantly, even reluctantly, revolutionaries and their opponents came to see that the relationship between politics and society was deeply problematic. Tradition lost its givenness, and French people found themselves acting on Rousseau's conviction that the relationship between the social and the political (the social contract) could be rearranged. As disagreement over the nature of the rearrangement became apparent, different ideologies were invented in order to explain this development. Socialism, conservatism, authoritarianism, and democratic republicanism were all practical answers to the theoretical question raised by Rousseau. Rather than expressing an ideology, therefore, revolutionary politics brought ideology into being. In the process of revolution, the French recast the categories of social thought and political action.

This is not to say, however, that the Revolution was only intellectual or that politics had primacy over society rather than vice versa. The revolution in politics was an explosive interaction between ideas and reality, between intention and circumstance, between collective practices and social context. If revolutionary politics cannot be deduced from the social identity of revolutionaries, then neither can it be divorced from it: the Revolution was made by people, and some people were more attracted than others to the politics of revolution. A better metaphor for the relationship between society and politics is the knot or the Möbius strip, because the two sides were inextricably intertwined, with no permanent "above" and "below." The politics of revolution appealed to certain individuals and groups, who in turn shaped the uses of revolutionary politics. The new political class (using class in a broad sense) was formed by its relationship to revolutionary politics as much as it formed them.

In order to reconstruct the logic of revolutionary action and innovation, it is thus essential to examine both the politics of revolution and the people who practiced them. My contention is that there was a fit or affinity between them, not that one can be deduced from the other. The political culture of revolution was made up of symbolic practices, such as language, imagery, and gestures. These symbolic practices were embraced more enthusiastically in some places and by some groups than in other places and groups. In many ways, the symbolic practices—the use of a certain rhetoric, the spread of certain symbols and rituals—called the new political class into existence; talk of national regeneration and festivals of federation, for instance, gave the new political elite a sense of unity and purpose. On the other hand, the differences in reception of the new practices also had their impact on the way revolutionary politics worked, and especially on its successes and failures. The rhetoric of universalism did not appeal to everyone, but it appealed to enough people to make its influence deep and lasting.

For analytical purposes, the politics and the people who practiced them have been separated. The three chapters in part I investigate the logic of political action as it was expressed symbolically: in the ways people talked, and in the ways they put the Revolution and themselves as revolutionaries into images and gestures. The chapters in part II establish the social context of the revolutionary experience and in particular the disparities in that experience. What were the geographical and social lines of division in revolutionary France; where was revolutionary political culture best received? In both parts the emphasis is on the creation of a new political culture, that is, on the ways in which "the Revolution" took shape as a coherent experience. There is no shortage of scholarly work showing that the Revolution meant different things to different people.[28] I have tried to show instead how it came to have some unity, even in its diversity. Unity and coherence came from several sources, which are discussed here under two general rubrics: the symbolic and the social. The symbolic sources of unity included the constant repetition of key words and principles, shared attitudes toward politics as an activity, and use of the same symbols, such as the liberty tree or female representations of the Republic. The social sources of coherence included the appearance of the same kinds of leaders in different places and the same kinds of places in the forefront of revolutionary action.

Although the subject of this book is politics, there is little in it about specific policies, politicians, partisan conflicts, formal institutions, or organizations. Emphasized instead are the underlying patterns in political culture that made possible the emergence of distinctive policies and the appearance of new kinds of politicians, conflicts, and organizations. Rather than focusing on the grain price maximum, Robespierre, or the Jacobin clubs, for instance, attention is drawn to the general principles of revolutionary language, to the operation of revolutionary symbols, and to the

---

[28] The emphasis on particularism is especially prominent in the works of those who are inspired by Richard Cobb and Alfred Cobban, e.g., Martyn Lyons, *Revolution in Toulouse: An Essay on Provincial Terrorism* (Berne, 1978) and Gwynne Lewis, *The Second Vendée: The Continuity of Counterrevolution in the Department of the Gard, 1789–1815* (Oxford, 1978).

pervasive concern with ritual and gesture. The investment of symbolic actions with political significance gave specific policies, individuals, and organizations greater impact than they would have had in nonrevolutionary times.

This method of proceeding relies on the work of three French historians who have pioneered in the study of revolutionary political culture (though they do not necessarily use the term themselves). The first is François Furet, who has done more than anyone else to revive the historiographical debates and point them in new directions. In a more specific vein Maurice Agulhon showed how images of the Republic on seals and statues actively shaped French political perceptions.[29] Similarly, Mona Ozouf demonstrated how revolutionary festivals were used to forge a new national consensus.[30] The studies of Agulhon and Ozouf show that cultural manifestations were part and parcel of revolutionary politics, and Ozouf in particular shows that there was a logic to revolutionary rituals. Historians can no longer assume that politics exists in a clearly separate realm from culture.

The chief accomplishment of the French Revolution was the institution of a dramatically new political culture. The Revolution did not startle its contemporaries because it laid the foundations for capitalist development or political modernization. The English found more effective ways to encourage the former, and the Prussians showed that countries could pursue the latter without democracy or revolution. Revolution in France contributed little to economic growth or to political stabilization. What it did establish, however, was the mobilizing potential of democratic republicanism and the compelling intensity of revolutionary change. The language of national regeneration, the gestures of equality and fraternity, and the rituals of republicanism were not soon forgotten. Democracy, terror, Jacobinism, and the police state all became recurrent features of political life.

The origins of the new political culture in the years or decades before 1789 were not very evident, and its outcome was not at first sight impressive: Napoleon and the Bourbons after him labored mightily to remove any remnants of that culture, and in many

---

[29] *Marianne au combat: L'Imagerie et la symbolique républicaines de 1789 à 1880* (Paris, 1979), English version (Cambridge, 1981).
[30] *La Fête révolutionnaire, 1789–1799* (Paris, 1976).

respects they appeared to succeed. Yet the new tradition of revolution, with its values and expectations, did not disappear. Even outside of France, it continued to have a vigorous life in the underground, and its specter was kept alive in the fears and writings of the defenders of that new ideology—conservatism. Even in the new police powers developed to contain it, the memory of revolution continued. Once revolutionaries acted on Rousseau's belief that government could form a new people, the West was never again the same.

THE POETICS
OF POWER

≪≋ 1 ≋≫

The Rhetoric
of Revolution

"Les mots, commes les choses, ont été des monstruosités."

AFTER the fall of Robespierre, the noted literary critic and author Jean-François La Harpe published a long reflection entitled *Du Fanatisme dans la langue révolutionnaire.*[1] La Harpe's arguments were not in themselves surprising: he traced the perversities of the Revolution back to the Civil Constitution of the Clergy, and he attributed the frenzy of "this abominable revolutionary spirit" to *philosophie* run riot. Most instructive, however, is La Harpe's conviction that the key to the Revolution's aberrations was its language. La Harpe, in fact, offered little analysis of this language itself; he was more interested in denouncing its consequences than in examining its causes or functioning. Yet his vitriolic pamphlet is nonetheless significant, because it shows that the revolutionaries themselves recognized the importance of language in the Revolution.

The crumbling of the French state after 1786 let loose a deluge of words, in print, in conversations, and in political meetings. There had been a few dozen periodicals—hardly any of which carried what we call news—circulating in Paris during the 1780s; more than 500 appeared between 14 July 1789 and 10 August 1792.[2] Something similar happened to the theater: in contrast to the handful of

Note: see forematter for a brief chronology of important revolutionary dates.

[1] *Du Fanatisme dans la langue révolutionnaire ou de la persécution suscitée par les Barbares du dix-huitième Siècle, contre la Religion Chrétienne et ses Ministres,* 3rd ed. (Paris, 1797), p. 14.

[2] Claude Bellanger et al., *Histoire générale de la presse française. 1: Des origines à 1814* (Paris, 1969), p. 434.

new plays produced annually before the Revolution, at least 1,500 new plays, many of them topical, were produced between 1789 and 1799, and more than 750 were staged just in the years 1792–94.[3] Political clubs proliferated at every level, and electoral assemblies seemed to meet almost continuously during the Revolution's first heady years. Added to these occasions were the countless festivals organized all over the country for the purposes of commemoration and celebration.[4] Everywhere, in short, talk was the order of the day.

Words came in torrents, but even more important was their unique, magical quality. From the beginning of the Revolution, words were invested with great passion. By the fall of 1789, *Etes-vous de la Nation?* had become the watchword of National Guard patrols.[5] As the king's sacred position in society eroded, political language became increasingly invested with emotional, even life-and-death, significance. Words associated with the Old Regime, names tainted with royalism, aristocracy, or privilege, became taboo. *Procureurs* and *avocats* (Old Regime legal types) became *hommes de loi* (simple "men of the law") if they wanted to continue legal practice; *impôts* were replaced with *contributions*, which sounded more voluntary. Wherever names were identified with Old Regime values, they were supplanted by new revolutionary (often Greek or Roman) appellations. Babies were named after classical heroes; the historic provinces were replaced with geographically identified departments; and rebellious towns were rechristened when they were retaken. At the height of the concern with names, in 1793, a deputation from one of the Paris sections suggested to the National Convention that it systematically rename streets and public squares

---

[3]For a suggestive analysis of the theater during the Terror, see Beatrice F. Hyslop, "The Theater during a Crisis: The Parisian Theater during the Reign of the Terror," *Journal of Modern History* 17 (1945): 332–55. Emmet Kennedy is working on a revision of many of Hyslop's views on this question. Another measure of the increase in volume of words, and especially political words, is the steady rise in the number of new political songs that appeared between 1789 and 1794: 116 in 1789, 261 in 1790, 308 in 1791, 325 in 1792, 590 in 1793, and 701 in 1794. Afterward, the number declined quickly from 137 in 1795 to only 25 in 1800 (Robert Brécy, "La Chanson révolutionnaire de 1789 à 1799," *AHRF* 53 [1981]: 279–303).

[4]Mona Ozouf, *La Fête révolutionnaire, 1789–1799* (Paris, 1976).

[5]The essential starting place is Ferdinand Brunot, *Histoire de la langue française des origines à 1900* 9 (La Révolution et l'Empire, in two parts) (Paris, 1937).

after "all the virtues necessary to the Republic." This would give the people "a silent course in ethics."[6]

Certain key words served as revolutionary incantations. Nation was perhaps the most universally sacred, but there were also *patrie*, constitution, law, and, more specific to the radicals, regeneration, virtue, and vigilance. Uttered in a certain context or included in soon-familiar formulaic expressions, such words bespoke nothing less than adherence to the revolutionary community. Revolutionaries placed such emphasis on the ritual use of words because they were seeking a replacement for the charisma of kingship. Primary among ritual words was the revolutionary oath, or what La Harpe derided as "an incurable mania for oaths."[7] As Jean Starobinski argues, the revolutionary oath of loyalty became an important ritual because it underlined the contrast between national sovereignty and the authority of kings. The kings received "the supernatural insignia of power" from a transcendent God during the ceremony of consecration; by contrast, the revolutionary oath of loyalty created sovereignty from within the community.[8]

Interpretations of revolutionary language do not precisely overlap with the three schools outlined in the introduction. There are Marxist and Tocquevillian positions on language, but there is as yet no developed revisionist position. Marxist interest in revolutionary language is relatively recent, and revisionist historians have until now followed the general lines of Tocqueville's analysis, when they have shown any interest in language at all. A third account of revolutionary language is what can be called a Durkheimian position, that is, an analysis that emphasizes the cultural and especially integrative functions of revolutionary language. All three positions proceed from the common assumption that the "real" significance of language is hidden in some fashion, and the task of analysis is most often construed as one of unmasking.

In Marxist analysis, political language is considered an expression of ideology. Revolutionary rhetoric, in this view, hides true social interests, in particular, the class aims of the bourgeoisie. Marx himself emphasized the false consciousness of the French revolu-

---

[6] As quoted by Bronislaw Baczko, *Lumières de l'Utopie* (Paris, 1978), pp. 366–67.
[7] *Du Fanatisme*, p. 71.
[8] *1789: Les Emblêmes de la Raison* (Paris, 1979), pp. 66–67.

tionaries: "in the classically austere traditions of the Roman republic its gladiators [those of bourgeois society] found the ideals
and the art forms, the self-deceptions that they needed in order to
conceal from themselves the bourgeois limitations of the content of
their struggles."[9] Nicos Poulantzas maintained this general position when he argued that "the bourgeois political aspect" of Jacobin
ideology "is masked by the fact that its language is an ethical and
not a political language."[10] In a similar vein, Jacques Guilhaumou
characterized the radical rhetoric of the Père Duchesne as camou-
flaging a bourgeois conception of democracy behind "a form which
wants to be sans-culotte."[11] In all these views, bourgeois discourse
only pretends to be something other than what it is—an ideological instrument of bourgeois political and social hegemony.

Recently, some Marxist historians have begun to move away from
this reductionist view of language. Guilhaumou himself has written
that Jacobin discourse cannot be reduced to masking and mystifica-
tion. Yet, though he and Régine Robin grant that language is something more than a reflection of social reality or a mechanism for its
reproduction, they still use a relatively inflexible framework of
analysis. They ground discourse in a particular "conjuncture" of
circumstances, which they define as "the unity of contradictions of a
social formation at a given moment, a unity overdetermined at the
political level."[12] This view may make the Marxist analysis of revolutionary language more complex, but it still relies on the implicit metaphor of sub- and superstructure; the social formation lies underneath the level of politics and language, and language expresses
those underlying social contradictions. Sense can only be made of
political discourse if reference is made to an "extra-linguistic" level.[13]

The Tocquevillian position does not make language an ideological instrument of class conflict, but it too emphasizes the element

[9] *The Eighteenth Brumaire of Louis Bonaparte* (New York, 1963), p. 16.

[10] *Pouvoir politique et classes sociales*, 2 vols. (Paris, 1971) 1: 191.

[11] "L'Idéologie du Père Duchesne: Les Forces adjuvantes (14 juillet–6 septembre
1793)," *Le Mouvement social*, no. 85 (1973): 115. The "Père Duchesne" was a popular
carnival figure used to adorn more than one revolutionary masthead. The most influential and enduring of the papers was the *Père Duchesne* of the radical Hébert. For
background, see F. Braesch, ed., *Le Père Duchesne d'Hébert*. 1: *Les Origines—La Constituante* (Paris, 1938).

[12] See their introduction, "Sur la Révolution française," *Bulletin du Centre d'Ana-
lyse du Discours de l'Université de Lille III* (Villeneuve d'Ascq, 1975), pp. 1–14.

[13] Régine Robin, *Histoire et linguistique* (Paris, 1973), p. 22.

of self-deception. In Tocqueville's view, the revolutionaries "nursed the foolish hope that a sudden, radical transformation of a very ancient, highly intricate social system could be effected almost painlessly, under the auspices of reason and by its efficacy alone." Their "fondness for broad generalizations, cut-and-dried legislative systems, and a pedantic symmetry" prevented them from seeing that they were in fact reproducing the absolute power of the Old Regime they hated.[14] In *Penser la Révolution française*, François Furet revives the Tocquevillian position and gives it a semiological twist. For Furet, the veil of language not only hides the truth of political continuity but also at the same time stands in for the realities of political competition: "speech substitutes itself for power," and thus, "the semiotic circuit is the absolute master of politics."[15] Because the normal relationship between society and politics has been disrupted, politics becomes a struggle for the right to speak on behalf of the Nation. Language becomes an expression of power, and power is expressed by the right to speak for the people. The inordinate importance of language in the Revolution was a sign of how untracked French society had become.

An alternative position has been forcefully presented by Mona Ozouf in her analysis of revolutionary festivals. Rather than unmasking the social content or the political deceptions of the festivals, she examines their ritual functions in Durkheimian fashion. Durkheim himself used the work of Albert Mathiez on revolutionary cults, and he frequently cited examples from the Revolution to illustrate his arguments on religion.[16] In Ozouf's view, the many, apparently conflicting festivals reveal a profound "identical conceptualization," "an identical collective need." The festivals accomplished "a transference of sacrality" to the new revolutionary community. Through the institution of the festival, "the discourse of the Revolution about itself" revealed an effort to form a new Na-

[14] Alexis de Tocqueville, *The Old Regime and the French Revolution*, trans. by Stuart Gilbert (New York, 1955), pp. 146, 147. For an analysis of Tocqueville's language, see Linda Orr, "Tocqueville et l'histoire incompréhensible: *L'Ancien Régime et la Révolution*," *Poétique* 49 (1982): 51–70.

[15] (Paris, 1978), pp. 71–72. I have discussed Furet's semiological interpretation at some length in *History and Theory* 20 (1981): 313–23.

[16] For example: "This aptitude of society for setting itself up as a god or for creating gods was never more apparent than during the first years of the French Revolution" (Emile Durkheim, *The Elementary Forms of Religious Life*, trans. by Joseph Ward Swain [New York, 1915], pp. 244–45).

tion on the basis of a new consensus.[17] The language of ritual and ritualized language served the function of national integration. It expressed the need for social solidarity.[18]

The historical analysis of language is especially susceptible to the trope of layers or levels; language, after all, is usually taken as expressing something else, something more "real" than the words themselves. The reading of revolutionary language commonly follows from some prior assumption: that language is an instrument of social conflict (the Marxist position), that language is a vehicle of political self-deception (the Tocquevillian position), or that language is a carrier of cultural integration (the Durkheiminian position). Each of these views has its merits, and they are not necessarily irreconcilable. But here a different point of departure is proposed: the rhetoric of the revolutionaries themselves. Rather than vertically peeling away the layers to get at what revolutionary language "really" meant, I propose to look at language more horizontally, that is, in terms of its internal patterns and its connections to other aspects of political culture. Rather than looking underneath or outside the words, as it were, for the meaning of political discourse, I will seek first to elucidate their rhetorical context.

Revolutionary language did not simply reflect the realities of revolutionary changes and conflicts, but rather was itself transformed into an instrument of political and social change. In this sense, political language was not merely an expression of an ideological position that was determined by underlying social or political interests. The language itself helped shape the perception of interests and hence the development of ideologies. In other words, revolutionary political discourse was rhetorical; it was a means of persuasion, a way of reconstituting the social and political world.

[17] *La Fête révolutionnaire*, pp. 35, 339; and Ozouf, "De Thermidor à Brumaire: Le Discours de la Révolution sur elle-même," *Revue historique* 243 (1970): 31–66.

[18] A functionalist analysis emphasizing the interaction between speaker and audience can be found in Hans Ulrich Gumbrecht, *Funktionen parlamentarischer Rhetorik in der Französischen Revolution* (Munich, 1978). Gumbrecht uses "reception theory" to analyze three rhetorical instances: Mirabeau's speech to the king on 16 July 1789, the development of group identities during the trial of the king, and the defense of institutionalized unanimity in the eulogies of Marat. His work illustrates the use of literary critical methods in a precise fashion. A functionalist analysis of revolutionary music can be found in Adelheid Coy, *Die Musik der Französischen Revolution: Funktionsbestimmung von Lied und Hymne* (Munich, 1978).

La Harpe recognized the rhetorical power of revolutionary language when he announced his intention to characterize the Revolution "by the examination of its language, which was its foremost instrument and the most surprising of all." He aimed "to demonstrate how the establishment, the legal consecration of this language, was a unique event, an unheard-of scandal in the universe, and absolutely inexplicable other than by divine vengeance." [19]

"Divine vengeance" is no longer a standard item in the repertory of historical explanations. In order to understand how political rhetoric could become "an unheard-of scandal" and the "foremost instrument" of the Revolution, I propose to treat revolutionary rhetoric as a text in the manner of literary criticism. Needless to say, however, there is no one manner of literary criticism; literary critics are at least as divided over their methodological approaches as historians. New critics, structuralists, post-structuralists, reception theorists, to name only a few, disagree on almost every point. [20] The debates within literary theory nevertheless open up many possibilities for historians. If the diverse utterances of revolutionary politicians are considered as constituting one text, for example, then the controversies about the nature of texts and the methods for their interpretation become directly relevant.

By its very nature, revolutionary rhetoric posed many of the same issues as those common in literary criticism today. Standards of political interpretation were as disputed in the 1790s as standards of literary interpretation are today. Just as literary critics are now concerned with the nature of authorship, audience, plot structures, and narrative functions, so too during the Revolution were political speakers concerned with authority, audience, and the correct interpretation of revolutionary history. When the deputies of the Third Estate resolved to call themselves, and whoever would join them, the "National Assembly," they challenged the traditional basis of monarchy and opened up general questions about

[19] *Du Fanatisme*, pp. 13–14.
[20] A useful place to start is Kenneth Burke, *A Rhetoric of Motives* (Berkeley, 1969). Recent critical essays with interesting implications for history can be found in W. J. T. Mitchell, *On Narrative* (Chicago, 1981) and Susan R. Suleiman and Inge Crosman, *The Reader in the Text: Essays on Audience and Interpretation* (Princeton, 1980). A useful review of post-structuralist positions can be found in Josué V. Harari, *Textual Strategies: Perspectives in Post-Structuralist Criticism* (Ithaca, N.Y., 1979).

the location of authority. The deputies claimed sovereignty for the Nation, but, in the years that followed, the question of who speaks for the Nation was never definitively settled in France.[21]

In other words, authority—the authorship of the revolutionary text—was uncertain. The charisma of the king, the traditional sacred center of society, steadily dwindled, but no one person, institution, or document succeeded in taking his place. Where was the sacred center of the Nation regenerate? Before Napoleon's rise to power, there were no individually charismatic leaders; France had no equivalent to George Washington, though there were candidates aplenty aspiring to the role, and the new Nation recognized no Founding Fathers. The Revolution had neither paternal origins nor a clear lineage. None of the many constitutions and national assemblies was able to make itself into the fixed reference point for the Nation. As a consequence of this constant displacement of political authority, charisma came to be most concretely located in words, that is, in the ability to speak for the Nation. Revolutionary language was "fanatical" in La Harpe's terms, because it had been invested with sacred authority.

Although the "text" of revolution was sacred, it was also constantly changing. There was no revolutionary Bible that could serve as a source of confirmation and sanctification of revolutionary practice. The French rhetoric of revolution had to provide its own hermeneutics: imbedded in the practice of politics and political discourse were the principles or canon against which that practice could be measured. The new rhetoric was not created all at once, however, nor were its principles ever definitively fixed. To compound the difficulty, those rhetorical principles were for the most part unexamined, despite or because of their self-proclaimed novelty. Revolutionaries fashioned their rhetoric in fits and starts after 1789, and it was only in the heat of political struggle that they clarified their principles.

Revolutionary rhetoric got its textual unity from the belief that the French were founding a new nation. The Nation and the Revolution were constantly cited as points of reference, but they came with no history. As one local revolutionary proclaimed,

[21] The importance of speaking for the Nation is emphasized in Furet, *Penser la Révolution française*, esp. pp. 70–76.

A revolution is never made by halves; it must either be total or it will abort. All the revolutions which history has conserved for memory as well as those that have been attempted in our time have failed because people wanted to square new laws with old customs and rule new institutions with old men. . . . REVOLUTIONARY means outside of all forms and all rules; REVOLUTIONARY means that which affirms, consolidates the revolution, that which removes all the obstacles which impede its progress.[22]

The will to break with the national past distinguished the French from previous revolutionary movements. The new community of American radicals was a living tradition; Americans had always inhabited a "new world" far from what they saw as the corruption of English politics. The English radicals referred to the purer community of their Saxon and dissenting pasts. French revolutionary rhetoric had nothing similar: the French did not have behind them a long-standing tradition of popular literacy motivated by religious dissent, and there were no recognized birthrights of the "free-born" Frenchman to sustain and animate revolutionary rhetoric.[23] Instead, the French harkened to what I will call a "mythic present," the instant of creation of the new community, the sacred moment of the new consensus. The ritual oaths of loyalty taken around a liberty tree or sworn en masse during the many revolutionary festivals commemorated and re-created the moment of social contract; the ritual words made the mythic present come alive, again and again.[24]

The mythic present was inherently undatable, and, as a consequence, the Revolution's own history was always in flux. The constant changes in revolutionary festivals testify to this temporal ambiguity; each regime and each faction expressed its interpretation

[22] A.N., F^{1c} III Meurthe 15, Correspondance et divers, 1789–an V, quoted from the "Discours prononcé à l'ouverture des séances du Comité des Sans-Culottes, par Marat-Mauger, président de ce Comité, et commissaire du Conseil éxécutif près le département de la Meurthe," 4 pp. (n.d., but, from the content and context, apparently late summer 1793). Note that Mauger had changed his name to Marat-Mauger to indicate his allegiance to the recently assassinated, radical journalist-deputy. For a discussion of the local role of such men as Mauger, see chap. 6.

[23] E. P. Thompson, *The Making of the English Working Class* (London, 1963), esp. part I.

[24] According to Starobinski, the oath "founded the future in the exaltation of an instant," yet the gesture also followed an archaic contractual model (*1789*, p. 67).

of the Revolution's historical logic by choosing different dates to celebrate.[25] Bastille Day (July 14) was always a strong candidate for the founding date of the new community because it was prior to all the others, but, as the Revolution progressed, other dates assumed equal and sometimes superior significance: the overthrow of the monarchy on August 10 (1792), the execution of the king on January 21 (1793), and the fall of Robespierre on 9 Thermidor (Year II). Yet, for all their differences, the festivals had in common the purpose of re-creating the moment of the new consensus. The festivals reminded participants that they were the mythic heroes of their own revolutionary epic.

Although it was enunciated with religious fervor, revolutionary language was nonetheless resolutely secular in content. As the battlelines with the church became clearer, as they did almost immediately, revolutionaries eliminated most positive references to Christianity from their vocabulary. This rejection of Christian or Catholic references was yet another way of announcing the revolutionary break with the French and European past. The new social contract needed no analogy to Biblical covenants; it was grounded in reason and the natural rights of man. Revolutionaries leaped over the French national past and turned to Roman and Greek models for inspiration. All of the educated men of the eighteenth century knew something of the classics, but the radical revolutionaries, men such as Camille Desmoulins, Saint-Just, and Robespierre, found in them lessons for instituting a new order; they "utopianized" classical history into the model of a new, innocent society, an ideal Republic.[26]

In the revolutionary view of history, the republicans of Greece and Rome had invented liberty, and the mission of France was to bring that good news to all men. The conservative editor of the *Gazette de Paris* recognized the implications of this view as early as July 1790. Commenting on the Festival of Federation, he declared: "[The Festival] is being compared to those given in Greece and Rome. People forget that one is always citing Republics as models. . . . We are a monarchy. . . . Be neither Romans, nor Greeks; be

[25] Ozouf, *La Fête révolutionnaire*, pp. 199–222.
[26] Ibid., pp. 330–31. On the educational background, see Harold Talbot Parker, *The Cult of Antiquity and the French Revolutionaries* (Chicago, 1937).

French." And the next day he laid out the conservative view of history:

> Ah! Let us not change our ancient formulas [*Vive le Roi* and *vive la Reine* were giving way to *Vive la Nation*]. Heirs of the *Franks*, who measured their own greatness against the even greater grandeur of their Chiefs, let us fight, love, live and die like them, faithful to the principles of our Fathers . . . we were one great family assembled together under the eyes of its Head. . . . Since we have all sworn to be brothers, we have a common father.[27]

The conservative position linked monarchy, tradition, and paternal authority with the historical model of the Franks, long a favorite reference point for those defending noble prerogatives against absolutist encroachment. And the conservative explicitly insisted on maintaining the traditional rhetoric—"our ancient formulas." Conservative papers devoted much space to parallels with past French history, and, in the Assembly, conservative orators relied on past examples to make their points.[28]

The radicals, in contrast, linked liberty, breaking with the past, and the model of the Ancients, which represented not so much the past as a model of a future society. As one radical document of 1793 proclaimed, "to be truly Republican, each citizen must experience and bring about in himself a revolution equal to the one which has changed France. There is nothing, absolutely nothing in common between the slave of a tyrant and the inhabitant of a free state; the customs of the latter, his principles, his sentiments, his action, all must be new."[29] The emphasis on newness sometimes went as far

[27] *Gazette de Paris*, 15 and 16 July 1790.

[28] On 15 July 1790, for instance, the conservative *L'Ami du Roi, des françois, de l'ordre, et surtout de la verité, par les continuateurs de Fréron* (the editor was the abbé Royou) reviewed a pamphlet analyzing the parallel between events in 1358 and 1789. The review concluded that both "revolutions" had originated in financial problems, and therefore "people are wrong who think that the revolution we are witnessing does not resemble any of those of past centuries" (no. 45). The use of historical precedents in conservative oratory can be seen in the speech given by abbé Maury to the National Assembly on 15 July 1790. The occasion was a dispute over the placement of the national flag. He opened by maintaining that "an historical summary, very short, will suffice to indicate to us the use which we should make of it." He argued that the flag should be entrusted to the king as supreme military commander (*L'Ami du Roi*, no. 46 [16 July 1790]).

[29] "Instruction adressée aux autorités constituées des départemens [sic] de Rhône

1. FESTIVAL OF LIBERTY, OCTOBER 1792

*The Statue of Liberty was placed on the pedestal which formerly held the
statue of Louis XV. Engraving from Revolutions de Paris, no. 171*
(Photo by Lynn Hunt)

as a denial of the authority of the Ancients as well. In his ground-breaking "Report and Project for a Decree on the General Organization of Public Education" of April 1792, Condorcet minced no words:

> Finally, since it is necessary to say everything, since all prejudices must today disappear, [I maintain that] the long, careful study of ancient languages . . . would be perhaps more harmful than useful. We are seeking an education that makes known truths, and these books are full of errors. We are seeking to educate reason, and these books can mislead it. We are so far from the Ancients, we are so far ahead on the road to truth, that it is necessary to have one's reason already well-braced in order for it to be enriched rather than corrupted by these precious remains.[30]

The radical break with tradition and with the justification of authority by reference to historical origins also implied the rejection of paternalist or patriarchal models of authority. On the official seal, in the engravings and prints representing the new republic, and in the *tableaux vivants* of the festivals, feminine allegorizations of classical derivation replaced representations of the king (see plate 1). These female figures, whether living women or statues, always sat or stood alone, surrounded most often by abstract emblems of authority and power. The Republic might have her children and even her masculine defenders, but there was never a Father present.[31]

The conservatives, on the defensive, recognized first that historical models, family metaphors, and the nature of authority were intimately connected in political rhetoric. It took longer to develop, much less weld together, the disparate elements of radical rhetoric. Yet from the beginning radicals found themselves overturning the traditional familial analogies to power. They seemed to be rhetor-

---

et de Loire, par la Commission temporaire" of Lyon (16 November 1793), reprinted in Walter Markov and Albert Soboul, eds., *Die Sansculotten von Paris: Dokumente zur Geschichte der Volksbewegung, 1793–1794* (Berlin, 1957), p. 224.

[30] Reprinted in M. J. Guillaume, ed., *Procès-verbaux du Comité d'instruction publique de l'Assemblée législative* (Paris, 1889), p. 200.

[31] I base this observation on my study of revolutionary prints in the collections of the Bibliothéque nationale and the Musée Carnavalet in Paris. See also Maurice Agulhon, *Marianne au combat: L'Imagerie et la symbolique républicaines de 1789 à 1880* (Paris, 1979), pp. 7–53; Hannah Mitchell, "Art and the French Revolution: An Exhibition at the Musée Carnavalet," *History Workshop Journal* 5 (1978): 123–45; and Lynn Hunt, "Engraving the Republic: Prints and Propaganda in the French Revolution," *History Today* 30 (1980): 11–17.

ically killing the king, their father, long before the Convention actually voted the death sentence. The radicals were brothers defending the virtue of *la Nation* and *la Liberté*, but there were no
French "Sons of Liberty." Local radicals in the distant department
of the Gers recognized this state of affairs when they proclaimed in
one of their addresses: "The French people wants to be and must
be only a family of brothers, equally cherished and protected by
their common mother."[32] In 1793 the implicit murder of the symbolic father became more explicit.[33] The king was executed, and
even the Christian God was challenged in the de-Christianization
movement. In Festivals of Reason all over the country, goddesses
of Liberty occupied the sacred places.

As revolutionaries cut themselves adrift from the moorings of
patriarchal conceptions of authority, they faced a dichotomous,
highly charged set of feelings: on the one hand, there was the ex-
hilaration of a new era; on the other, a dark sense of foreboding
about the future. A mythic present and charismatic language were
fragile underpinnings for a new community whose boundaries
were ill defined. The reverse side of the mythic present of national
regeneration was an enormous, collective anxiety about the solid-
ity of the new consensus. The Puritans of early seventeenth-century
England had been convinced of their "calling" and their special,
"elect" status long before they had an opportunity to act in the national political arena.[34] Radical Americans of the late eighteenth
century enjoyed at least a decade of intense political education and
practice before they actually attempted to separate the colonies
from England, and as they embarked on that path they spoke the
language the English Whigs and radicals had developed before
them.[35] French radicals, in contrast, found themselves in the midst

[32] The quote comes from an address written in March 1794, cited in G. Brégail,
"L'Eloquence révolutionnaire dans le Gers," *Bulletin de la Société archéologique du Gers*
20 (1919): 119.
[33] The symbolic murder of the father is briefly discussed in Michel Vovelle, *Idéologies et mentalités* (Paris, 1982), p. 301.
[34] Michael Walzer, *The Revolution of the Saints: A Study in the Origins of Radical Politics* (Cambridge, Mass., 1965).
[35] J. R. Pole, *Political Representation in England and the Origins of the American Republic*
(Berkeley, 1966); Gordon S. Wood, *The Creation of the American Republic, 1776–
1787* (New York, 1969), esp. chap. 1; and J. G. A. Pocock, "1776: The Revolution
against Parliament," in Pocock, *Three British Revolutions: 1641, 1688, 1776* (Princeton,
1980), pp. 265–88.

of revolution before they had much occasion to reflect on their precarious position.

The novelty of French revolutionary rhetoric did not stem from its formal properties, that is, from its rhetorical structure in the narrow, classical sense of the term. The clerical *collèges* of the Old Regime had provided revolutionaries and nonrevolutionaries alike with a store of classical and neoclassical commonplaces.[36] Almost all of the speeches given at the tribune in the various national assemblies were written out ahead of time, and they usually followed the order or *dispositio* set out by Quintilian: first the *exordium* or general introduction; then the statement of the case, customarily taking the form of a narration of events; followed by the arguments in favor of the speaker's position and a refutation of the points made by opponents; and finally the peroration, in which the speaker summed up his case and tried to sway the audience in his favor by appealing to their emotions.[37] Not surprisingly, this classical order derived from judicial oratory, precisely the kind of training most useful to the lawyers who dominated national politics during the Revolution. The order of speeches, the use of figures and paradigms, and the reliance on classical examples can be traced back to schoolboy rhetorical exercises.[38]

The political ideas expressed in this classical rhetorical form were decisively shaped by seventeenth- and eighteenth-century intellectual and political developments. As Kingsley Martin explained over fifty years ago, "the new creed, which had been shaping itself piecemeal in the minds of scientists and men of letters in the seventeenth century, had become religion to the deputies who met in the States-General."[39] Locke, Newton, Bayle, Fénelon, and the *philosophes* had prepared the way. Even the aristocratic courts had used the language of Enlightenment in their efforts to oppose the

[36] Marc-Eli Blanchard, *Saint-Just & Cie: La Révolution et les mots* (Paris, 1980), pp. 42–51.

[37] Peter France, *Rhetoric and Truth in France: Descartes to Diderot* (Oxford, 1972), pp. 10–11. France describes here the rhetorical training given in Old Regime French schools. Anyone who has read a number of revolutionary parliamentary speeches will recognize the common structure.

[38] Some useful observations on this issue are provided in Blanchard, *Saint-Just & Cie*, pp. 25–68. See also Roger Chartier et al., *L'Education en France du XVIe au XVIIIe siècle* (Paris, 1976), pp. 196–99.

[39] *The Rise of French Liberal Thought: A Study of Political Ideas from Bayle to Condorcet*, 2nd ed. (New York, 1954), p. 2.

crown; beginning in the 1770s and then more dramatically in the 1780s, the Parlement of Paris remonstrated on behalf of the rights of "citizens" and "the Nation." [40] Nor were the issues of republicanism and democracy or the language of virtue versus corruption invented by the French; they were part of what J. G. A. Pocock calls "the Atlantic Republican Tradition," which he traces back to Renaissance Florence. [41]

French revolutionaries learned the language of reform and opposition from the *philosophes* and *parlementaires* (high court magistrates), but they had to invent the language of revolution for themselves. The sparsely populated colonies across the ocean in America declared their independence; the most populous nation in Western Europe was self-consciously making something radically new in the world, a revolution, a word that before 1789—even in America—usually stood for a return back to a previous state rather than for a leap into the future. [42] There was no historical or religious Golden Age in the French past that the radicals might hope to recapture; there was only bravery in the face of an unpredictable future and unstable present.

The uncertainty about the course of the Revolution can be seen in the transformation of narrative structures that informed revolutionary rhetoric. In the first months of the Revolution, most rhetoric was unconsciously shaped by what Northrup Frye terms the "generic plot" of comedy. [43] Comedy turns on a conflict between an older social order (the phrase *ancien régime* was invented in these early days) and a new one, and this conflict is often represented as one dividing a son who wants freedom from his more arbitrary and conventional father. In the plot of comedy, the "blocking characters" (the father, in France, the king) are usually reconciled rather than repudiated altogether. The final reconciliation, the happy

---

[40] Bailey Stone, *The Parlement of Paris, 1774–1789* (Chapel Hill, N.C., 1981), esp. chaps. 3 and 6. However, Jacques Godechot argued that "la Nation" only became charged with revolutionary significance during the electoral campaign of 1789 ("Nation, patrie, nationalisme et patriotisme en France au XVIIIe siècle," *AHRF* 43 [1971]: 481–501, esp. p. 495).

[41] *The Machiavellian Moment: Florentine Political Thought and the Atlantic Republican Tradition* (Princeton, 1975).

[42] See the entry under "Revolution" in *The Compact Edition of the Oxford English Dictionary* (1971).

[43] *Anatomy of Criticism: Four Essays* (Princeton, 1957), pp. 163–86. For another use of Frye's categories by an historian, see Hayden White, *Metahistory: The Historical Imagination in Nineteenth-Century Europe* (Baltimore, 1973), esp. pp. 1–42.

emergence of the new society, is signaled by a festive ritual, which often takes place at the end of the action.

Nothing better reveals the structure of comedy in revolutionary rhetoric than the commentaries on the Festival of Federation of 14 July 1790 (see plate 2). Whether by conservatives or budding radicals, the descriptions of the Paris Festival all emphasize the desire for reconciliation and happy reunion: "On the route, at windows, on the rooftops, everywhere men were beside themselves, elated with a judicious joy that resembled in no way the unrestrained joy of slaves."[44] Subjects had become citizens, and the king himself seemed to endorse the emergence of a new society. Led by Lafayette, the new officials, the National Guard, troops of the line, and even battalions of children aged eight to ten took a common oath to be forever faithful to the Nation, the Law, and the King. Thanks were publicly given for "this inseparable bond between all the French, regardless of sex, age, station in life, or occupation."[45] Even the influential conservative newspaper, *L'Ami du Roi*, referred to the Federation as celebrating "the most astonishing epoch in our history." The editor recounted several incidents that demonstrated "the innate love in the hearts of all French people for the person of the King and for the royal family."[46] The Festival brought the French family back together again, with the recognition that the father had given in to the pressing demands of his sons.

The reconciliation did not last, however, and the narrative of Revolution did not come to a close in 1790. The king had acquiesced only in appearance, and the radicals were not satisfied with the restoration of family harmony. As the radicals began to dominate discourse in 1792, especially after the declaration of the Republic in September, the generic plot shifted from comedy to romance. Now the Revolution seemed more like a quest, in which the heroes were the brothers of the revolutionary fraternity, who faced a series of life-and-death struggles with the demonic forces of counterrevolution.

As Frye characterizes it, romance does not favor complex or subtle characters: on the one side are the almost mythical heroes, and

[44] Anon., *Description fidèle de tout ce qui a précédé, accompagné et suivi la cérémonie de la Confédération nationale du 14 juillet 1790* (Paris, n.d.), p. 16.

[45] Anon., *Description de la Fête du Pacte fédératif, du 14 juillet, fixée par la ville, avec le réglement de la police* (Paris, n.d.).

[46] No. 56 (26 July 1790) and no. 57 (27 July 1790).

2. FESTIVAL OF FEDERATION, PARIS, JULY 1790

(Photo from Cabinet des Estampes, courtesy of the Bibliothèque nationale)

on the other are the villains, the cowards, the dragons.[47] Republicans in 1792 and 1793 emphasized the titanic nature of their struggle to free France, their distance from the past, the virtues of their efforts, and the utter villainy of their opponents. There was no longer one happy family, but there was still great confidence in the ability of republicans to remold France in the image of virtue. One little-known deputy captured the urgency of the quest when he proclaimed, "The moment of catastrophe has arrived. All prejudices must fall at once. We must annihilate them, or we will be crushed. We must, between 10 August [1792] and 1 January 1793 traverse the space of several centuries with daring and courage."[48] He made this statement in mid-December 1792, just before the expiration of his presumed deadline. In it, he exhorted his fellow deputies to just those virtues so characteristic of romance: daring, courage, and headlong movement.

As the expected leap into the future met increasing obstacles, as the "enormous gap between what we are and what we could be" that Grégoire saw in January 1794 (see the introduction) failed to narrow, an undercurrent of the third generic plot came to the surface. In tragedy, the half-human, half-divine hero (in France, the increasingly isolated republican leadership) has had an extraordinary destiny almost within his grasp, and the glory of his efforts never quite fades. The tragedy is that the goal was so right, yet the quest for it inevitably failed. The heroes who nevertheless made the attempt were making a noble sacrifice of themselves for the sake of the community. As a consequence, in Frye's terms, "the rhetoric of tragedy requires the noblest diction."[49] At the end of 1793 and the beginning of 1794, republicans spoke their most dramatic lines. In an important speech in early May 1794, for example, Robespierre (see plate 3) sounded many tragic notes in the midst of continuing themes of romance:

> Everything has changed in the physical order [thanks to the conquests of science]; everything must change in the moral and political order. Half of the world's revolution is already complete; the other

---

[47] *Anatomy of Criticism*, p. 195.

[48] From a speech by Jacob Dupont quoted in a report on the National Convention's session of 14 December 1792, *Réimpression de l'Ancien Moniteur* 14 (Paris, 1847), no. 744 (16 December 1792).

[49] *Anatomy of Criticism*, p. 210.

3. MAXIMILIEN ROBESPIERRE
Lithograph by Préval, 1849
(Photo from Cabinet des Estampes, courtesy of the Bibliothèque nationale)

half must be accomplished. . . . We will teach [Europe] the names
and virtues of the heroes who died fighting for liberty . . . we will
tell them the hour in which the death of the world's oppressors was
sounded. . . . I am French, I am one of your representatives. . . .
Oh! Sublime people! Receive the sacrifice of all my being. Happy is
he who was born in your midst! Even happier is he who can die for
your happiness![50]

It seemed as if he knew his own end was coming only a few weeks
later.

The narrative shift from comedy, to romance, and then to tragedy was propelled by the French revolutionary obsession with
conspiracy. If the mythic present of the regenerated national community was the Garden of Eden of the revolutionaries, then conspiracy was its Evil Spirit. The enemies of the Revolution ruined the

[50] From his speech "Sur les rapports des idées religieuses et morales avec les prin-
cipes républicains, et sur les fêtes nationales," in *Oeuvres de Maximilien Robespierre* 10
(Discours: 27 juillet 1793–27 juillet 1794) (Paris, 1967): 445. Vovelle asserts that the
Revolution was experienced by its actors as tragic (*Idéologies et mentalités*, p. 301).

apparent reconciliation of 1790. The enemies of the Republic constantly thwarted the quest for moral and political regeneration. No sooner was a conspiracy uncovered than others emerged to take its place. The French obsession with conspiracy was not, however, unique in itself. American colonials of the 1760s and 1770s acted on the conviction that corrupt ministers in England were plotting to deprive them of their natural and traditional rights.[51] Yet, though the rhetoric of conspiracy was not peculiar to the French Revolution, it continued to dominate political discourse in France even after the break with the Old Regime had occurred. In America conspiracy presumably pitted the colonials against a distant mother country, and, after the break had been made, American revolutionaries became much more concerned with the problems of representing the interests of different regions and social groups in the new order.[52] In France, conspiracy was fraternal and hence fratricidal, and the preoccupation with it only grew more intense after 1789. As Furet has argued, the obsession with conspiracy became the central organizing principle of French revolutionary rhetoric.[53] The narrative of Revolution was dominated by plots.

Because they were haunted by the lurking specter of conspiracy, revolutionaries talked incessantly about unmasking. Radical journalists, such as Marat and Hébert, specialized in this rhetoric of denunciation, but people talked a similar language at every political level from the beginning of the Revolution. Already in July 1789 there was a newspaper entitled *Le Dénonciateur national*. By 1793 the phraseology of conspiracy had become a regular, required part of revolutionary discourse. A semiliterate, anonymous placard captured the vagaries of the notion:

> Sans-culotte it is time to sound the alarm. . . . Beware, it is time, civil war is making ready you are the toy of all the scoundrels who supposedly govern the Republic. They are all conspirators and all of the merchants of Paris, I denounce them. Several of those who are going to read my two words described, which is the pure truth, are going to say that I am a conspirator because I tell the truth.[54]

[51] Bernard Bailyn, *The Ideological Origins of the American Revolution* (Cambridge, Mass., 1967).
[52] Wood, *The Creation of the American Republic*, and Pole, *Political Representation*.
[53] *Penser la Révolution française*, pp. 78–79.
[54] From an "Hébertist" placard reported to the police on 9 March 1794, reprinted in Markov and Soboul, *Die Sansculotten*, p. 203.

The revolutionary tribunals of 1793–94 gave the rhetoric of conspiracy legal form, but they did not invent its usage.

The revolutionary obsession with conspiracy had two distinct social sources, one in popular culture, the other in "patriot" fears of "aristocratic" counterrevolution in 1789. Conspiracy in France was an age-old popular fixation that was fostered by the rigidities of a subsistence economy and easily sustained by a community dependent on oral transmission of news. Popular belief in hidden treasures inspired tales of aristocratic caches of arms, secret correspondence, or hoarded grain.[55] Hunger and the threat of starvation made fears of conspiracy all the more compelling.[56] Dearth was nothing new, and the popular response of outrage at presumed speculation and spontaneous price fixing had a long history. In the last decades of the Old Regime, however, talk of hoarding and speculation became increasingly bound up with national political issues. In the 1760s and 1770s the crown alternately tried to liberalize the grain trade and shore it up with unpublicized government intervention. Critics of the government accused leading ministers and even the king himself of fomenting artificial famines for profit, and in retaliation the government launched its own propaganda campaigns to portray recalcitrant magistrates as the authors of crisis.[57] The cross fire of allegations at the highest level of government fanned the flames of popular mistrust, and even highly placed people believed that the vital supply of grain was subject to political manipulation.

In 1789 popular suspicion about rising grain prices was aroused in the midst of a constitutional crisis. As the deputies of the new National Assembly saw thousands of troops move into Paris and Versailles, they too became convinced of the existence of an aristocratic conspiracy, this one of a political rather than of a social nature. One deputy wrote home on June 24 describing what he saw as an attempt to "tighten the chains of our slavery."[58] On July 10 the

[55] Richard Cobb, "Quelques aspects de la mentalité révolutionnaire (avril 1793–thermidor an II)," in Cobb, *Terreur et subsistances, 1793–1795* (Paris, 1965), pp. 20–21.

[56] Georges Lefebvre, "Foules révolutionnaires," reprinted in Lefebvre, *Etudes sur la Révolution française*, 2nd ed. (Paris, 1963), pp. 371–92.

[57] A comprehensive account is in Steven L. Kaplan, *Bread, Politics and Political Economy in the Reign of Louis XV*, 2 vols. (The Hague, 1976).

[58] A.N., W 306, "Dossier de l'abbé de Champagne," letter of 24 June 1789 written by Camusat de Belombre, deputy from the Third Estate of the bailliage of Troyes.

same deputy (a merchant from Troyes and a political moderate) wrote that "everyone is convinced that the advance of troops covers some violent design," and he attributed that design to the "infernal intrigue" of "the Aristocracy, which rules us with an iron rod."[59] The dismissal of the minister Necker, who was regarded as favorable to the demands of the National Assembly, brought popular and bourgeois fears of conspiracy together into a new and potent combination.

The rhetoric of conspiracy permeated revolutionary discourse at every political level, but it was above all the watchword of the radicals. In the conservative analysis of events, the authors of evil were not conspirators, but rather the monsters, scoundrels, barbarians, and cannibals unleashed by the breakdown of traditional social bonds. In January 1792 the editor of the *Gazette de Paris* concluded that it was "our vile Innovators" who were leading the people astray: "*Propaganda* has risen up in the midst of all the Peoples of the Earth . . . her flanks have opened up and thousands of serpents have been transformed into men. This new family brings with it the morals, the character, and the genius of the monster which conceived them."[60]

It was not long, however, before conspiracy rhetoric invaded all varieties of political discourse in France. By 1791 right-wing newspapers were publishing their own exposés of Protestant and Freemason plots, intrigues imputed to the Duke of Orleans, and insidious efforts to dupe the people.[61] The most influential conservative conspiracy accounts were written after the fall of Robespierre, however, and they were offered as explanations of the whole revolutionary process rather than as day-to-day commentaries in the manner of radical commentators.[62] Radical brochures written for popular consumption, articles in radical newspapers, Jacobin speeches on the Convention floor, and the indictments of radical-dominated

[59] Ibid.
[60] *Gazette de Paris*, 4 and 6 January and 15 April 1792.
[61] W. J. Murray, "The Right-Wing Press in the French Revolution (1789–1792)," Ph.D. diss., Australian National University, 1971. Murray does not trace this theme in particular, but he gives many instructive examples.
[62] On the Protestant plot, see *Les Véritables auteurs de la Révolution de France de 1789*, attributed to Sourdat of Troyes (Neufchâtel, 1797); and, on the Freemason plot, Abbé Barruel, *Mémoires pour servir à l'histoire du jacobinisme*, 5 vols. (Hamburg, 1798). For an overview, see Jacques Godechot, *The Counter-Revolution, Doctrine and Action, 1789–1804*, trans. by Salvator Attansio (New York, 1971).

revolutionary tribunals were all packed with lengthy, minute examinations of the political acts and words of those under fire.[63] What began as a response to fears of price manipulation and secret aristocratic maneuvering developed into a systematic and obsessive preoccupation that pervaded every aspect of public political life.

Contemporary observers (and historians ever since) were most struck by the combination of vagueness and particularity in denunciations of conspiracy. Anyone was a potential enemy, perhaps especially one's own friends. Once a traitor had been discovered within the midst of the supposed friends of the Revolution, no effort was spared to reread the history of his actions in a new light. When Saint-Just itemized the charges against Danton and his friends in the spring of 1794, for example, he felt it necessary to examine everything Danton had done and everyone he had known since the beginning of the Revolution. If the traitorous general Dumouriez had praised Fabre-Fond, who was the brother of Fabre d'Eglantine, who was the friend of Danton, then "can one doubt your criminal concert to overthrow the Republic?"[64] The threads of conspiracy could be discovered almost everywhere, and every such discovery required a rewriting of history.

The centrality of conspiracy in revolutionary rhetoric cannot be sufficiently explained in historical terms. It was more than a traditional resentment of hunger, more than a carryover from court intrigues, more than an age-old moral sensibility shaped by the Christian belief in evil as a hidden force.[65] All of these factors contributed to making conspiracy believable and emotionally compelling. But conspiracy only became a systematic obsession when the revolutionaries confronted the novelties of mass politics. Furet describes this dilemma as the two sides of the "democratic imaginary of power": for him, "like the will of the people, the plot is a delir-

[63] I have benefited from many illuminating observations on the differences in style between radical, moderate, and conservative or counterrevolutionary newspapers in Suzanne Desan, "'Avec des plumes': Parisian Journalism in 1791–1792," unpublished senior thesis, Princeton University, April 1979, loaned to me by the author. See also Jack Richard Censer, *Prelude to Power: The Parisian Radical Press, 1789–1791* (Baltimore, 1976).

[64] "Rapport sur la conjuration ourdie pour obtenir un changement de dynastie; et contre Fabre d'Eglantine, Danton, Philippeaux, Lacroix et Camille Desmoulins," *Oeuvres complètes de Saint-Just*, intro. and notes by Charles Vellay, 2 vols. (Paris, 1908) 2: 305–32, quote p. 319.

[65] Furet suggests the importance of religious sensibility in shaping plot theories in *Penser la Révolution française*, p. 78.

ium on power." [66] On the one side, democracy, the people's will, the Revolution; on the other, the plot, the anti-principle, the negation. This formulation of the problem tends to make the connection between democracy and conspiracy philosophical and necessary. However, the American experience at the same time showed that the connection was not necessary; the American Republic was not undermined by a continuing preoccupation with conspiracies against the Nation. The difference was that in France all organized politics were conflated with conspiratorial plotting.

To a great extent, the ambivalence toward organized politics was shared by educated men on both sides of the Atlantic in the eighteenth century. Everyone seemed to fear back-room politicking, secret machinations, and factionalism. But in France there was no "Whig science of politics," no familiarity with the ins and outs of ministerial turnovers, no practice with patronage systems and interest group formations. [67] The transition from the constricted polity of the Old Regime to the seemingly limitless participation in the new one was particularly sharp and disjointed. The French had more to explain to themselves than a change in policy by ministers far away or even ministers right at home. They had more to fear than a change in court allegiances or a slight rise or dip in "country" control of national policy. The struggle between the regenerated French nation and her presumed enemies was particularly divisive, thanks to the combination of the novelty of political mobilization, the intensity of social antagonism (as exemplified in talk of famine plots), and the unparalleled emphasis on doing something entirely new in the world. If Americans and Englishmen found it difficult to accept the emergence of party politics and factional competition, then the French refusal to sanction such developments was all the more determined. And the consequences of such a refusal were all the more disastrous.

While American republicans were working their way, however fitfully, toward party politics and the representation of interests, the French found themselves denying the possibility of "liberal" politics in spite of their best intentions. [68] The social or even political

---

[66] Ibid., p. 79.

[67] For the American background, see Wood, *The Creation of the American Republic*.

[68] On the American side, see Pole, *Political Representation*. It is worth noting that similar studies of ideological and political development during the First Republic in France have not been attempted.

differences between a Jefferson or a Madison and a Robespierre or a Saint-Just were minimal. The salient difference between them was the context in which they spoke. They grew up learning the same rhetorical skills and reading many of the same books. But when Robespierre or Saint-Just or one of the many others like them came to the speaker's podium of the Convention, words and rhetoric had a different significance. French political orators were speaking in two registers at once: one political and the other sacred. In the absence of a common law tradition or any acceptable sacred text of reference, the voice of the nation had to be heard constantly. Speaking and naming took on enormous significance; they became the source of significance.[69] In America, as J. R. Pole concludes, the written instrument of the Constitution acquired supremacy, and political discourse thereafter revolved around issues of interests, property, rights, representation, and checks and balances.[70] In France, the spoken word retained its supremacy (at least until 1794, perhaps until 1799), and political discourse was structured by notions of transparency, publicity, vigilance, and terror.

In France in the 1790s, factional politics was synonymous with conspiracy, and "interests" was a code word for betrayal of a nation united. Nothing particular (and all "interests" were by definition particular) was supposed to divide the general will. Constant vigilance and the publicity of all politics were the ways to prevent the emergence of particular interests and factions. Behind these notions was the revolutionary belief in the possibility and desirability of "transparency" between citizen and citizen, between the citizens and their government, between the individual and the general will.[71] Accordingly, there should be no artificial manners or conventions separating men from each other and no institutions block-

---

[69] This emphasis on the power of the spoken word can be found in both Furet, *Penser la Révolution française*, and Blanchard, *Saint-Just & Cie.*

[70] *Political Representation*, p. 511.

[71] I have taken the notion of transparency from Jean Starobinski, *Jean-Jacques Rousseau: La Transparence et l'obstacle* (Paris, 1957). Furet uses the notion when discussing the relations between the people and power (or representations of power), but he does not extend it to the relationship of citizens to each other (e.g., *Penser la Révolution française*, pp. 86, 103). According to Marc Richir, "In a profound sense, all of 'revolutionary' thought is animated by the belief in a transparency of society to itself in the 'moment' of Revolution." In his introduction, "Révolution et transparence sociale," to J. G. Fichte, *Considérations destinées à rectifier les jugements du public sur la Révolution française* (Paris, 1974), p. 10.

ing free communication between citizens and their delegates. Transparency, in this sense, gave meaning to the civic oath and to the revolutionary festival, both of which depended on enthusiastic adherence, that is, on the abolition of the distance between citizen and citizen and between individual and community. Community, in essence, was this transparency between citizens, another word for the manifestation of the mythic present.

Politically, transparency meant that there was no need for politicians and no place for the professional manipulation of sentiments or symbols; each citizen was to deliberate in the stillness of his heart, free from the nefarious influences of connections, patronage, or party. Hébert's *Père Duchesne* was the rough-and-ready sans-culotte version of the model patriot, pure of heart and free of artifice. He expressed only the most simple and definite emotions, usually either "great joy" or "wrath." On 1 September 1791 Père Duchesne gave his advice on the coming elections: "Citizens, if you don't want to be betrayed, beware of appearances. Put no faith in golden tongues. . . . Don't let yourself be dazzled by beautiful promises. . . . If you know a citizen who is obscure and without ambition, that's the one you should choose."[72]

Radical deputies spoke a more refined language, but they too placed a premium on authentic emotion. They linked oratorical eloquence with purity and virtue of the heart. Among the virtues Robespierre thought necessary to a representative of the people, he gave high priority to "the eloquence of the heart without which one cannot succeed in persuading."[73] In the oratory of the Convention, in particular, the verb *frémir* (tremble, quiver, shake) appeared again and again; orators spoke directly to the hearts of the auditors (though rarely extemporaneously!), and they expected to produce in them immediate emotion.[74] This expectation was the translation into political practice of Rousseau's notion of authenticity, the condition in which citizens are transparent to each other.[75]

Heart-to-heart politics were meant to take place in public; each citizen and all of his elected representatives were expected to per-

[72] Braesch, ed., *Le Père Duchesne*, no. 72, p. 751.

[73] Pierre Trahard, *La Sensibilité révolutionnaire (1789–1794)* (Paris, 1936), p. 189.

[74] Ibid., p. 186. See also F.-A. Aulard, *Les Orateurs de la Révolution: L'Assemblée Constituante* (Paris, 1905).

[75] Starobinski, *Jean-Jacques Rousseau*.

form their deliberations in public, in front of the other citizens. The true patriot could have nothing to hide. The meetings of the humblest neighborhood militants and those of the country's chosen legislators shared the quality of compulsive publicity. Neighborhood clubs elected "censors" to patrol the meeting hall and prevent "private conversations."[76] The sans-culottes carried publicity, "the safeguard of the people," furthest: contrary to law, several Parisian sections insisted on voice voting in elections and even on voting by acclamation. They maintained that this was the way free men, republicans, voted.[77] The publicity of politics made vigilance possible, and vigilance was necessary because it was hard to believe that men so recently and incompletely regenerated could sustain political transparence; recurrent conspiracies showed this to be true. The infallible sign of vigilance at work was denunciation. There had been informers and denunciations to the police under the Old Regime, of course, but during the Revolution, denunciation was elevated to a virtuous act, a civic duty.

Public vigilance and denunciation were institutionalized in the Terror. As Robespierre explained,

> in this situation the first maxim of your policy must be to guide the people with reason and the people's enemies with terror. . . . Terror is nothing other than justice, prompt, severe, and inflexible; it is therefore an emanation of virtue. . . . Break the enemies of liberty with terror, and you will be justified as founders of the Republic. The government of the revolution is the despotism of liberty against tyranny.[78]

The Terror was an emanation of virtue for Robespierre and the other radicals, because it was required for the security of the new republic. In a sense, then, it followed logically from the presuppositions of revolutionary language.[79] If the Revolution was in the

[76]See, for example, "Réglement pour la Société populaire de la Section de la République," reprinted in Markov and Soboul, *Die Sansculotten*, pp. 258–67.
[77]Albert Soboul, *Les Sans-culottes parisiens en l'an II*, 2nd ed. (Paris, 1962), pp. 549–61.
[78]From his "Rapport sur les principes de morale politique qui doivent guider la Convention nationale dans l'administration intérieure de la République," 5 February 1794, in *Oeuvres* 10: 356–57.
[79]For Furet, the Terror is the logical consequence of revolutionary discourse and its "illusion of the political" (*Penser la Révolution française*, esp. pp. 229 and 259). Patrice Higonnet takes a position similar to Furet's but without the Tocquevillian affiliation; he emphasizes the inherent contradiction between "bourgeois individualism"

first instance the founding of a new community, then Robespierre's "government of the revolution" was the enforcer of communitarian discipline—"the despotism of liberty against tyranny." It was not conceived as the arbiter of conflicting interests (agriculture vs. commerce, for example), but rather as the mechanism for ensuring that individual wills were forged into one, single, general, or national will.

Contrary to the views of scholars such as J. L. Talmon, however, the government during the Terror was not a totalitarian, one party-state, but rather a communitarian state without party.[80] The principles of revolutionary rhetoric prevented the Jacobins themselves from becoming a behind-the-scenes agent of rule. The Jacobin clubs did not take over the revolutionary state; they were more or less absorbed by the state and reduced to serving as a sounding board for government policy.[81] Because the Jacobins more than anyone else accepted the principles of revolutionary rhetoric, they did not organize opposition to the restrictions placed on them after the fall of Robespierre. Indeed, some legal restraints were welcomed as dissipating "the phantom . . . that the popular societies wished to become an intermediary power between the people and the Convention."[82] After years of trying to organize legally in the face of increasing repression and persecution, the Jacobins finally began to change their position late in 1799. They started defending themselves in print as a party and as a loyal opposition.[83] A month later Bonaparte ended that experiment along with many others.

---

and the communitarian side of "bourgeois universalism" (*Class, Ideology, and the Rights of Nobles during the French Revolution* [Oxford, 1981]).

[80] *The Origins of Totalitarian Democracy* (New York, 1965). Furet seems close to Talmon in his judgment of the Terror, but his explanation for it is different. Talmon emphasizes the intellectual lineages of totalitarianism: the deductions from Enlightenment philosophy. Furet emphasizes the philosophical problems of democracy as they are worked out in practice (following Tocqueville and Cochin).

[81] There are many illuminating remarks on this issue in Crane Brinton, *The Jacobins: An Essay in the New History* (New York, 1930), e.g.: "The Jacobin Clubs, then, when they cease to be in opposition to the government and a bureaucracy wholly manned by their own members, cease to practice the tactics associated with their name . . . one may say that in general the final role of the clubs as such is that of auxiliary administrative bodies" (p. 129).

[82] The deputy Crassous, as quoted in Isser Woloch, *Jacobin Legacy: The Democratic Movement under the Directory* (Princeton, 1970), pp. 15–16.

[83] This issue is discussed at some length in Lynn Hunt, David Lansky, and Paul Hanson, "The Failure of the Liberal Republic in France, 1795–1799: The Road to Brumaire," *Journal of Modern History* 51 (1979): 734–59, esp. p. 755.

Although the Terror followed logically from the principles enunciated in revolutionary rhetoric, it was not the only possible deduction from those principles. The history of the Revolution between 1795 and 1799 and even after the rise of Napoleon shows this to be true. The Directory regime failed in large measure because it too resisted the possibility of organized politics. Despite the efforts of some of its leaders to organize a center party, most supporters of the regime feared that political organization would only benefit the Jacobins and/or the royalists. As a result, they refused to allow the formation of any organized opposition and purged the legislature whenever either the left or the right seemed to win the elections. At the same time, the Directorials could not bring themselves to give up frequent elections or to install a one-party state of their own.[84]

Under Napoleon, the ambivalence toward organized politics took the form of repressing all political activity worthy of the name. Both the Directorial and the Napoleonic "solutions" to the antinomies of revolutionary rhetoric merely reflect the power of that rhetoric in the first place. Transparency, publicity, and vigilance did not give way to a principled representation of interests (though some Directorial politicians hoped that would be possible); the original revolutionary principles were rejected as unworkable or even dangerous, but no other rhetoric was convincing enough to take their place. The Directorial government tried to rule without principles or with a watered-down version of the original revolutionary principles; government under the Directory aimed to be neither royalist nor terrorist, but it was never able to go far beyond an enunciation of what it did not want to be. Napoleon, in contrast, declared his adherence to the principles of revolutionary rhetoric but announced himself to be the voice of the people. In his view, there was no problem about the location of the Nation, charisma, or society's center.

Revolutionary rhetoric was in some sense defeated by its inherent contradictions. While being political, it refused to sanction factional politicking. While showing the power of rhetoric, it denied the legitimacy of rhetorical speech. While representing the new community, it pushed toward the effacing of representation (in

[84] Ibid.

the name of transparency between citizens). While referring to a mythic present, revolutionary rhetoric also had to explain the failures of the present, which it could only lay at the door of conspiracy-politics. In short, as a text, it was constantly subverting its own basis of authority.[85] Yet at the same time the French Revolution set the foundations for much of modern politics, for our notions of political practice, and for many different, conflicting political ideologies.

French revolutionary rhetoric broke through the confines of past politics by positing the existence of a new community (rather than the revival of a purer, former one) and by insisting that it could be realized through politics (rather than through the true religion, a return to past tradition, or an adherence to some previously made social contract). It could be argued that revolutionary politics was restrictively defined in terms of communitarian discipline, since the Revolution did not directly foster the development of liberal politics. Yet those "narrow terms" were in another sense remarkably broad; politics hereafter concerned not just ministers, parliaments, constitutions, interests, or government, but rather the very nature of social relations.[86] Politics was not an arena for the representation of competing interests. It was rather an instrument for reshaping human nature, making citizens out of subjects, free men out of slaves, republicans out of the oppressed.

Even though the integrative functions of revolutionary rhetoric were ultimately stymied, the belief in the possibility of a radically new community proved fruitful beyond all imagining. Despite the failures of 1794 and 1799, an alternative, egalitarian and republican tradition was established, which permanently recast the terms of French political debate and social struggle. For this reason, the Durkheimian position contains an important insight into the working of revolutionary rhetoric. The travails and setbacks of the new community did not make the notion itself a delusion. Or, to re-

---

[85] The analysis presented here of the revolutionary political text can be compared to Derrida's analysis of writing in *Of Grammatology*, trans. by Gayatri Chakravorty Spivak (Baltimore, 1976), esp. part II. Derrida's "metaphysics of presence" and threat of the violence of writing have the same relation of tension as the mythic present (the transparency of the community, the fullness of speech) and the violence of conspiracy-politics. In this sense, revolutionary rhetoric was constantly "deconstructing" itself, that is, at once positing the possibility of a community without politics and inventing politics everywhere.

[86] Some suggestive passages are to be found in Claude Lefort's review of Furet, "Penser la révolution dans la Révolution française," *AESC* 35 (1980): 334–52.

phrase the Tocquevillian line, if the revolutionaries were acting on behalf of an "imaginary ideal society," this did not mean that the results of their so acting were "imaginary" in the least.

Revolutionary rhetoric cannot be explained in the classic Marxist terms: capital, profit, labor, and class were not the structuring principles in revolutionary rhetoric. Nor was the discourse of revolution fashioned by a class in the Marxist sense. But it might nevertheless be termed a "language of class struggle without class." Revolutionary rhetoric was distinctly anti-aristocratic, and it was developed in the first place as an instrument of attack on the old society. Indeed, one of the initial accomplishments of the new rhetoric was its invention of the *ancien régime*. Once French society was rhetorically divided, as it were, into a new Nation and an "old" or former regime, the revolution had been put in motion.[87] The purpose of revolution was to make the cleavage between the two absolute.

Revolutionary rhetoric can be taken as "bourgeois," then, in that it expressed the will to break with the past of aristocratic domination. Revolutionaries did not do this in the name of capitalism, and, in fact, the radicals in particular continued to be deeply troubled by the corruption associated with commerce.[88] Implicit in the desire to break irrevocably with the past was a new valuation of innovation itself. Revolutionize meant to innovate, and self-styled revolutionaries were not afraid of being called "vile innovators." This preoccupation with making things anew may have prevented the revolutionaries from seeing how they fostered a silent aggrandizement of state power in France, but the rhetoric of innovation was not for that reason hallucinatory. Just as the belief in community had opened the way for a tradition of egalitarian and republican politics in France, so too the belief in the radically new character of their experience made possible a continuing tradition of revolutionary politics. After all, Marx got his own faith in the possibility of remaking society through revolution from the French example, but he failed to appreciate the irony and significance of the source of this conviction; the rhetoric of political innovation and

[87] On the invention of the term, see Pierre Goubert, *The Ancien Régime: French Society 1600–1750*, trans. by Steve Cox (New York, 1974), esp. chap. 1.

[88] It would be fruitful to develop Pocock's "Machiavellian Moment" in the French context.

revolution was not the product of the most advanced industrial society, England. The language of revolution was French.

American revolutionary rhetoric did not foster the development of a revolutionary tradition; instead, it fed into constitutionalism and liberal politics. The difference in France was the emphasis on rejecting all models from the national past. Imagine the difficulties of teaching history in republican schools. One elementary text captured the problem in these words: "When leafing through the book of History, or rather the registers of the unhappiness of humanity, the young man will continually encounter kings, great nobles, and everywhere the oppressed, on each page the people counted like a herd of animals."[89] To counter that history of unhappiness, the republicans could only offer the isolated examples of republican Rome, Athens, and Sparta and, closer to their own present, the Swiss and the Americans. None of them had gone as far as the French or had faced as many obstacles. Rousseau, the prophet of revolution, appeared as a kind of miracle—the lone voice of reason and nature in a century of frivolity and cynicism. But that previous history of oppression only served to mark off the magnitude of the revolutionary achievement.

As La Harpe in his cranky fashion recognized, language was the Revolution's "foremost instrument and the most surprising of all." The rhetoric of political innovation made the Revolution "an unheard-of scandal in the universe," for it prompted revolutionaries to embark on uncharted waters seeking the shores of national regeneration and the republic of virtue. Revolutionaries invented new words, but, most important, they gave them new meaning by speaking them in the context of, and for the purpose of, radical political change. It was the persuasive force of their speaking—the rhetoric, not the lexicon—and the exhortation of new secular values, that enabled the Revolution as an experience to jolt the world. Tradition would find its defenders, but, like the other new ideologies, it could never again go unspoken.

[89] As quoted in Louis Trenard, "Manuels scolaires au XVIIIe siècle et sous la Révolution," *Revue du Nord* (1973): 107. See also Jean-François Chassaing, "Les Manuels de l'enseignement primaire de la Révolution et des idées révolutionnaires," in Jean Morange and Jean-François Chassaing, *Le Mouvement de réforme de l'enseignement en France, 1760–1798* (Paris, 1974), esp. pp. 142–43.

$\approx 2 \ll$

Symbolic Forms
of Political Practice

THE FALL of the Bastille, the flight to Varennes, the massacre at the Champ de Mars, the attack on the Tuileries, the fall of the monarchy, the fall of the Girondins, the fall of Robespierre, the purge of the royalists, the purge of the Jacobins, the rise of Napoleon—the succession of revolutionary turning points, the rising and falling of factions, were vertiginous. Each in turn required proclamations, addresses, reports, and eventually festivals and revisions of festivals. Many different kinds of accounts are to be found in these endless productions of words. An instructive local example can be found in a typical proclamation from 1797. In this document, the government's agent (the commissioner of the Executive Directory attached to the departmental administration) in the Isère department published his official commentary on the local reactions to the recent purge of the national legislature. Many deputies had been arrested as supposed royalists, and the elections of scores of others were annulled.

> On learning of *the triumph of the Republic and the Constitution of the Year III* over the *ROYALIST CONSPIRATORS* and of their *escape from the rage of those who wished to destroy them*, it is obviously permitted to every good citizen to show his joy. But why on this occasion were there menaces and provocations between citizens because of dress or different opinions? It is a contravention of the constitutional charter . . . to insult, provoke, or threaten citizens because of their choice of clothing. Let taste and propriety preside over your dress; never turn away from agreeable simplicity. . . . RENOUNCE THESE SIGNS OF RALLYING, THESE COSTUMES OF REVOLT, WHICH ARE THE UNIFORMS OF AN ENEMY ARMY.[1]

[1] A.N., F^{1c} III Isère 9, Correspondance, 1791–1853, "Adresse du Commissaire du

In Grenoble the association of dress with politics had become explosive in 1797. The government's agent wanted to warn against taking dress too seriously, but at the same time he could not help recognizing the power of dress himself. So he concluded with his own warning to those who had taken to wearing the frills and colors associated with the revival of royalism.

The problem of costume was neither new nor limited to Grenoble. Politics were not confined to verbal expression, to the selection of deputies, or to the public debate in clubs, newspapers, and assemblies. Political meaning was closely woven into a variety of symbolic expressions, in which words were only the "foremost instrument," as La Harpe claimed. Different costumes indicated different politics, and a color, the wearing of a certain length of trousers, certain shoe styles, or the wrong hat might touch off a quarrel, a fistfight, or a general street brawl. During the Revolution, even the most ordinary objects and customs became political emblems and potential sources of political and social conflict. Colors, adornments, clothing, plateware, money, calendars, and playing cards became "signs of rallying" to one side or another.[2] Such symbols did not simply express political positions; they were the means by which people became aware of their positions. By making a political position manifest, they made adherence, opposition, and indifference possible. In this way they constituted a field of political struggle.

In revolutionary rhetoric, power came from the Nation (or the people), yet it was never clear how the Nation's will was to be recognized in practice. As Benjamin Constant declared in 1796, "Revolutions efface nuances . . . a torrent levels everything."[3] In the rushing forward of revolutionary events, it was difficult to locate the legitimacy of any government. To "have" power in this situation meant to have some kind of control, however brief, over the articulation and deployment of outward manifestations of the new nation. Speakers in clubs and assemblies tried to claim the right to speak for the nation, but individual voices were often easily

---

pouvoir exécutif près l'administration centrale du département de l'Isère," 2e jour complémentaire an V.

[2] For an overview of the politicization of everyday objects, see Serge Bianchi, *La Révolution culturelle de l'an II: Elites et peuple (1789–1799)* (Paris, 1982).

[3] *De la force du gouvernement actuel de la France et de la necessité de s'y rallier* (1796), p. 10.

overwhelmed. More enduring, because more collective and repro-
ducible, were the symbols and rituals of revolution: liberty trees
and liberty caps, female figures of liberty and the Republic, and ritual occasions as diverse as festivals, school contests, elections, and
club meetings. The ritual forms were as important as the specific
political content. Political symbols and rituals were not metaphors
of power; they were the means and ends of power itself.

The exercise of power always requires symbolic practices. There
is no government without rituals and without symbols, however
demystified or unmagical government may seem.[4] Governing cannot take place without stories, signs, and symbols that convey and
reaffirm the legitimacy of governing in thousands of unspoken
ways. In a sense, legitimacy is the general agreement on signs and
symbols. When a revolutionary movement challenges the legitimacy of traditional government, it must necessarily challenge the
traditional trappings of rule as well. Then it must go about inventing political symbols that will express accurately the ideals and
principles of the new order.

The French Revolution brought the process of symbol making
into particularly sharp relief, because revolutionaries found themselves in the midst of revolution before they had the opportunity to
reflect on their situation. The French did not start out with an organized party or coherent movement; they had no banners and only
a few simple slogans. They invented their symbols and rituals as
they went along. From the *philosophes*, the revolutionaries had
learned that other societies had different kinds of symbols and rituals. But no previous society seemed entirely worthy of emulation.
As Robespierre proclaimed, "The theory of revolutionary government is as new as the revolution which brought it into being. It is
not necessary to search for it in the books of political writers, who
did not foresee this revolution, or in the laws of tyrants, who, content to abuse their power, occupied themselves little with establishing its legitimacy."[5] The past, with its absurd practices, could offer
few guidelines.

[4]Clifford Geertz, "Centers, Kings, and Charisma: Reflections on the Symbolics
of Power," in Joseph Ben-David and Terry Nichols Clark, eds., *Culture and Its Creators: Essays in Honor of Edward Shils* (Chicago, 1977), pp. 150–71. These "reflections"
are more fully developed (though in ways less relevant to Europe) in Geertz, *Negara:
The Theatre State in Nineteenth-Century Bali* (Princeton, 1980).

[5]From his "Rapport sur les principes du gouvernement révolutionnaire," 25 De-

Nevertheless, the French monarchy had demonstrated the power of symbols. The Bourbons had not only drastically circumscribed the political reponsibilities of French subjects, as Tocqueville argued; they had also succeeded in making power virtually coterminous with the symbolic apparatus of monarchy, especially the monarch's person. Power was measured by proximity to the body of the king. To regain their own political responsibilities as citizens, to take power for themselves, the French had to eliminate all of those symbolic connections to monarchy and the king's body. Eventually this took the form of putting the king on trial and executing him in public. Because the Bourbons had emphasized the symbolic trappings of rule, revolutionaries were particularly sensitive to their significance.

The rhetorical matrix of revolutionary politics also enhanced the import of symbolic forms. In the face of ambivalence toward organized politics, especially in the form of parties or factions, new symbols and ceremonies became the most acceptable medium for working out political attitudes. It was not "factional" to plant a liberty tree or wear the colors of the new nation. In the symbolic arena, political conflicts could be engaged without invoking parties or politicians by name. Thus the revolutionaries' passion for the allegorical, the theatrical, and the stylized was not simply a bizarre aberration, but rather an essential element in their effort to mold free men. In the long run, moreover, symbolic forms lent the revolutionary experience psycho-political continuity. Its symbols and rituals gave the Revolution a *longue durée*; they were the tangible reminders of the secular tradition of republicanism and revolution.

In some respects, however, revolutionaries simply expanded on the political practices of the Old Regime. Tocqueville observed long ago that the revolutionaries did not so much smash the monarchical state as they improved on its bureaucracy and administrative powers. The modernizing dreams of the monarchy became reality under the Republic.[6] On the local level as in the national ministries, moreover, there was much continuity between old regime and new; city officials, for example, though elected by a larger por-

---

cember 1793, in *Oeuvres de Maximilien Robespierre* 10 (Discours: 27 juillet 1793–27 juillet 1794) (Paris, 1967): 274.

[6] See, most recently, the lucid book by Clive H. Church, *Revolution and Red Tape: The French Ministerial Bureaucracy, 1770–1850* (Oxford, 1981).

tion of the citizenry than before, still had to take minutes, hold debates, choose committees, pass ordinances, and generally police local life.[7] The minutes of any revolutionary city council have the same tone of dutiful concern as the proceedings of their Old Regime counterparts.

Outside the realm of administration, political activities proliferated despite the revolutionary distaste for politicians and political maneuvering. Clubs, newspapers, pamphlets, posters, songs, dances (all the usual manifestations of political interest "out of doors") developed rapidly between 1789 and 1794. Yet, the large number of newspapers and clubs, however dramatic the contrast with prerevolutionary times, did not make the politics of the Revolution revolutionary; the multiplication of politics outside the halls of government only made France seem more like England or the new United States. What made the French different, what made them seem to themselves and to observers alike "this new race," was their profound conviction that they were establishing a new human community in a present that had no precedent or parallel.

Because revolutionary rhetoric insisted on a complete break with the past, it called into question all customs, traditions, and ways of life. National regeneration required nothing less than a new man and new habits; the people had to be re-formed in the republican mold. Every nook and cranny of everyday life therefore had to be examined for the corruption of the Old Regime and swept out in preparation for the new one. The other side of the coin of the rhetorical refusal of politics was the impulse to invest politics everywhere.[8] Because politics did not take place in a defined sphere, it tended to invade everyday life instead. This politicization of the everyday was as much a consequence of revolutionary rhetoric as the more self-conscious rejection of organized politics. By politicizing the everyday, the Revolution enormously increased the points from which power could be exercised and multiplied the tactics and strategies for wielding that power.[9] By refusing the specifically

[7] An excellent study of municipal government during the Revolution can be found in Christiane Derobert-Ratel, *Institutions et vie municipale à Aix-en-Provence sous la Révolution, 1789–an VIII* (Aix-en-Provence, 1981).

[8] This impulse has been suggestively described by François Furet: "La Révolution française est cet ensemble de pratiques nouvelles qui surinvestit le politique de significations symboliques" (*Penser la Révolution française* [Paris, 1978], p. 73). However, Furet offers little analysis of those "pratiques nouvelles" themselves.

[9] Michel Foucault's analysis of power is potentially more fruitful than Tocqueville's

political, revolutionaries opened up undreamt-of fields for the play of power.

Politics did not invade the everyday all at once, but from the beginning participants and observers alike perceived that something untoward was happening in France, and they experienced and explained those happenings via symbols. In his letter of 16 July 1789 to the English government in London, the Duke of Dorset referred to "the greatest Revolution that we know anything of," and he illustrated this observation by describing the appearance of the cockade in everyone's hat.[10] On 22 July he reported that "the Revolution in the French Constitution and Government may now I think be looked upon as compleated," because the king had recently been forced to visit Paris. In a symbolic procession of acquiescence to the July revolution, "He was actually led in triumph like a tame bear by the Deputies and the City Militia."[11] Symbolic acts such as the donning of the patriotic cockade and the "humiliating" entry of the king into Paris were the clearest signposts of revolutionary change; they were also the first hesitant steps in the making of revolutionary politics.

The potential for political and social conflict became apparent as soon as the first symbols were invented. The cockade is a good example. According to the Duke of Dorset, the first cockades were made of green ribbons, but these were rejected because green was the color of the livery of the Count Artois, the king's much-maligned younger brother.[12] They were soon replaced by a combination of red, white, and blue. Once the tricolor cockade became

---

in this context, but Foucault never analyzes power in a political arena. This chapter develops what might be termed a Foucaultian analysis of politics as the creation of new strategies and tactics for wielding power. The French Revolution, in my view, is a particularly privileged example of this process. For Foucault's definition of power, see his *The History of Sexuality*. 1: *An Introduction* (New York, 1978), esp. pp. 94–95.

[10] PRO, FO 27, France, 32, May–August 1789, letter no. 39.

[11] Ibid., letter no. 42.

[12] Ibid., letter no. 39 (16 July 1789). Dorset claimed that red and white were substituted for green because they were the colors of the Duke of Orleans. Most people assumed, however, that the tricolor cockade or rosette combined the colors of monarchy and those of Paris. See, for example, Albert Mathiez, *Les Origines des cultes révolutionnaires, 1789–1792* (Paris, 1904), p. 30. Whatever the reason for the tricolor combination, the cockade is a good example of the invention of revolutionary symbolism, which Mathiez describes in these terms: "Le symbolisme révolutionnaire, qui s'est formé comme au hasard, sans idées préconçues et sans plan d'ensemble, avec une spontanéité remarquable, au cours des années 1789, 1790 et 1791, fut l'oeuvre commune de la bourgeoisie et du peuple" (p. 29).

4. ENGRAVING ENTITLED "ORGY OF THE GARDES DU CORPS
AT VERSAILLES, OCTOBER 1789"
From Révolutions de Paris, *no. 13. The soldiers are
trampling the tricolor cockade and saluting white and black ones,
according to the accompanying text*
(Photo by Library Photographic Services, University of California, Berkeley)

widely accepted, it took on enormous political significance. Louis'
life quite literally depended on donning it, and rumored "out-
rages" against it precipitated the fateful march of women to Versailles in October 1789. No doubt the women knew they were defending the Revolution when they marched to Versailles, but no
speech about "the Revolution" could have mobilized them the way
the cockade did. They marched when they heard that the soldiers
at Versailles had trampled the tricolor cockade and worn in its place
the white of the Bourbons or the black of the aristocratic counterrevolution. Plate 4 shows the offending scene as it was pictured by
an anonymous engraver. The inclusion of the print in a newspaper
account of the "October days" demonstrates the emotional importance of the symbol. When "the sacred sign of French liberty" was
trampled underfoot, the Nation itself was insulted.[13] Even in these

[13] Quote from the article, "Détails du 3 au 10 octobre 1789: Conjuration formée
par les aristocrates contre notre liberté: Preuves et suite de cette conjuration." *Révolutions de Paris,* no. 13 (article accompanied the engraving, plate 4), vol. 1.

first months of the Revolution, opposing sides in the struggle were given clarity, if they were not actually called into being, by symbols.

Like the cockade, the liberty cap, the patriotic altar, and the liberty tree all appeared in the first months of the Revolution. Each symbol had a different genealogy, but all of them came to be widely accepted. Once invented and broadly diffused, they did not cease to engender contests and confrontations of various sorts. Opponents of the Revolution tore out liberty trees or vandalized them, for instance, and local governments replanted them. The symbols of power were caught up not only in the political struggles of the moment, but also in the more subterranean tensions between officialdom and popular enthusiasms. Officials sometimes tried to get hold of popular symbols by tracing their origins back to the individual who presumably invented the usage. In the Year II, for example, Grégoire wrote an "Historical and Patriotic Essay on the Trees of Liberty" in which he asserted that the first one had been planted in May 1790 by a parish priest in rural Poitou. Historians have now shown, however, that the first "trees" were the maypoles planted by the peasants of the Périgord during their insurrection against local lords in the winter of 1790. The insurrectionary poles often looked like gallows and frequently were hung with menacing slogans. Priests, notables, and national commissioners sent to inquire considered these maypoles "insulting witnesses," "symbols of revolt," and "monuments of insurrection."[14] Before long, nevertheless, the liberty tree became a general symbol of adherence to the Revolution, and, by May 1792, 60,000 liberty trees had been planted all over France.[15]

Once symbols proved their popularity by wide diffusion, they were taken up in more official fashion. All men were *required* to wear the tricolor cockade after 5 July 1792. A few days earlier, the Legislative Assembly had asked every commune to set up a patriotic altar for the reception of newborns. Jacobin clubs and local governments took over the planting of liberty trees and made it into their own kind of ceremony. Ordinances were passed forbidding excessive displays; in Beauvais, for example, officials were dis-

---

[14]Mona Ozouf, *La Fête révolutionnaire, 1789–1799* (Paris, 1976), pp. 280–90.
[15]On the spread of revolutionary symbolism generally, see Maurice Dommanget, "Le Symbolisme et le prosélytisme révolutionnaire à Beauvais et dans l'Oise," *AHRF* 2 (1925): 131–50; 3 (1926): 47–58, 345–62; 4 (1927): 127–34; 5 (1928): 46–57, 442–56; 6 (1929): 372–91; 7 (1930): 41–53, 411–42.

tressed by the practice of dragging opponents to the newly planted tree and forcing them to pay homage.[16] Fences were erected to mark off the sacred ground and regulate its access. The fences, the decrees, and the incorporation of such symbols into official ceremonies and festivals all marked the disciplining of new forms of popular power.

The most telling example of this process of discipline was the systematization of festivals, described so brilliantly by Mona Ozouf.[17] Born in the days of fear, panic, and joy of late 1789 and early 1790, the first "savage" festivals were simple, extemporaneous acts of union either against imagined plots or for the imposition of the new revolutionary symbolism, for example, to plant a liberty tree, to force the wearing of the cockade, or to take an oath of loyalty to the Revolution. The festivals of Federation in 1790 marked the first step in regularization, and, significantly, men in uniform were at the heart of the ceremony. All over France at noon, soldiers, national guards, and officials were to take the oath, which included promises to protect people and property, and to assure the free circulation of grain and the collection of taxes.[18] The popular classes gathered around the edges of the ceremonial space to watch as the tricolor cockade, the patriotic altar, and the other signs of liberty were sanctified by their use in the new state ritual. (See plate 2.) The people's enthusiasm had invested those symbols with meaning in the first place; now official ceremonies regularized them. In this fashion, the popular contribution was at once recognized and partially defused.

As the festivals became more elaborate, a host of increasingly obscure symbols were incorporated into them—some Biblical or Catholic in inspiration, but more often antique or Masonic, and thus inherently less "popular" in resonance. The Masonic level became the symbol of equality, the Roman fasces the symbol of union, the Roman and Gallic laurel the sign of civic virtue, the Egyptian eye the emblem of vigilance, and a host of female goddesses represented not only liberty but also reason, nature, victory,

---

[16] Ibid. 3 (1926).

[17] *La Fête révolutionnaire.* See also Michel Vovelle, *Les Métamorphoses de la fête en Provence de 1750 à 1820* (Paris, 1976).

[18] Anon., *Description de la Fête du Pacte fédératif, du 14 juillet, fixée par la ville, avec le réglement de la police* (Paris, n.d.).

5. SEAL OF THE REPUBLIC, 1792
(*Photo courtesy of the Archives nationales*)

sensibility, pity, charity, and the like.[19] Long processions carried didactic banners and visited edifying, allegorical "stations." Replacing the saints of Catholicism were the new representations of revolution; replacing the priests and vicars of the church were the
officials and pageant-masters of the new regime.[20]

Just as the Counter-Reformation church of the late seventeenth
century had tried to discipline popular religious festivity, so too the
officials of the revolutionary regime tried to discipline popular political festivity. Officials incorporated popular symbols into organized festivals and ceremonies, and they devised their own symbols for popular consumption. The goddess of Liberty is the best
known example, also the most successful. When Liberty was
chosen for the seal of the Republic in 1792 (see plate 5; this choice is
discussed in more detail in chap. 3), she was not an unknown fig-

[19]Revolutionary iconography is most fully deciphered in Jules Renouvier, *Histoire de l'art pendant la Révolution considéré principalement dans les estampes* (Paris, 1863).
See also Dommanget, "Le Symbolisme."

[20]David Lloyd Dowd, *Pageant-Master of the Republic: Jacques-Louis David and the
French Revolution* (Lincoln, Neb., 1948).

ure in French iconography. In 1775 Moreau painted her as a young woman dressed in Roman style with a liberty cap on top of her pike.[21] Liberty evidently appeared first during the Revolution on a medal commemorating the establishment of a new municipal government in Paris in July 1789. Until her elevation in September 1792, she was overshadowed by such figures as the "génie" of France, which appeared on the reverse of the new royal coins released in 1791, Mercury, Minerva, and female figures representing the city of Paris.[22] By the end of the decade, however, Liberty was indelibly associated with the memory of the Republic she had represented. In collective memory, *La République* was "Marianne." The name first given Liberty—the Republic—in derision by opponents of the Revolution soon became a familiar nickname of affection, and her image reappeared in every subsequent republic.[23]

Liberty's poised demeanor on the seal of 1792 evoked little of the frantic violence of the various revolutionary "days" of popular mobilization. Like a Counter-Reformation saint, she represented the virtues so desired by the new order: the transcendence of localism, superstition, and particularity in the name of a more disciplined and universalistic worship. Liberty was an abstract quality based on reason. She belonged to no group, to no particular place. She was the antithesis of those "ridiculous usages, gothic formulas, absurd and puerile etiquette, and the right usurped by the clergy," which radicals had already denounced in 1790.[24] Once Liberty had received official recognition and widespread diffusion, however, she also became more accessible to popular uses. The movement of revolutionary political practice, like that of Counter-Reformation religion, was not one-directional toward discipline.[25]

The most striking example of the malleability of symbols, and of Liberty in particular, was the notorious "Festival of Reason." By

[21] Renouvier, *Histoire de l'art*, p. 401.

[22] Michel Hennin, *Histoire numismatique de la Révolution française*, 2 vols. (Paris, 1826) 1: 32–33.

[23] Maurice Agulhon, *Marianne au combat: L'Imagerie et la symbolique républicaines de 1789 à 1880* (Paris, 1979).

[24] These were the words used to describe "cette fête bisarre [sic] instituée à l'avènement au trône," i.e., the coronation ceremony, by an observer of the Festival of Federation in 1790 (Anon., *Description fidèle de tout ce qui a précédé, accompagné et suivi la cérémonie de la Confédération nationale du 14 juillet 1790* [Paris, n.d.]).

[25] My parallels to Counter-Reformation religion are based on Keith Phillip Luria, "Territories of Grace: Seventeenth-Century Religious Change in the Diocese of Grenoble," Ph.D. diss., University of California, Berkeley, 1982.

decision of the radical Paris city government, the festival in honor of Liberty planned for 10 November 1793 was transformed instead into a "Triumph of Reason." Scheduled originally for the former Palais Royal, the event was moved to Notre Dame to make the attack on Catholicism more explicit. The festivities themselves incorporated a strange mixture of elite and popular themes, which might be expected since the Paris *commune* or city government fancied itself as a kind of mediator between the rationalist vision of the deputies in the Convention and the more down-to-earth concerns of the Parisian lower classes.[26] In the center of the former cathedral sat a mountain, symbol of the left in the Convention. Gracing the mountain was a small temple, engraved with *À la philosophie*. Lining the entry of the temple were busts of the *philosophes*. As one of the organizers noted:

> This ceremony had nothing that resembled Greek and Latin mummery; it went directly to the soul. The instruments did not howl like the snakes of churches. A Republican musical ensemble, placed at the foot of the mountain, played in common language [*en langue vulgaire*], the hymn that the people understood all the better because it expressed natural truths and not mystical and chimerical adulations.[27]

Two rows of young girls dressed in white and crowned with laurel wreaths descended the mountain with torches in their hands and then made their way back up again. At that moment, Liberty, "represented by a beautiful woman," came out of the temple and sat on a throne of greenery to receive the homage of republicans present (see plate 6).

The astounding innovation of the festival and the most unexpected was the appearance of a living woman as Liberty. Three days before, when the city government voted to change the location of the event, it still had in mind the usual presentation of a statue: "the statue of Liberty will be erected in place of that of the

[26] See the analysis in F.-A. Aulard, *Le Culte de la Raison et le culte de l'Etre Suprême (1793–1794)* (Paris, 1892). See also M. J. Guillaume, ed., *Procès-verbaux du Comité d'Instruction publique de la Convention Nationale* 2 (3 juillet 1793–30 brumaire an II [20 novembre 1793]) (Paris, 1894): 803–6.

[27] According to Guillaume (n. 26), the only good description of the festival was that of the *Révolutions de Paris* attributed to Momoro, a departmental administrator and one of the organizers of the festival. Quote from *Procès-verbaux du Comité d'Instruction publique* 2: 805.

6. FESTIVAL OF REASON, NOVEMBER *1793*
Engraving from Révolutions de Paris, *no. 215*
(Photo by Library Photographic Services, University of California, Berkeley)

'former Holy Virgin.'"[28] We do not know how this change came about, but it was mimicked in many provincial towns.[29] Behind the appearance of a living vignette of Liberty (or Reason, or Nature, or Victory—in many places, even in Paris, the distinctions were not always clear to the participants or to the organizers)[30] was the desire for a transparent representation, one that would be so close to nature that it would evoke none of the old fanatical strivings after false images. As one newspaper commented:

> One wanted from the first moment to break the habit of every species of idolatry; we avoided putting in the place of a holy sacrament an inanimate image of liberty because vulgar minds might have mis-

[28] The decision of the Commune was reported in the *Feuille du salut public*, quote in ibid., pp. 803–4
[29] The festivals of reason in the provinces were the highwater mark of the de-Christianization campaign. They were often accompanied by the renunciation of priestly functions, marriages of priests, burning of religious books and artifacts, in short, by a conscious assault on Catholicism as well as by the effort to establish a new civic cult. They are described in detail by Aulard, *Le Culte de la Raison*, pp. 112–94.
[30] Ozouf, *La Fête révolutionnaire*, pp. 116–17.

understood and substituted in place of the god of bread a god of stone . . . and this living woman, despite all the charms that embellished her, could not be deified by the ignorant, as would a statue of stone.

Something which we must never tire of saying to the people is that liberty, reason, truth are only abstract beings. These are not gods, for properly speaking, they are parts of ourselves.[31]

Liberty was to look like an ordinary woman, not like a superstitious icon. Almost everywhere, however, the Liberty chosen was much like a Carnival queen—the most beautiful woman of the village or the neighborhood. The people had made her their own queen for a day. In this way, the radical didactic impulse to repress all idols was appropriated and inverted by popular rituals of festivity. The Convention had had no part in this, at least not officially, and so, once the festival had been presented, the participants marched off to the Convention to invite the deputies to a repeat performance. The people, guided by their local government in Paris, had put on their own play.

The Festival of Reason, as it soon came to be called, showed the complexities at work in the field of symbolic power. The Convention, the Paris city government, local militants, and the general Parisian population all had their own interests and aspirations. The Convention had introduced the Roman goddess of Liberty as an appropriate French replacement for the king as the central symbol of the government and its legitimacy. The deputies wanted an abstract symbol that had little or no resonance with the French monarchical past. At the time of the Festival, the Paris city government was looking for ways to challenge the hold of Catholicism; Liberty was secular, easily associated with reason (both were represented iconographically as female figures), and opposable to the central female figure of Catholicism, the Virgin Mary. The people present were able to convert the abstract, secular goddess into a living Carnival queen, who called to mind the queens of traditional, popular religious rituals. Yet the people only got their living goddess in a decor provided by the Opera, with the participation of the members of the Opera ballet and music from the Opera repertory.[32] The

---

[31] *Les Révolutions de Paris*, no. 215 (23–30 brumaire an II), vol. 17.

[32] Judith Schlanger, "La Représentation du bien," reprinted in Schlanger, *L'Enjeu et le débat* (Paris, 1979), esp. pp. 123–27.

people made Liberty their own only to discover that she was an actress, playing a role for their edification.

The use of symbols to fight political struggles and develop political positions was by no means limited to supporters of the Revolution. In May 1799 the city administration of Toulouse wrote to the Minister of Police in Paris to complain about local demonstrations inspired by a statue of the Black Virgin. The black wooden statue of Notre-Dame-la-Noire had played a prominent part in local religious ceremonies for centuries, and as late as 1785 she had been escorted by the city council in a public procession organized to pray for rain. In 1799 the statue was brought out of hiding and shown again in a local church: "The collections produced immense sums, and all the ridiculous benedictions used by the priests were renewed; everyone wanted a handkerchief, a ring, or a book that had touched the Madonna." The administrators were outraged that "at the end of an enlightened century, we have seen reproduced in our commune those miserable means of fanaticism which only owed their deadly success to the times of ignorance and superstition." The statue was burned a few days later.[33]

In addition to the revival of traditional religious symbols, opponents of revolutionary innovations also revitalized popular Carnival practices. Just before Lent local communities had organized parades, processions, and dances that frequently spilled over into boisterous, even riotous challenges to local authorities. It was common in these festivities to wear masks and dress up in women's clothing. After 1794 members of "anti-terrorist" squads frequently used such means to hide their identities from the authorities. In January 1797 the departmental administration of the Gironde at Bordeaux passed a decree forbidding the use of disguises or masks and in particular outlawed the wearing of "clothes of another sex than one's own." The commissioner of the Executive Directory explained the need for this decree:

> It is under the mask that vengeance audaciously directs its daggers; it is under the mask that vicious people insult and mistreat with impunity those they regard as their enemies; it is under the mask that

[33] A.M., Toulouse, 2D4, "Correspondance de l'administration municipale," letter of 7 prairial an VII. For the history of the statue, see Abbé Degert, "Origine de la Vierge noire de la Daurade," *Bulletin de la Société archéologique du Midi de la France*, no. 31 (1903): 355–58.

the thief and crook find it easy to despoil those whose fortune they envy; it is under the mask that one gives oneself over to the last degree of imprudence in those unrestrained games that bring ruin and desolation to families.[34]

In the official view, masks and disguises facilitated, if they did not actually bring about, virtually every political and moral evil known to man.

These kinds of symbolic resistance to the Revolution were rooted in traditional popular culture. In the sixteenth and seventeenth centuries, local populations used Carnival masks and local saints to defend their collective identities against the incursions of reforming bishops and aspiring local notables. At the end of the Old Regime, such battles lost their bitter edge, but the Revolution revived them with an infusion of new political content. In the eyes of some disgruntled locals, revolutionary ideologues and republican notables had simply taken over from the bishops and landowners of the Old Regime. To convinced republicans, in contrast, Carnival masks and Black Virgins represented everything the Revolution was trying to overcome: royalism, fanaticism, ignorance, superstition, in short, everything reprehensible about the French past. Black Virgins insulted the goddess of Liberty; Carnival masks flew in the face of the transparent citizen.

Republicans knew that these symbolic battles were far from "merely" symbolic, and they frequently took up their symbolic cudgels with a rationalistic vengeance. In 1796 the resolutely republican city administration of Toulouse requested permission to buy a chapel for use as a grain storage facility; later in the same year they tried to turn the former Carmelite convent into a botanical museum; and in 1798 they asked to convert the convent into a grain market.[35] It is not hard to imagine that some people ostentatiously patronized the local Black Virgin in order to demonstrate their rejection of such de-Christianizing measures. Republicans were often mystified by the depth of antagonism these symbolic conflicts aroused. When accused of being a "terrorist," for example, one Toulousain administrator explained, "I have always demonstrated opinions

---

[34] A.N., F^7 3677^9, Police générale, Gironde, "Arrêté de l'administration centrale du département de la Gironde, qui prohibe les Masques et les Travestissements: Séance du 21 nivôse an V de la République française, une et indivisible."

[35] A.N., C 400 (no. 290), 402 (no. 327), 432 (no. 175).

based on the most mellow philanthropy"; and he cited Rousseau, Voltaire, and Helvétius as the source of his "moral principles."[36] Such principles led ineluctably to battles with the Catholic church and Old Regime symbols.

Revolutionaries could only hope to win their "symbolic" battles if they succeeded in educating their public. An intense course in political education was necessary to teach the people to distinguish between the Liberty of their republican present and the Black Virgin of their royalist past. As a consequence, the political practice of republicans was fundamentally didactic; republicans had to teach the people how to read the new symbolic text of revolution. Teaching began most obviously with the nation's children. A new generation of true republicans could only be created through a system of organized, national, lay public instruction. As Romme maintained in his report of 1793, "the constitution will give to the nation a political and social existence; public instruction will give it a moral and intellectual existence."[37]

Accordingly, the various assemblies of the Revolution developed ambitious projects for the restructuring of all levels of education. The Catholic Church's control over education was broken, and primary education was opened to all children, regardless of social background. The school "master" was replaced by a secular, state-paid instructor (*instituteur*, literally, the one who would found new values).[38] Although most of these plans were left hanging due to lack of time and money, and the more radical notions of equality and free schooling were abandoned after 1795, scores of instructional manuals and "republican catechisms" were published and distributed to the new schoolteachers.[39] In theory, schoolchildren

[36] A letter from Jacques Vaysse to the local right-wing paper, *L'Anti-Terroriste*, 2 *messidor an III* (20 June 1795).

[37] *Rapport sur l'instruction publique considérée dans son ensemble, suivi d'un projet de décret . . . présentés à la Convention Nationale, au nom du comité d'instruction publique, par G. Romme* (Paris, 1793).

[38] The best summary of the legislation on primary education can be found in Maurice Gontard, *L'Enseignement primaire en France de la Révolution à la loi Guizot (1789–1833)* (Lyon, 1959), pp. 79–188.

[39] For a general discussion of catechisms, see Jean-François Chassaing, "Les Manuels de l'enseignement primaire de la Révolution et les idées révolutionnaires," in Jean Morange and Jean-François Chassaing, *Le Mouvement de réforme de l'enseignement en France, 1760–1798* (Paris, 1974), pp. 97–184. See also Emmet Kennedy, "The French Revolutionary Catechisms: Ruptures and Continuities with Classical, Chris-

were supposed to learn the Declaration of the Rights of Man and Citizen, the territorial divisions of the Republic, republican poems and hymns, and the principles of republican government in addition to French grammar, reading, and writing, a little natural history, and the examples provided by previous republics. The local administrators who were charged with supervising education often found, however, that teachers were lacking in numbers and preparation and all too often lacking in enthusiasm for the new order as well.[40]

In any case, republicans could not afford to wait for the formation of a new generation, so they put most of their efforts into the re-formation of adults. One of the most important "Jacobin schools" was the army of 1792–94.[41] Deputies were sent on mission from the Convention to each of the armies in the field to supervise the republican discipline of the soldiers and their officers. They arrested presumed traitors, set up revolutionary tribunals, and distributed bulletins, addresses, proclamations, instructions, and even newspapers. The government subsidized five thousand subscriptions to the Jacobin paper, *Journal des hommes libres*, and over nine months sent as many as one million copies of the *Père Duchesne* directly to the army. At the zenith of its propaganda efforts, the Convention sent the army 30 thousand newspapers a day.[42] In addition, there were victory festivals planned especially for the army's benefit, and many civic festivals included the military in great numbers. The assessment behind these efforts was made clear by a lieutenant who wrote to an official in the War ministry asking for yet more newspapers: "The soldier is good-hearted, but he needs to be enlightened."[43]

---

tian, and Enlightenment Moralities," *Studies on Voltaire and the Eighteenth Century* 199 (1981): 353–62.

[40] On the realities of education, see G. Chianéa, "L'Enseignement primaire à Grenoble sous la Révolution," *Cahiers d'histoire* 17 (1972): 121–60. A more positive view of the Revolution's accomplishments can be found in Emmet Kennedy and Marie-Laurence Netter, "Les Ecoles primaires sous le Directoire," *AHRF* 53 (1981): 3–38.

[41] Jean-Paul Bertaud, *La Révolution armée: Les Soldats-Citoyens et la Révolution française* (Paris, 1979), pp. 194–229.

[42] Marc Martin, *Les Origines de la presse militaire en France à la fin de l'Ancien Régime et sous la Révolution (1770–1799)* (Paris, 1975), pp. 149–227.

[43] The lieutenant requested in particular the *Père Duchesne* and *L'Ombre de Marat* (Arthur Chuquet, *Lettres de 1793* [Paris, 1911], pp. 162–63).

Even revolutionary officials had to be educated for their new roles. To this purpose, the national government poured out an unending stream of bulletins of information and detailed explanations of bureaucratic duties and rationales. The national government demanded regular accounts of its agents in the departments, who in turn demanded reports from their agents in the municipalities. The regular, uniform collection of information insured that the government would keep in touch with public opinion and, at the same time, keep its agents and the lower levels of the bureaucracy reminded of its loyalties. A letter from the Directory's commissioner in the Vendée department captures the spirit of this enterprise. He wrote to the commissioners attached to the municipal administrations of the department reminding them that they were to send in "an analytical account" of the situation in their area every *décade* (every ten days according to the new revolutionary calendar). He complained of the lack of zeal shown by many and insisted, "I have the right to expect a methodical precision from you, reasoned results, a few new views, and especially, exactness." To encourage them, he sent along printed forms divided into columns with spaces for each query. As he concluded, the zeal (a word he used several times in the letter) of officials was essential to the "perfectioning of the political machine."[44]

National education, propagandizing in the army, and the enforcement of bureaucratic routine were strategies for the extension of power. They contributed to the "perfectioning of the political machine" by incorporating officials and ordinary citizens alike into the republican state. Never before had such an ambitious program of political discipline been undertaken. After the declaration of the Republic in September 1792, republican officials saw the potential for struggle between the forces of regeneration and the forces of counterrevolutionary conspiracy almost everywhere. Newspapers, army uniforms, bureaucratic forms, and schoolbooks were political symbols as much as cockades and liberty trees. But now even the measures of space, time, and weight came into question. Everyone should speak the same language, use the same weights and measures, and turn in the old coinage. A commission worked on establishing the metric system, and the Convention instituted a new cal-

[44] A.N., F^{1c} III Vendée 7, Correspondance et divers, 1789–1815, letter dated 28 prairial an VI.

endar. In place of the seven-day week, there would be a ten-day "decade," with no variation from month to month. In place of the names of the "vulgar epoch," the names of months and days would reflect nature and reason. Germinal, Floréal, and Prairial (late March–late June), for instance, called to mind the buds and flowers of springtime, while primidi, duodi, etc. ordered the days rationally without the help of saints' names.[45] In Toulouse, city officials went so far as to contract with a clockmaker to "decimalize" the clock on city hall.[46] Even clocks could offer witness to the Revolution.

The government of the Revolution had an hierarchical arrangement that was accentuated when the radicals took over after 1792. The assembly (in 1792–95, the National Convention) in Paris organized the central government, and it expected authority to flow down from it to the departments and ultimately to the municipalities. Yet, even though the Convention passed the laws and decrees restructuring education, the army, and the bureaucracy, the strategies and tactics of power did not simply trickle down and outward from Paris. Just as some revolutionary symbols came out of popular practices, so too some of the tactics of political reeducation originated locally. In 1789, local governments developed bureaucratic procedures on their own before the deputies in Paris had even considered reorganizing the bureaucracy.[47] In some departments, local administrations tried to reorganize public education before the Convention agreed on a plan.[48] Moreover, the success of government activities in these areas depended in large measure on the "zeal" of locals.

During most of the Revolution, but especially in 1792 and 1793, political mobilization took place primarily outside of regular, offi-

---

[45] For a brief account, see Bianchi, *La Révolution culturelle de l'an II*, pp. 198–203. The revolutionary years began on 22 September (23 September in Year VIII and IX). The names of the months (from September) were Vendémiaire, Brumaire, Frimaire, Nivôse, Pluviôse, Ventôse, Germinal, Floréal, Prairial, Messidor, Thermidor, and Fructidor. The five extra days (each month had 30 days) were called *jours complémentaires*. In the Year II they were celebrated as *sans-culottides*.

[46] M. J. de Rey-Pailhade, "Etude historique sur l'emploi du calendrier républicain et sur le temps décimal à Toulouse pendant la Révolution," *Bulletin de la Société de Géographie de Toulouse* 27 (1908): 429–57.

[47] Lynn Hunt, *Revolution and Urban Politics in Provincial France: Troyes and Reims, 1786–1790* (Stanford, 1978), pp. 81–82.

[48] The department of the Gers, for example, passed a detailed decree in November 1793 setting the course of instruction in primary schools (G. Brégail, *L'Instruction publique dans le Gers pendant la période révolutionnaire* [Auch, 1899], pp. 3–6).

cial government channels. The clubs, the popular societies, and the newspapers took on themselves the responsibility for converting local populations, including local army garrisons, to the republican cause. Women's clubs and societies of artisans and shopkeepers explicitly devoted themselves to republican self-improvement. A "patriotic society" of artisans and shopkeepers was formed in Bordeaux in 1790, for example, because "since every man is a member of the state, the new order of things can call anyone to the public administration." The purpose of the society was to educate every man to those potential responsibilities by discussing the decrees of the national assembly and reading newspapers and periodicals.[49]

In short, the power of the revolutionary state did not expand because its leaders manipulated the ideology of democracy and the practices of bureaucracy to their benefit; power expanded at every level as people of various stations invented and learned new political "microtechniques."[50] Taking minutes, sitting in a club meeting, reading a republican poem, wearing a cockade, sewing a banner, singing a song, filling out a form, making a patriotic donation, electing an official—all these actions converged to produce a republican citizenry and a legitimate government. In the context of revolution, these ordinary activities became invested with extraordinary significance. Power, consequently, was not a finite quantity possessed by one faction or another; it was rather a complex set of activities and relationships that created previously unsuspected resources. The surprising victories of the revolutionary armies were only the most dazzling consequence of this discovery of new social and political energy.

Although revolutionary political practice multiplied the strategies and tactics of power, it also incorporated the same tensions that beset revolutionary rhetoric. Most important was the tension between the belief in the possibility of transparency and the need

[49]Pierre Bécamps, "La Société patriotique de Bordeaux (1790–1792), " *Actes du 82e Congrès-National des sociétés savantes. Bordeaux. 1957* (Paris, 1958), pp. 255–83, esp. p. 257.

[50]See the analysis of Michel Foucault, *Discipline and Punish: The Birth of the Prison*, trans. by Alan Sheridan (New York, 1979), esp. pp. 135–94. The microtechniques of political power can be compared to Foucault's "hundreds of tiny theatres of punishment" (p. 113) except that, in the French Revolution, these techniques were as potentially liberating as they were incarcerating.

for didacticism. If the truth and justice of the people's will were self-evident, that is, engraved in all men's hearts, then the people's will had only to be voiced in order for virtue to reign supreme. Political mechanisms were therefore secondary, if not irrelevant, at least in theory. As Robespierre claimed, "Virtues are simple, modest, poor, often ignorant, sometimes coarse; they are the attribute of the unfortunate, and the patrimony of the people."[51] If every heart was transparent, then virtue would shine. And if men were virtuous, then a republic of virtue followed almost automatically. Politics were only necessary in corrupt societies; indeed, the very existence of politics was a sign that society was corrupt. The practice of revolution could only consist, then, in freeing the people's will from the fetters of past oppression.

Yet the experience of the Revolution showed that ignorance and superstition were not so easily overcome. Robespierre himself recognized this problem when he confessed, "We have raised the temple of liberty with hands still withered by the irons of despotism."[52] At the end of the decade, Madame de Staël concluded that "the Republic arrived in France before the enlightenment which should have prepared the way for the Republic."[53] As a consequence, revolutionaries had to place great faith in their ability to reshape society and the individual in a very short time. To this end, they mobilized enormous pedagogical energies and politicized every possible aspect of daily life. Transparency could only work if didacticism prepared the way.

The tension between transparency and didacticism can be seen in the elaboration of symbols of power. Popularly "invented" symbols, such as the cockade and the liberty tree, had to be incorporated into the symbolic repertoire because they seemed to represent the voice of the people. But at the same time officials worked to discipline these popular forms and to impose their own (such as Liberty, the female representation of the Republic) in order to further the education of the people in their rights and duties. Governmental discipline was only legitimate, however, if it promised to re-

---

[51] *Oeuvres* 10: 278.

[52] As quoted in Alfred Cobban, "The Political Ideas of Robespierre, 1792–5." *Aspects of the French Revolution* (New York, 1968), p. 192.

[53] *Des Circonstances actuelles qui peuvent terminer la Révolution et des principes qui doivent fonder la République en France*, ed. by John Viénot (Paris, 1906), p. 33.

store the voice of the people and the values dictated by nature and reason. Didacticism was justified by the belief in transparency.

At times the tension between transparency and didacticism was expressed as a contrast between words and images, between verbal and visual representations. Republican leaders attached extraordinary significance to words, especially in extended prose form. A peasant might hang his maypole with a menacing slogan, and poor journeymen and dayworkers in the city were able to understand rough placards that threatened grain merchants. Republican leaders expected much more from words; they were the sign and the guarantee of liberty, but they were also a means of discipline through interpretation. Spontaneous popular festivities required no proclamations, but every one of the organized Parisian festivals was accompanied by printed programs, banners of identification, and images engraved with words. Judith Schlanger calls this the "discursive foundation of political didacticism": "the inscriptions manifest the belief in the superiority of the clarifying function [*l'explicitation*] of saying over the pregnancy of showing."[54]

Verbal explanation was essential because the symbolic framework of the Revolution required constant clarification. Revolutionary political culture was by nature continually in flux; the mythic present was always being updated. New symbols and images appeared every few months, and "old" images went through frequent modifications. In the fluid political situation of the Revolution, the "normal" uncertainty involved in reading images and symbols was exacerbated, and as a consequence verbal texts seemed all the more necessary as supplements. The speeches, the banners, and the inscriptions directed the attention of participants and spectators; they repressed unwanted readings and elicited "correct" ones.[55] In addition the speeches and the texts ensured the continuity of revolutionary experience. Although offices changed hands repeatedly (see chapters 5 and 6), and many symbols were altered, the principles of interpretation remained much the same.

No other issue demonstrates the tension between transparency and didacticism more dramatically than the question of revolution-

[54] "Le Peuple au front gravé," in *L'Enjeu et le débat*, pp. 163–64.

[55] On the relationship between words and images, see Roland Barthes, "Rhetoric of the Image," in his *Image, Music, Text*, trans. by Stephen Heath (New York, 1977), pp. 32–51.

ary dress. From the beginning of the Revolution, clothing was invested with political significance. When the Estates General opened with a ceremonial procession on 4 May 1789, for example, many observers were struck by the court's insistence on different costumes for the different orders: the deputies of the Third Estate were to wear somber black, while the nobles wore gold braiding, white hose, lace cravats, and gracious white plumes in their hats.[56] As the visitor John Moore remarked, the distinction in dress not only caused offense but also precipitated a revolution of sorts in political apparel: "So that in a short time a little black cloak on a brown thread-bare coat became respectable; and afterwards, when the cloaks were laid aside . . . a great plainness or rather shabbiness of dress was . . . considered as a presumption of patriotism."[57]

In the early years after 1789 revolutionaries emphasized the elimination of odious distinctions of dress. Religious costumes were abolished, and the only distinction allowed municipal officers, for example, was a tricolor scarf.[58] At the same time, certain aspects of personal decoration might signal adherence or antipathy to the Revolution; the color of one's cockade and even the material of the cockade (wool was less pretentious than silk) were significant. After 1792, social equality became an increasingly important consideration in dress. Some aspiring politicians began to wear the short jacket, long trousers, and even the clogs of the sans-culottes, the urban popular classes.[59] Militants of the sections in Paris frequently wore the red Phrygian bonnet or liberty cap (in wool, of course), though most bourgeois leaders disdained such displays and continued to wear breeches and ruffled shirts.

In May 1794 the concern with dress culminated in a request to the artist-deputy David; the Committee on Public Safety asked him to present his views on improving national costume and on ways

[56] *Costume de Cérémonie de Messieurs les Députés des trois Ordres aux Etats-généraux* (Paris, 1789).

[57] *A View of the Causes and Progress of the French Revolution*, 2 vols. (London, 1795) 1: 150.

[58] Religious costume was addressed in October and November 1790, March 1791, and August 1792. The scarf for municipal officials was decreed 20 March 1790. See Yves-Claude Jourdain, *Table générale alphabétique des matières contenues dans les décrets rendus par les assemblées nationales de France, depuis 1789, jusqu'au 18 brumaire an 8* (Paris, an X).

[59] Jennifer Harris, "The Red Cap of Liberty: A Study of Dress Worn by French Revolutionary Partisans, 1789–1794," *Eighteenth-Century Studies* 14 (1981): 283–312.

to make it more appropriate to republican and revolutionary character. The most rational way to ensure the appearance of equality and to eliminate the expression of political differences through dress was to invent a national civil uniform.[60] The committee liked his designs well enough to order 20,000 copies of the engravings for distribution to public officials all over the country. In a recent study of revolutionary dress, Jennifer Harris concluded that David drew from historical, theatrical, and contemporary sources for his civil costume. The short, open tunic worn with close-fitting hose seemed to recall Renaissance fashion; the cloaks were reminiscent of classical drapery.[61]

Even more striking than the eclecticism and classicism of David's design is his obvious avoidance of the dress of the sans-culottes. If all men were to look alike, they were to do so in a suitably high-minded fashion. The leveling, if it was to take place, was to take place upward and not downward. Rather than representing a radical impulse toward equality, David's designs expressed a bourgeois fantasy of playing out the classics. In practice, it was obvious that only a bourgeois elite could afford to take on the role, and David's costumes were never manufactured. Nevertheless, the committee's request and David's response to it have more than anecdotal interest. They were part of an ongoing quest for the look of the republican. Dress, the mode of appearance, was an important aspect of the definition of revolutionary practice.

The search for an appropriate revolutionary costume incorporated all the ambiguities of revolutionary politics. Not only was David's project for civilian costume very different from the dress of the sans-culottes, but it was also only one part of a larger endeavor to provide distinctive costumes for military, legislative, judicial, and administrative functions as well. Six thousand copies of each of the engravings of these official costumes were ordered at the same time.[62] Although official costume was designed by David to look much like civilian costume, it was nonetheless distinct. Judges and legislators, for example, were to wear ankle-length cloaks.[63]

[60]Ibid., p. 299. A.N., AF II 66, Comité de Salut Public, Esprit public, Dossier 489: "Arts, Caricatures, Costume national, 1793-an III," piece no. 15, signed by Barère, Collot d'Herbois, Prieur, Carnot, Billaud-Varenne, and Robespierre.
[61]"The Red Cap," p. 307.   [62]A.N., AF II 66, piece no. 19.
[63]Harris, "The Red Cap," p. 307.

The people were supposed to be able to recognize their representatives. Dress seemed to inevitably entail difference and differentiation. Two contradictory impulses were involved in David's project. On the one hand, the deputies or representatives of the people were supposed to be simply a transparent reflection of the people, that is, just like them, because part of them. For this reason, everyone was supposed to wear a new national uniform that would efface differences. On the other hand, the representatives were obviously other, different, not like the people exactly because they were the teachers, the governors, the guides of the people. Accordingly, the uniforms of officials were to be just distinct enough to permit recognition.

After the fall of Robespierre and the end of the Terror, the idea of civilian costume faded away. But official costume continued to preoccupy legislators. In October 1794 the reconstituted Committee of Public Safety agreed to pay the engraver Denon for his reproductions of David's designs; he was paid almost 20,000 francs for a total of nearly 30 thousand prints.[64] One of the last acts of the Convention was to pass a law prescribing official costume for the new Directory government: costumes were to be designed for the members of the two Councils, the Executive Directory, the ministers, state messengers, bailiffs, the judiciary, justices of the peace, and departmental and municipal administrations (25 October 1795).[65]

The law on official costume adopted in 1795 was based primarily on Grégoire's report of 14 September 1795. He provided the clearest rationale for official dress: "The language of signs has an eloquence of its own; distinctive costumes are part of this idiom for they arouse ideas and sentiments analogous to their object, especially when they take hold of the imagination with their vivid-

[64] A.N., AF II 66, pieces nos. 40–50.
[65] The deputy Boissier opened the session with a new presentation by the Committee on Public Instruction on costumes, but his project was denounced on the floor as resembling the dress of a Jacobin. Chénier declared that current dress would not do: "Les tableaux ou les statues ne supporteront jamais la mesquinerie de notre habit actuel, et le retreci de nos draperies. C'est cette forme de nos habits qui a rendu presque inéxécutable le beau tableau du Serment du Jeu de Paume." Chénier's view reveals much of the thinking behind costumes; the deputies felt it necessary to dress the part of great men and this was only possible in the costume of ancient times. Hearing this, the Convention voted to adopt Grégoire's project instead. *Réimpression de l'Ancien Moniteur* 26:165 (12 brumaire an IV [3 November 1795]).

ness."[66] Costumes were not disguises or masks, but rather a means of enhancing the perception of natural truths. "The costume of the public official says to the citizens: Here is the man of the law. . . . A free people does not want an idol, but in everything it wants order, good customs, justice; a free people honors itself, respects itself, when honoring, respecting its legislators, its magistrates, in other words, its own work [*ouvrage*]."[67] Costumes for public officials would serve two related purposes: they would help delineate a specific political sphere by marking off public officials from the rest of the population, and in the process they would serve to establish greater political discipline, or what Grégoire called respect for legislators. The people would know they were represented and would be encouraged to honor and respect that representation as both distinct from themselves and emanating from their will.

When Grégoire spoke in 1795, he was concerned to avoid the democratic "excesses" associated with the reign of Terror:

> The costume will have not only the advantage of distinguishing in a certain manner the legislators, but also without doubt that of fixing a little French vivacity: from now on, the site of sessions will no longer be an unstable scene whose corridors are blocked without cease by those who are going in and out; the sessions will be perhaps less frequent or less long. . . . And this whirlwind of events and passions that in the space of three years has given birth to fifteen thousand decrees will be dissipated. Then we will save more time, which is the most precious thing after truth and virtue. All the sessions will be full of things, and the legislature, by the gravity of its bearing and the dignity of its costume, will recall the majesty of the nation.[68]

In this passage, Grégoire reveals how much the deputies expected from something as seemingly trivial as a toga [see plate 7]. By fixing the identity of the legislator, the costume would sharply differentiate between represener and represented, between the representatives of the nation and the people. Sessions would no longer be disturbed by those in the gallery who imagined themselves to have equal voice and who in the past were dressed much like those on

[66] *Du Costume des fonctionnaires publics: Rapport fait par Grégoire (Séance du 28 fructidor an III).*
[67] Ibid.
[68] Ibid.

7. SESSION OF THE COUNCIL OF ANCIENTS, *1798–99*
(Photo from Cabinet des Estampes, courtesy of the Bibliothèque nationale)

the floor. In other words, political differentiation and political order were to be produced by official costume. While debating about
cloaks and hats, the deputies were developing their notions about
politics, representation, and hierarchy.

Official costume continued to occupy the deputies for several
years. Grégoire's report called for long robes of different colors and
velvet hats [see plate 8]. Red, white, and blue were not surprisingly
the dominant colors, and all the cloth was supposed to come from
France. In November 1797 the Councils recognized that Grégoire's
project was too difficult to complete, so they simplified the task by
making the costumes of all deputies the same: a "French" coat of
"national blue," a tricolor belt, a scarlet cloak *à la grecque*, and a velvet hat with tricolor aigrette.[69] Despite some difficulties with deliv-
eries, the deputies were able to begin wearing their costumes in

[69] A.N., C 519 (no. 194). "Extrait du procès-verbal des séances du Conseil des
Cinq-Cents," 29 brumaire an VI.

8. OFFICIAL COSTUMES, 1798–99
(Photo from Cabinet des Estampes, courtesy of the Bibliothèque nationale)

February of the following year.[70] The public reception was not as enthusiastic as Grégoire had hoped. The *Moniteur* observed that "this great quantity of red clothing fatigues the eyes extremely; yet it must be admitted that this costume has in it something beautiful, imposing and truly senatorial." Nevertheless, the editor warned, only regular and consistent wearing of the outfit would stifle possible sarcasm.[71] One foreign visitor to Paris found the legislative costume "quite noble and picturesque; but, as it is too far removed from ordinary dress, it has a theatrical air . . . and this defect keeps it from being, at least for now, seriously dignified and truly imposing."[72]

Under the Directory regime (1795–99), the concern with civilian

[70]The cloaks were mistakenly confiscated in Lyon as English contraband! (A.N., C 521 [no. 225], "Résolutions du Conseil des Cinq-Cents approuvées par le Conseil des Anciens," 27 nivôse an VI).

[71] *Réimpression de l'Ancien Moniteur* 29: 158 (3 ventôse an VI [21 February 1798]).

[72]Henri Meister, *Souvenirs de mon dernier voyage à Paris (1795)* (Paris, 1910), p. 106.

dress did not disappear, even though the legislature had given up on the notion of a civilian uniform. Dress had never ceased being a personal freedom (it was declared a right by the Convention on 29 October 1793), yet as late as December 1798 the Council of Five Hundred discussed the possibility of punishing those who did not wear the national cockade and forbidding foreigners to wear it at all.[73] Outside the halls of the legislature, the "signs of rallying" continued to be as potentially divisive as ever. In 1798 an illustrated brochure entitled *Caricatures politiques* described the five "classes" of men who could be found among republicans.[74] The classes were distinguishable by their principles, their banners, and their mottos, that is, their politics. But they were even more readily recognizable by their everyday dress or costume and by their "genres," or demeanor in the world.

The "independents" were clearly the true republicans; they were "well-educated and capable of great things." In appearance, they had a proud and noble look, an assured demeanor, clean clothes, white linen; and they usually wore close-fitting pants of fine cloth, ankle boots, morning coats, and round hats (plate 9). In contrast, the "exclusives" were of a brusque, "suspecting," and restless humor (plate 10). Their eyes did not accommodate well to the daylight; they felt more at home in darkness (a none-too-subtle reference to their less-than-civilized nature). Their hair was ordinarily neglected; their clothing sometimes dirty. They wore short jackets, pants of common wool, and shoes tied with leather straps. They donned outlandish hats and most of the time could be found smoking short clay pipes, which gave them horribly bad breath. The "exclusives" were the militant leaders of the sans-culottes.

You could tell a good republican by how he dressed. The right dress was a sign of virtue, and dress in general made manifest the political character of the person. The costume of a true republican was predictable, whereas the "sell-outs" (*les achetés*) never had their own look, the "systematics" changed every two weeks, and the "fat cats" (*les enrichis*) wore whatever pleased them as long as it was glittering and luxurious. This refinement of categorization based on dress was most typical of political concerns under the Di-

[73] Reported in the *Moniteur* on 15 frimaire an VII (5 December 1798) and 7 nivôse an VII (27 December 1798).
[74] Signed Beauvert, an VI.

9. "THE INDEPENDENT"
(Photo courtesy of the Bibliothèque nationale)

rectory. After the fall of Robespierre, political distinctions became
more and more complicated, and as a result ascertaining the look
of a republican became an increasingly delicate and subtle operation. Even among republicans, there were five classes of men.

Civilian and official costume became such a focus of concern because dress was a political sign. Under the Old Regime, the different orders and many professions and trades had been identified
by their clothing: nobles, clergymen, judges, and even masons
were known by what they wore. Revolutionaries wanted to break
with the system of invidious social distinctions, but they continued
to believe that dress revealed something about the person. Dress
was, as it were, politically transparent: you could tell a person's political character from the way he or she dressed. At its most extreme, this conviction led to the search for an appropriate civilian
uniform. If virtue was to be found equally in every class or group,

10. "THE EXCLUSIVE"
(Photo courtesy of the Bibliothèque nationale)

then there was no justification for social or political distinctions of dress. All true republicans should look alike.

On the other hand, republicans recognized the distance their new nation had to travel before becoming truly free. The people had to be recast first in the republican mold. Dress in this perspective was not a reflection of character; it was a way of remaking character. Wearing a national civil uniform would make citizens more national, more uniformly republican, just as speaking French rather than dialect would make them more nationally minded and civic spirited. Wearing red togas would make legislators more serious in their bearing and consequently make the political process itself more successfully republican. Dress was not so much the measure as the maker of the man.

The uncertainties about the political meaning of dress were made even more acute by the republican confusions about equality.

The Directory politicians knew they had to confront this issue head-on because they wanted to avoid what they considered the excesses of the previous regime. Hence the author of the *Caricatures politiques* explicitly distanced the good republicans ("the independents") from the sincere, but brutish, sans-culottes ("the exclusives"). The bourgeois social element in this distinction was not hard to detect; good republicans dressed like good bourgeois, without the pretensions associated with the aristocracy of the Old Regime. Even in the midst of the Terror, the deputies in the Convention had worried about the deterioration of standards of dress and personal behavior. Grégoire spoke for the Jacobin government when he denounced "this practice of foul talk whose contagion has even overtaken many women. . . . This degradation of the language, of taste and of morality is truly counterrevolutionary. . . . A decent, careful [*soigné*] language is alone worthy of the exquisite feelings [*sentiments exquis*] of a republican." [75] He might as well have substituted dress for speech in this passage. If there was hope for the lower classes, it was the hope that they would learn to emulate their betters; their betters did not wish to degrade themselves.

The chief confusion about equality was not social, however, but political. Few if any of the Jacobin leaders believed that everyone should be or could be socially equal; few of them wanted to look like sans-culottes. Like Rousseau, the Jacobins believed that extremes of inequality were dangerous, but they did not imagine that the government could do other than ameliorate gross inequities. The more pressing problem was posed by democracy and in particular by the relation between the people and its representatives. Even the Directorials believed that the people should participate in government through frequent elections; the representatives should be, as Grégoire said, their *ouvrage*. But what were the limits on this relationship? As the Revolution moved forward, there seemed to be none. A constant stream of petitions, letters, and addresses brought the people's demands to the attention of the deputies. When the Assembly moved to Paris in October 1789, the legislators found themselves face to face with the people of Paris, who were not reluctant to vocalize their likes and dislikes within the precincts of the legislature. In mid-May 1793 the Convention moved to new

[75] *Rapport sur les inscriptions des monuments publics, par le citoyen Grégoire (séance du 22 nivôse an 2).*

quarters in the *Salle de Spectacle* of the Tuileries, making audience participation all the more possible. Even then, Robespierre was not satisfied; he suggested that the Convention build a meeting place large enough to hold 12 thousand spectators, for only then would the general will, the voice of reason, and the public interest be heard.[76] Popular participation was to be taken quite literally.

After the experience of extended democracy in 1793–94, one of the primary concerns of the writers of the new Constitution of the Year III (1795) was to limit the number and role of spectators.[77] Robespierre's successors believed that the lines between the people and their representatives had to be more clearly drawn. The political arena had to be more sharply delineated if political life was to have any prospect of stability. As Grégoire claimed, official costumes would distinguish the legislators "in a certain manner" and eliminate the "unstable scene" that disturbed the working of legislative sessions. Official costume was not justified because it would reestablish social hierarchy but because it would encourage proper republican (political) respect. Legislators, judges, administrators, and military officers were not necessarily socially better, at least not in theory, but they were politically different. The deputies hoped that official costumes would stabilize the system of political signs and eliminate the constant uncertainties in political interpretation. Official dress would identify the voice of the nation.

The costumes did not instill new political habits as quickly as the deputies hoped, and the bright red togas did not prevent the rise of Napoleon. Among those in scarlet robes were the men who brought Bonaparte into the corridors of power. Republicanism was indeed a state of mind more than a fashion. Yet, for all the outlandishness and bombast of these efforts, republicans had learned an important and enduring set of truths. The apprenticeship of republicanism did require new habits and new customs, if not new costumes. The Republic could not survive without a circumscribed political arena, respect for legislators, and a politically educated populace. The survival of republicanism after the fall of the Re-

[76] Joseph Butwin, "The French Revolution as *Theatrum Mundi*," *Research Studies* 43 (1975): 141–52, esp. pp. 144–45.
[77] Although the sessions of the Councils were open to the public, the number of spectators was limited to half the number of deputies (*Projet de Constitution pour la République française et discours préliminaire prononcé par Boissy-D'Anglas, au nom de la Commission des Onze, dans la séance du 5 Messidor an III* [Niort, n.d.], pp. 93–94).

public and the remarkable similarities between political practice under the Directory and politics under the long-lived Third Republic show that the republicans of the 1790s were not utopian dreamers. Their red togas did not catch on, and many Black Virgins survived. But Marianne, political banquets, red caps, the tricolor flag, and "Liberty, Equality, Fraternity" all became part of a standard repertoire of opposition and contestation. At the time, who could have predicted which would last and which would fade? It was only in the strife of the moment, the helter-skelter of republican politics, that the symbols and rituals of republicanism were tried, tested, and ultimately chosen. Without them, there would have been no collective memory of republicanism and no tradition of revolution.

$\backsim 3 \backsim$

The Imagery
of Radicalism

ALL POLITICAL AUTHORITY requires what Clifford Geertz calls a "cultural frame" or "master fiction" in which to define itself and make its claims. The legitimacy of political authority depends on its resonance with more global, even cosmic cultural presuppositions, for political life is "enfolded" in general conceptions of how reality is put together.[1] Many anthropologists and sociologists insist, in addition, that every cultural frame has a "center," which has sacred status.[2] The sacred center makes possible a kind of social and political mapping; it gives the members of a society their sense of place. It is the heart of things, the place where culture, society, and politics come together.

French political authority under the Old Regime fits this model well; under the monarchy, the king was the sacred center, and the cultural frame of his authority was firmly fixed in long-standing notions of a Catholic, hierarchical order.[3] Kings stood between mere mortals and the Christian God in the great chain of being, and kingship was therefore mystical and quasi-divine. As late as January 1792, a conservative newspaper gave this explanation: "Just as the Eternal attaches from his all-powerful hand, to the foot itself of his Throne, the first link in the great chain, which ties all

[1] Clifford Geertz, "Centers, Kings, and Charisma: Reflections on the Symbolics of Power," in Joseph Ben-David and Terry Nichols Clark, eds., *Culture and its Creators: Essays in Honor of Edward Shils* (Chicago, 1977), pp. 150–71.

[2] Ibid., and Edward Shils, *Center and Periphery: Essays in Macrosociology* (Chicago, 1975).

[3] I do not mean to imply that the Old Regime cultural frame was static, because it too went through a long process of development. See, for example, Ernst H. Kantorowicz, *The King's Two Bodies: A Study in Mediaeval Political Theology* (Princeton, 1957). Kantorowicz shows how central the king's body was to the monarchical cultural frame; it was the focus of most "political" discussion.

the beings created by him, from the thousands of spheres which rotate over our heads to the moving mound of earth on which we live, so too the paternity of Kings reascends to that of God himself."[4] Until 1789 the cultural frame of this authority seemed so perdurable that it was considered "traditional"; it needed no self-conscious justification and for the most part received none, other than its repeated ceremonial reenactments in coronations, entry ceremonies, and the like.

When the French Revolution challenged the political authority of the Old Regime, it therefore also called into question its cultural frame. Ardent republicans eventually embraced the political side of this challenge with enthusiasm, but they were less certain about its cultural aspects. Where would their confrontation lead them? Radicals rejected the traditional model of authority; they exposed to themselves and everyone who watched the fictionality of the Old Regime's "master fiction" and in the process created a frightening vacuum in their social and political space. By refusing to recognize the charisma of the king, they decentered the frame of traditional authority. As the same conservative newspaper editor claimed, "In order to make people forget this sacred lineage . . . they disputed God's right to the incense of the Earth, Kings' rights to the tributes of their Subjects, and Fathers' rights to the respect of their Children."[5]

Where was the new center of society, and how could it be represented? Should there even be a center, much less a sacred one? Could the new democratic Nation be located in any institution or any means of representation? By opening up these fundamental questions, the French Revolution became more than just another example of how politics is shaped by culture; the experience of the Revolution showed for the first time that politics was shaped by culture, that a new political authority required a new "master fiction," and, most important, that the members of society could invent culture and politics for themselves. French revolutionaries did not just seek another representation of authority, a replacement for the king, but rather came to question the very act of representation itself.

The crisis of representation only emerged gradually. In the exhil-

[4] *Gazette de Paris*, 6 January 1792.
[5] Ibid.

arating days of 1789–90, it was enough to hold a festival and swear
a common oath. The new community seemed to spring into action
almost effortlessly, creating and re-creating its own sacred presence, and making manifest the Nation as a counterpoise to monarchy. As the monarchy as an institution came increasingly into
question, most revolutionaries agreed that the symbols of the Old
Regime had to be effaced, though there was dispute over how public and explicit this effacement had to be. At the inaugural meeting
of the National Convention on 21 September 1792, one deputy argued that no official declaration of the abolition of royalty was necessary: "I think neither of the king nor of royalty; I concern myself
entirely with my mission [to establish a new government] without
thinking that such an institution [as royalty] *could ever have existed*." [6] There was no need to officially declare the abolition of royalty because the reality of the institution was already in the past.

In countering this argument, the deputy Grégoire (plate 11) expressed a nearly unanimous opinion; the institutions of the Old
Regime might be gone, but the tangible reminders of them had to
be rooted out of popular consciousness: "Certainly, none of us will
ever propose to conserve the deadly race of kings in France . . . but
we must fully reassure the friends of liberty; it is necessary to de-
stroy this word 'king,' which is still a talisman whose magical force
can serve to stupefy many men. I demand therefore that by a sol-
emn law you consecrate *the abolition of royalty*." [7] After a spontaneous demonstration in support of Grégoire's proposal, the Convention went on to approve a new seal for its records: replacing the
king as the insignia of the official seal of state was "a woman lean-
ing with one hand on a fasces, holding in the other hand a lance
topped by a liberty cap, with the legend 'Archives de la République
française.'" [8] Soon after, this seal (plate 5) became the seal for all
branches of public administration, and the Convention ordered

---

[6] *Archives Parlementaires*, 1st ser., 52: 81 (italics mine).

[7] Ibid. (italics in original).

[8] The *Moniteur* did not carry any mention of this decision about the seal until
September 26; then it only reported that the "sceau de l'état portera un faisceau sur-
monté du bonnet de la liberté," with no mention of the female figure (*Réimpression
de l'Ancien Moniteur* 14, 26 September 1792). The account given in the *procès-verbal* is
identical to the one in the *Archives Parlementaires*, and neither of them mentions the
rudder that appears in the seal. See, however, the account given in Maurice Agulhon,
Marianne au combat: L'Imagerie et la symbolique républicaines de 1789 à 1880 (Paris, 1979),
p. 29.

11. HENRI GRÉGOIRE
Grégoire (1750–1831), the son of a poor tailor, became a priest
in 1775 and a leader of the movement for religious tolerance in the 1780s.
He sat in almost every revolutionary legislature and distinguished himself
as one of the deputies most sensitive to questions of culture and political
legitimacy. He served in Napoleon's legislative councils as well and even-
tually became a count.
(Photo from Cabinet des Estampes, courtesy of the Bibliothèque nationale)

that all public acts be henceforth dated Year I of the French Republic. Two weeks later, the deputies decreed that the seals of royalty, the scepter, and the crown all be broken into pieces, trans-
ported to the mint, and melted down into republican coins. The
markings of the old cultural frame had been transmuted into the
material for a new one.

The debate about the abolition of royalty brought to the surface
a growing concern with the proper place of symbols and images in
political life. In the years that followed, the seal of state would
serve as a kind of barometer of the crisis of representation. Once
royalty and its symbols had been abolished, what, if anything, was

to take their place? Should a sign or insignia be necessary to republican government? In a report given to the Council of Five Hundred more than three years after the initial discussion on seals, the ubiquitous Grégoire referred to a "strange question" that had been posed: "Is it necessary that there be a seal of the Republic? In the beginning, seals, they tell us, were only employed to compensate for the ignorance or the imperfection of writing."[9] In the most radical view, a people with access to print and public discussion needed no icons. As one writer asserted, "The metaphysical principles of Locke and Condillac should become popular, and the people should be accustomed to see in a statue only stone and in an image only canvas and colors."[10] Once the Nation had liberated itself from the superstitious symbols and images of the past, it had no need to create new ones.

This extreme rationalist position was in fact rarely taken, and Grégoire's answer of 1796 was much more common. He argued that all civilized people found that "a sign, a type, was necessary to give a character of authenticity" to all public acts. In essence, the Nation was only recognized by its representation in some kind of public symbol. The use of a seal of state was founded on reason, in Grégoire's view, because a seal was more easily recognized than a signature, more permanent, and more difficult to counterfeit. The seal made authority public rather than private; it represented something much more general than a man's signature ever could. True, Grégoire admitted, "the ridiculous hieroglyphs of heraldry are now for us only historical curiosities." The seal of a republic should not be superstitious and obscure like the insignia of aristocracy and royalty. But this did not mean that symbols should be thrown out completely.

> When one reconstructs a government anew, it is necessary to republicanize everything. The legislator who ignores the importance of signs will fail at his mission; he should not let escape any occasion for grabbing hold of the senses, for awakening republican ideas. Soon the soul is penetrated by the objects reproduced constantly in

[9] Corps législatif, *Rapport fait au Conseil des Cinq-Cents, sur les sceaux de la République, par Grégoire: Séance du 11 pluviôse an IV* (31 January 1796).

[10] As quoted in E. H. Gombrich, "The Dream of Reason: Symbolism of the French Revolution," *British Journal for Eighteenth-Century Studies* 2 (1979): 190. The quote comes from an article in the *Annales Patriotiques*.

front of its eyes; and this combination, this collection of principles, of facts, of emblems which retraces without cease for the citizen his rights and his duties, this collection forms, in a manner of speaking, the republican mold which gives him a national character and the demeanor of a free man.[11]

Grégoire offered here his own interpretation of Condillac's psychology; for him, the sign and the symbol, when correctly chosen, could serve the purpose of political propaganda by "grabbing hold of the senses" and penetrating the soul. The seal, then, was not only a representation of public authority but also an instrument of education, an element in the "republican mold." As part of a new cultural framework, new symbols could make new men.

Even Grégoire's spirited defense of a seal was not without its uncertainties, however. Grégoire gave his long report in 1796, because the deputies were once again reconsidering their choice of a seal. The decision in September 1792 had been almost haphazard, and the seal proposed was designed initially for the Convention's archives. At the time, the deputies had no clear sense of where their desire for a new political authority would take them. In 1796, after three years of experimenting with the "republican mold," the seal was still in limbo. Despite Grégoire's efforts, it remained so until the advent of Napoleon. Although most deputies could agree that some kind of insignia was necessary, they did not agree for long on what it should be. Both the structure of political authority and its cultural representations remained uncertain.

The controversies over the choice of seal reveal the importance revolutionaries attached to their central symbols. The seal was never definitively fixed, because the Revolution itself was always in flux. Debate was most intense at the three major turning points of the Revolution: when the Republic was first established in September 1792, during the Terror (summer 1793–summer 1794), and just after the inauguration of a new, more moderate legislative system in late 1795 and early 1796. The debates on seals can be read in two ways: as a tracer of immediate political conflicts and as a dramatic arena for working out the role of representation more generally. These two aspects cannot be neatly separated, just as political authority cannot be separated from its cultural frame. Debates over

---

[11] *Rapport . . . sur les sceaux . . . 11 pluviôse an IV.*

the signs of authority called the function of signs and symbols themselves into question, and every decision about signs and symbols had its own, sometimes unintended, political consequences.

In September 1792 when royalty was abolished and the Republic declared, the choice of a new insignia seemed almost automatic. The archivist proposed the choice of Liberty, and none of the accounts of the discussion mention any controversy about the type chosen for the new seal. In his study of the "feminine civic allegory," Maurice Agulhon offers several reasons for this virtually reflexive identification: in iconographic tradition, most qualities and, in particular, the different principles of government, even monarchy, were represented by female figures; the Phrygian bonnet or liberty cap of the goddess provided a particularly clear contrast with the crown of royal authority (and the female figure reinforced that contrast); Catholicism made the French more receptive to a Marian figure (the sobriquet Marianne was certainly semantically close to Mary, mother of Jesus); and the French Republic could find in the feminine allegory a figure suitably distant from the real-life heroes-turned-villains of the revolutionary process. Where Mirabeau, Lafayette, and many others had disappointed their followers and passed from the historical scene, Marianne endured, thanks to her abstraction and impersonality.[12]

Agulhon has traced, in addition, the political implications of different ways of representing Marianne. The seal of 1792 showed her standing, young, and determined, though not exactly aggressive. She held the lance of popular revolution, capped by the Phrygian bonnet of liberation. This figuration was in many ways an intermediate one, straddling the line between the more radical poses of Liberty marching bare-breasted and fierce of visage, which were current in 1793, and the more conservative poses favored by later governments in the 1790s and in the nineteenth century in which Liberty appeared seated, stolid, tranquil, and often without lance or liberty cap.[13] The same choices between radical and conservative

[12] Agulhon, "Esquisse pour une archéologie de la République: L'Allégorie civique feminine," *AESC* 28 (1973): 5–34; and *Marianne au combat*.

[13] Hannah Mitchell, "Art and the French Revolution: An Exhibition at the Musée Carnavalet," *History Workshop Journal* 5 (1978): 123–45; and Lynn Hunt, "Engraving the Republic: Prints and Propaganda in the French Revolution," *History Today* 30 (1980): 11–17.

Liberty figures would be posed again in 1848 and after 1871, under the Second and Third Republics.

After generations of controversy over the republic and, as a consequence, over its emblem, Marianne, the feminine civic allegory was not only accepted but widely diffused in France. But during the Revolution her dominance was much less certain.[14] The first challenge to Marianne came from within the ranks of republicans. In October 1793 after the arrest of the Girondin deputies (who opposed the growing power of the Paris districts and their radical Jacobin leaders) and in the midst of desperate efforts to recast the Republic in a more radical mold, the Convention decreed that the seal and the coins of the Republic should henceforth carry the ark of the constitution and the fasces as their emblem. The seal's new legend, "Le peuple seul est souverain" (The People Alone is Sovereign), underscored the new reliance on popular support. Within a month, however, the Convention changed its mind again. In early November 1793 the artist-deputy David proposed that the Convention order the erection of a colossal statue to represent the French people. Ten days later the Convention voted to make the statue the subject of the seal of state.[15] The deputies had chosen a giant Hercules as the emblem of the radical Republic.

The intention of the Convention was reaffirmed on at least two other occasions in the Year II: in February 1794 and again in April 1794.[16] The Musée Carnavalet in Paris has several sketches by the official engraver Dupré that match the guidelines laid down by the Convention for the new seal (plate 12).[17] Although this seal was not used to the exclusion of others, it does appear at the end of official decrees published in the *Bulletin des lois de la République* from June

[14]Here I part company with Agulhon's otherwise admirable analysis. He presents Marianne as a virtually inevitable figure.
[15]The Committee on Public Instruction and the Committee on Moneys were supposed to collaborate on the question of seals and coins. At first the former favored the ark of the constitution, and the latter preferred the female figure of France. David's proposition resolved the dispute, at least temporarily. M.J. Guillaume, ed., *Procès-verbaux du Comité d'Instruction publique de la Convention Nationale* 2 (3 juillet 1793–30 brumaire an II [20 novembre 1793] (Paris, 1894): 667–68, 714, 742, 772, 778–79, 808–11.
[16]Ibid., 3 (1 frimaire an II [21 novembre 1793]–30 ventôse an II [20 mars 1794]) (Paris, 1897): 465, 493, 499; and 4 (1er germinal an II [21 mars 1794]–11 fructidor an II [28 août 1794]) (Paris, 1901): 107–10.
[17]The Dupré collection in the *Réserve* of the Musée Carnavalet was the essential basis for this chapter.

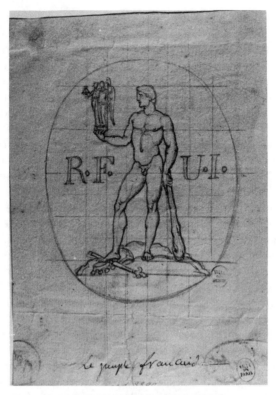

12. SKETCH OF HERCULES BY DUPRÉ
From the collections of the Musée Carnavalet
(Photo by Lynn Hunt)

1794 (prairial an II) until June 1797 (prairial an V).[18] That David had Hercules in mind as the model for the statue-seal is made clear both by the iconography of Dupré's sketch—the figure holds the distinctive club and his lionskin lies just beside him—and by David's original text: "This image of the people *standing* should carry in his other hand the terrible club with which the Ancients armed their Hercules!"[19] A giant, mythic, male figure now dwarfed Marianne.

[18] A.N., Collection of the *Bulletin des lois*. The seal resembles in every iconographic aspect the Dupré sketch in plate 12.
[19] *Procès-verbaux du Comité d'Instruction publique* 2: 779 (David's speech of 17 brumaire an II [7 November 1793]). A slightly different version is given in the *Révolu-*

The political meaning of the Hercules figure is revealed most clearly by the circumstances of its appearance. The first major public use of the figure came on 10 August 1793 during an elaborate festival planned by David.[20] Although the festival was held on the first anniversary of the uprising that brought down the monarchy, it was explicitly designed to celebrate the defeat of federalism, the revolt of the summer of 1793 in support of the arrested deputies known as the Girondins. At this critical moment, David orchestrated a festival that aimed at nothing less than a review of the Revolution's development. It was a morality play with a set of striking allegorical messages. Four "stations" retraced the major turning points in the Revolution in preparation for the final ceremony of consecration of the new constitution: a figure of Nature sat on the site of the fall of the Bastille; an arch of triumph was dedicated to the heroines of October 1789; a statue of Liberty (much like, if not identical to plate 1) memorialized the execution of the king in January 1793; and finally, a colossus representing the French people (plate 13) used its club to smash the hydra of federalism. The figure in the festival was not referred to officially as Hercules, but the iconography did not escape educated participants. One of the best-known Herculean "labors" was the killing of the Hydra, which had been emblematic over the centuries of various sorts of evil from sophism to vice, from ignorance to the nation's enemy in war.[21] An engraver who visited the site earlier on the day of the festival referred to "the colossal figure of Hercules, twenty-four feet high. . . . This Hercules had his left foot on the throat of the [figure representing] counterrevolution."[22]

The placement of Hercules relative to Liberty is particularly relevant. The statue of Liberty came just before Hercules in the celebratory procession. By implication Liberty was important, but repre-

---

tions de Paris, no. 217 (10–18 frimaire an II): "Que cette image du peuple *debout* tienne dans son autre main cette massue terrible et réelle, dont celle de l'Hercule ancien ne fut que le symbole."

[20] *Recueil complet de tout ce qui s'est passé à la Fête de l'Unité et l'Indivisibilité de la République Française* (Paris, n.d.), B.N., under 8° Z Le Senne 9.438. The first part of the pamphlet reproduces David's program for the festival.

[21] Marc-René Jung, *Hercule dans la littérature française du XVIe siècle: De l'Hercule courtois à l'Hercule baroque* (Geneva, 1966), esp. pp. 129–31. See also Leopold D. Ettlinger, "Hercules Florentinus," *Mitteilungen des Kunsthistorischen Institutes in Florenz* 16 (1972): 119–42, esp. p. 127.

[22] *Mémoires et Journal de J.-G. Wille, graveur du Roi*, 2 vols. (Paris, 1857) 2: 387.

13. ENGRAVING ENTITLED "THE FRENCH PEOPLE OVERWHELMING
THE HYDRA OF FEDERALISM," AUGUST 1793
From the collections of the Musée Carnavalet
(Photo by Lynn Hunt)

sentative of only one particular moment, a moment now passed. At the statue of Liberty, delegates from the departments put the torch to the hateful symbols of monarchy and thus reenacted the ritual sacrifice of the monarch to the goddess of the Republic (the king was executed in January, nine months before). At the next stop, there was nothing for the delegates to do; Hercules–the French people was the only actor. He gathered the fasces, symbol of unity, in one hand, while he crushed the monster of federalism (half-woman, half-serpent, according to observers)[23] with the club in his other hand. The political meaning of the progression was evident: the representatives of the people established liberty when they punished Louis XVI for his crimes, and then the people themselves protected the Republic against the monster of disunity and fac-

[23] Ibid.

tionalism. Hercules did not need the help of the deputies, though he planted himself firmly on the mountain, which stood, however inertly, for the righteous deputies within the Convention (including, of course, David). Without this intervention by the people, the Republic and its constitution could not be safely enshrined at the last station—the Revolution could not be fully realized. In comparison to Liberty, then, Hercules represented a higher stage in the development of the Revolution—one characterized by the force and unity of the people, rather than by the sagacity of its representatives.

When David proposed the erection of the colossal statue three months after the festival, the political circumstances were different. The federalist crisis had passed, but new issues had arisen to take its place. At the beginning of September the Convention, surrounded by angry and hungry sans-culottes, had officially agreed to make terror "the order of the day." A general maximum on prices was declared, and executions by the Revolutionary Tribunal in Paris accelerated. On October 16 the queen was guillotined. Then in November the most divisive issue of all gathered steam: de-Christianization. During the same session at which David first made his proposal (7 November 1793), several priests and bishops among the deputies publically abjured their clerical offices.[24] Three days after David's proposal and just a week before the Convention decided to make the colossus the subject of the seal, the notorious Festival of Reason was held in Notre Dame Cathedral, now dubbed the Temple of Reason. The radical deputies introduced Hercules as a symbolic response to this set of political and cultural crises.

Hercules faced a set of tasks worthy of his name. The most radical deputies and their followers wanted nothing less than a cultural revolution that would repudiate all Christian antecedents. The revolutionary calendar introduced in October 1793 was a striking manifestation of this desire (see chap. 2). The five extra days in the year were called sans-culottides and consecrated to national festivals of Genius, Work, Virtue, Opinion, and Recompense.[25] The calendar, the Festival of Reason, and Hercules were all meant to be

---

[24] *Procès-verbaux du Comité d'Instruction publique* 2: 775–82. For the general historical background, see Georges Lefebvre, *The French Revolution: From 1793 to 1799*, trans. by John Hall Stewart and James Friguglietti (New York, 1964), esp. chap. 2.

[25] For a brief account, see Serge Bianchi, *La Révolution culturelle de l'an II: Elites et peuple (1789–1799)* (Paris, 1982), pp. 198–203.

part of a new symbolic language fashioned for the newly mobilized masses. Robespierre, David, and the other Jacobin leaders had to respond to the desire for radical innovation (and the popular demands for a punitive, interventionist government), but at the same time they wanted to gain firmer control of a movement that threatened to alienate a large segment of the still fervently Catholic population. From the beginning, therefore, David's Hercules had to represent radical aspirations, while at the same time curbing them.

David's immediate political intentions were evident in the formal speech he gave on 17 November 1793, the day the Convention voted to adopt his statue as the prototype of the seal. The statue was to be a monument to the "glory of the French people" and a remembrance of the people's triumph over despotism and superstition. The "double tyranny of kings and priests" would be overcome symbolically in the construction of the statue's base, which would be made up of the debris from the statues of kings knocked off the porticos of Notre Dame. Thus would the Convention, with its "liberating energy," free the present, the future, and even the past from the "shame of a long servitude."[26] The statue would represent the power of the people in the most literal possible fashion; at forty-six feet in height, Hercules would overshadow memories of even the most popular kings, such as Henry IV, whose merely life-size image he would replace on the Pont-Neuf.

The choice of the giant Hercules at once embodied and strained to transcend the ambiguities in the radical view of representation. David explicitly emphasized the opposition between people and monarchy; Hercules was chosen, after all, to make this opposition more evident. But David's speech, and the image itself, implicitly referred as well to the uneasy tension between the people and the Convention, the new sovereign and its representatives. When they chose Hercules for the seal of the Republic, the radicals committed themselves to the view that some sort of representation of sovereignty was necessary. In Hercules they sought the most "transparent" representation possible, a kind of diminishing point of representation. Because they wanted an image that would convey the sovereign majesty of the people united, the statue contained no obvious reference to the deputies or to the Convention. Yet even this pared-down representation was constantly subverted by its nature

[26] *Procès-verbaux du Comité d'Instruction publique* 2: 806–11.

as an image. It was an image-representation of the people provided by the people's representatives, and as such it inherently included the representatives' interpretation of the people. This implicit interpretive element threatened to reestablish in cultural form the very relationship of political authority (authority outside the people) that the radicals were promising to abolish. Thus, even as the image proclaimed the supremacy of the people, it reintroduced the superiority of the people's representatives.

When speaking to the Convention, David sought to underline the simplicity of his conception. "Your Committee [of Public Instruction, for which David spoke] believed that, in the proposed monument, everything, both the materials and the forms, ought to express in a sensitive and forceful manner the great memories of our revolution." The statue itself would be made out of bronze furnished by the victories of the French armies. And, "since it is a kind of national representation, it could not be too beautiful." The enormous size of the figure would impose a "character of force and simplicity," the virtues of the people.[27] In one of his monumental hands, the colossus (now no longer referred to explicitly as Hercules by David) would hold little figures of both Equality and Liberty, pressed close together, which showed, as David claimed, that they depended entirely on the genius and virtue of the people.

In the present of 1793–94 the giant male figure had potent resonances. The new radical republic had no need of the "small and vain men" whom Robespierre denounced as the natural enemies of the Revolution; the Revolution had brought forth a new, heroic man of mythological proportions:

> The French people seem to have advanced two thousand years beyond the rest of humankind; one would be tempted even to regard it, from within its midst, as a different species. Europe kneels before the shadows of the tyrants we are punishing. . . . Europe cannot conceive that one could live without kings, without nobles; and we, that one could live with them. Europe spills its blood to rivet the chains of humanity; and we spill ours to break them.[28]

Who else but a colossus could break those chains of humanity?

[27] Ibid., pp. 778–79 and 806–11.
[28] "Sur les rapports des idées religieuses et morales avec les principes républicains, et sur les fêtes nationales," *Oeuvres de Maximilien Robespierre* 10 (Discours: 27 juillet 1793–27 juillet 1794) (Paris, 1967): 455.

The Herculean metaphor had appeared in radical discourse before David ever thought of using the image in his festival of 10 August. At the end of June 1793 Fouché described the victory of the people of Paris over the Girondins in this fashion:

> the excess of oppression broke through the restraints on the people's indignation. A terrible cry made itself heard in the midst of this great city. The tocsin and the cannon of alarm awakened their patriotism, announcing that liberty was in danger, that there wasn't a moment to spare. Suddenly the forty-eight sections armed themselves and were transformed into an army. This formidable colossus is standing, he marches, he advances, he moves like Hercules, traversing the Republic to exterminate this ferocious crusade that swore death to the people.[29]

Fouché's remarkable statement reveals the compelling force of the Hercules image for the radicals in Paris; this figure was nothing like a Marianne. As Fouché slips back and forth between the people and the colossus, between the past and the present tense, between "them" and "him," we can almost see the startling transformation taking place, as a kind of "terrible" (i.e., awe-inspiring and "sublime") monster rises from the depths of the city and its people to wreak its vengeance on the people's enemies. Where is the sacred center now? With democracy it has become a field of forces rather than a fixed point: "the people" is everywhere, but when it is assembled, when it comes together in a critical mass, it is transformed into a powerful new energy. "The Terror" was a radical, emergency form of government established to confront a series of life-threatening crises, but we can see in this passage how it was also a real and disturbing experience for the men who supposedly invented it. The Terror was the people on the march, the exterminating Hercules. Hercules, the people, was in the eyes of the radicals who had called it into being a potential Frankenstein.

The terrifying monster image only began to appear within radical discourse during the Terror, when the power of the people assembled became more visibly awesome. Before the Revolution, Hercules had a long iconographic history which was no doubt well known to bourgeois political leaders. Hercules was not a "popular"

[29] The quote is from a declaration by Fouché to the citizens of the department of the Aube, dated 29 June 1793 (Troyes) (*Archives Parlementaires* 68: 73 [proceedings of the Convention, 2 July 1793]).

figure; he did not appear, for instance, in the repertory of popular woodcuts (*imagerie populaire*), which were widely circulated in the kingdom under the Old Regime.[30] Instead, Hercules appeared most commonly as the mythological representation of French kings, the Gallic Hercules (*Hercule gaulois*). This figuration dates from the French Renaissance. In 1549, for example, the triumphal arch designed for Henry II's entry into Paris was capped by a Gallic Hercules representing Henry's predecessor Francis I.[31] Like many Renaissance versions of Hercules, this one had chains extending from his mouth to his companions' ears, because it was supposedly characteristic of Hercules that he led by persuasion rather than by force.[32]

By the time of the French Revolution, Hercules had gone through something of an iconographic metamorphosis. Louis XVI, last of the Bourbons, was evidently never associated with Hercules.[33] At some point, the figure migrated to America. Sometime after 1776, our same engraver Dupré struck a medal for Benjamin Franklin that had the head of a young girl with the device, *Libertas Americana*, on the front, and on the reverse had a young child strangling two serpents. This Baby Hercules was being attacked by a leopard, which a goddess holding a shield with a border of fleur-de-lys was about to strike with her lance.[34] Here royal France was protecting the new republican Hercules in America. When a committee was set up on 4 July 1776 to prepare a device for a seal of the United States of America, one of its members, John Adams, proposed Gribelin's engraving of "The Judgment of Hercules," which served as the frontispiece to Shaftesbury's widely read tract on the need for clarity in art (1723).[35] In America, too, the choice of seal was not

[30] Jean Mistler, François Blaudez, and André Jacquemin, *Epinal et l'imagerie populaire* (Paris, 1961).

[31] The arch is described in Lawrence M. Bryant, "*Parlementaire* Political Theory in the Parisian Royal Entry Ceremony," *Sixteenth Century Journal* 7 (1976): 15–24. I am indebted to the author for calling this to my attention. This early appearance of the Hercules figure is not mentioned in J.-B. Gaignebet, "Essai sur le cheminement d'Hercule au cours de l'histoire de France," *Provence historique* 25 (1975): 111–24.

[32] Jung, *Hercule dans la littérature française*, esp. pp. 73–93.

[33] Gaignebet, "Essai," p. 121.

[34] Ibid. This was not Dupré's only contribution to American revolutionary art. See the medal pictured in Joshua C. Taylor, *The Fine Arts in America* (Chicago, 1979), p. 30. On Dupré's prerevolutionary career, see Charles Saunier, *Augustin Dupré: Orfèvre, Médailleur, et Graveur-Général des Monnaies* (Paris, 1894).

[35] Frank H. Sommer, "Emblem and Device: The Origin of the Great Seal of the United States," *Art Quarterly* 24 (1961): 57–76, esp. pp. 65–67.

effortless. The final decision was not made until 1782, after six years of deliberation and false starts. Then the choice of an imperial eagle was, as one art historian claims, "obscure, 'aenigmatical' [in Shaftesbury's sense], and far beyond the comprehension of all but the middle- and upper-class gentlemen who had invented [it]." The eagle was the emblem of Charles V, Holy Roman Emperor, and it had been taken from a German book of emblems and devices.[36]

Hercules appeared on a few prints and engravings in revolutionary France before 1793, but David (perhaps on the urging of Dupré) was almost single-handedly responsible for reviving and transforming him into a powerful new symbol in the revolutionary repertory. Hercules had long since lost his association with rhetoric and persuasion; in the major dictionary of iconology printed in the first years of the Revolution, Hercules appeared only under the entries "Courage" and "Force."[37] The remarks on "Force" indicate, moreover, how allegories had been feminized: "The iconologists represent Force with the figure of a woman covered by a lionskin and armed with the club of Hercules."[38] David was not so much continuing an iconographic tradition as he was choosing certain elements in it and inverting their meaning. In the eyes of the educated elite, Hercules had stood in French history for the power of individual kings; in the revolutionary present, David turned him into the representation of a collective, popular power. He took one of the favorite signs of monarchy and reproduced, elevated, and monumentalized it into the sign of its opposite.

It is impossible to know exactly what the deputies of the Convention had in mind when they chose Hercules for the seal, because the choice aroused little official comment. They may not have been struck by his iconographic history, especially since that history had been attenuated in the last generations of the Old Regime. However, they were almost certainly attracted to the masculinity of the figure, since they had already voted to replace the female goddess of Liberty on the seal. This decision was in the first instance

[36] Ibid., pp. 73–74.

[37] B.N., Réserve. *Iconologie ou Traité de la Science des Allegories à l'usage des Artistes en 350 Figures, Gravées d'après les dessins de M.M. Gravelot et Cochin: Avec les explications relatives à chaque sujet* (Paris, n.d.). According to the "Avis de l'Editeur" at the front of the work, it was published in 1791.

[38] Ibid. 2: 55. The feminine representation of "Force" appears as the Queen of Spades in one edition of revolutionary playing cards published in 1792 (Henry-René D'Allemagne, *Les Cartes à jouer, du XIVe au XXe siècle*, 2 vols. [Paris, 1906] 1: 131).

political: choosing Hercules enabled the Jacobins to distance themselves iconographically from their opponents, the Girondins. Hercules stood for the people on whom the Jacobins were dependent
for their precarious superiority in national politics.

More was involved here, however, than just a straightforward
political message. David's Hercules recaptured and rehabilitated a
distinctly virile representation of sovereignty, a concept that had
connotations of domination and supremacy in any case. Yet Hercules was not a paternal emblem of authority; in the David-Dupré
figuration he was a powerful brother protecting the sister figures of
Liberty and Equality. The masculinity of Hercules reflected indi-
rectly on the deputies themselves; through him they reaffirmed the
image of themselves as the band of brothers that had replaced the
father-king. In addition to supplanting the king, Hercules dwarfed
his female companions. In this way, the introduction of Hercules
served to distance the deputies from the growing mobilization of
women into active politics. On the grounds that women's active
participation in politics would lead to "the kinds of disruption and
disorder that hysteria can produce," the Convention had outlawed
all women's clubs at the end of October 1793.[39] That action pre-
ceded David's proposal for a gargantuan statue by only a few days.
In the eyes of the Jacobin leadership, women were threatening to
take Marianne as a metaphor for their own active participation; in
this situation, no female figure, however fierce and radical, could
possibly appeal to them. Hercules put the women back into perspective, in their place and relationship of dependency. The monumental male was now the only active figure.

Like all powerful symbols, Hercules was multivalent; he trans-
mitted more than one message at once. He could be "popular," fraternal, parricidal, and antifeminist even while he was a transposed
and magnified sign of monarchy itself. Hercules reflected Jacobin
and radical aspirations; he symbolized the alliance between radical
deputies and the popular classes of Paris and served as a weapon

[39] As quoted in Jane Abray, "Feminism in the French Revolution," *American Historical Review* 80 (1975): 57. See also Darline Gay Levy, Harriet Branson Applewhite,
and Mary Durham Johnson, *Women in Revolutionary Paris, 1789–1795* (Urbana, Ill.,
1979). Levy first drew this issue to my attention and suggested that it might be related to the appearance of Hercules. For a provocative view of a similar revolutionary situation in 1848, see Neil Hertz, "Medusa's Head: Male Hysteria under Political
Pressure," *Representations* 4 (1983): 27–54.

in their ideological armory. Hercules could be taken as a barely veiled warning to the educated and as a reminder of the ways in which their world had been transformed by the Revolution. The people, the new, formidable giant, had become king. Even the deputies were answerable to it-him. Yet, what did Hercules mean to the people? The colossus—officially unnamed—was only an enormous giant to the popular classes. The resonance for them was not with the classics or with French history, but with the monsters, heroes, and perhaps even with the saints of popular tales.[40]

The interpenetration of elite and popular images of Hercules can be seen in the festival of 21 January 1794 at Grenoble. The festival celebrated the death of the king the year before. On a platform sat a manikin representing Louis Capet (with a crown and the horns of a cuckold!), on his right sat the "so-called" pope, and on his left a figure representing the nobility. When the crowd gathered in the square cried out for vengeance, two "French Hercules" appeared from behind the figures to finish them off with clubs. Then the fallen figures were dragged through the mud and trampled underfoot by the participants.[41] For the elite, the *Hercule français* replaced the *Hercule gaulois*; he was now a true national figure and not one limited to monarchy. For the popular classes, the *two* Hercules figures became part of a revived carnival scene, which was filled with derision and the inversion of traditional roles. Just as the maypole of tradition had been transformed from a statement of homage to authority into a sign of sedition and peasant power,[42] so too the Hercules of kingly power had been recast as the sign of the people's power.

The cultural origin of Hercules was, however, very different from that of the liberty tree. The maypole was a "popular" symbol with deep roots in peasant culture in France, at least in southwestern France.[43] By contrast, Hercules came more directly out of elite

[40] See, e.g., Geneviève Bolleme, *La Bibliothèque bleue: Littérature populaire en France du XVIIe au XIXe siècle* (Paris, 1971).

[41] Auguste Prudhomme, *Histoire de Grenoble* (Grenoble, 1888), pp. 640–41. The same account is given in Albin Gras, *Deux années de l'histoire de Grenoble, depuis la suspension de Louis XVI (10 août 1792) jusqu'à la chute de Robespierre (9 thermidor an II [27 juillet 1794])* (Grenoble, 1850), pp. 65–66.

[42] Some interesting remarks on the maypole are made in J. Boutier, "Jacqueries en pays croquant: Les Révoltes paysannes en Aquitaine (décembre 1789–mars 1790)," *AESC* 34 (1979): 760–86, esp. p. 764.

[43] Ibid.

culture, even if he could be construed as an image with attraction for the popular classes. The transformation of Hercules, moreover, was not one effected by the popular classes; he was reinvented by the radicals in the Jacobin government of Paris. Consequently, Hercules can be read as an expression, not only of the radicals' attempt to restructure society along more popular lines, but also of their ambivalence about the sources of their power. For Hercules never appears as an intelligent giant. In Fouché's account, he is a mighty force, crying with the pain of betrayal, fierce when aroused; he reacts more like an injured animal than like an agent of his own destiny. David's plan for the statue underscores this aspect in a curious way: he called for the engraving of several key words on the giant's body. On his brow would be inscribed "light" (a rather weak reference to intelligence); "nature" and "truth" were to appear on his chest; "force" and "courage" on his arms; and "work" on his hands.[44] Hercules brings light and truth to the world in David's vision, not through his intellect or cleverness, but through his strength, courage, and "labor."

David's choice of words made the radical view of the people explicit. The giant was a force of nature; his transparency made him nature's medium for truth and light. Apparently without reason, he had no second thoughts, no secrets, no potential for those most-feared combinations—conspiracies against the Revolution. His contribution was not in the realm of ideas, obviously, but rather as soldier and worker; his was the courage and strength without which the radical cause would have been doomed. He was the backbone of that "terror, without which virtue is powerless."[45] And, perhaps most important, the giant represented those who worked with their hands, the "sans-culottes," those who wore long trousers rather than the breeches of the leisured classes. Work under the Old Regime had been devalued; working with one's hands

---

[44] In his first speech to the Convention on 7 November 1793, David did not include "travail," at least according to the account given in the *Moniteur*. But ten days later the official decree did include mention of "sur ses mains, *Travail*" (*Procès-verbaux du Comité d'Instruction publique* 2: 778–79, 806). Judith Schlanger includes a fascinating discussion of "the ideographic dimension of the written word" in her essay on this aspect of David's project, "Le Peuple au front gravé," *L'Enjeu et le débat* (Paris, 1979), pp. 155–68.

[45] Quote from Robespierre's speech of 5 February 1794 on the "Moral and Political Principles of Domestic Policy," trans. by Philip Dawson, *The French Revolution* (Englewood Cliffs, N.J., 1967), p. 135.

made one a member of the "vulgar mechanic classes."[46] The radicals were trying to revalue work as a source of pride and dignity; nothing was more despised by them than the idle rich. Yet David's Hercules undermined this revaluation while attempting to memorialize it; "work" on his hands became yet another sign of the giant's status as dumb force. Only David's words could make him speak.

The proposed inscription was only one example of the ambiguity involved in the effort to represent the people to themselves. The sheer mass of the statue was supposed to convey an unmistakable message: the people was monumental and awesome, overwhelming in its force. And the people stood alone. Yet it was the people's representatives who provided the interpretations, and in that capacity they kept creeping back into the picture. When Hercules first appeared in the festival of 10 August 1793, he was simply labeled the "Colossus of the Invalides," because his statue was erected on the square of that name (place des Invalides). As the participants gathered in front of the station, the president of the Convention explained just what the people were to see in him: "French people! Here you are looking at yourself in the form of an emblem which is rich in instructive lessons. The giant whose powerful hand reunites and reattaches in one bundle the departments which make up its grandeur and its strength, that giant is you!"[47] The deputies had arranged the allegory in order to show the people their own image, but their recognition of its import depended on speeches provided by their representatives. The visual image only worked correctly in the context of words.

Hercules as radical image was taken a step further in a newspaper editorial commenting on David's original speech about the statue. The editor of the *Révolutions de Paris* immediately grasped the political import of the image: "We will see the people standing, carrying the liberty that it conquered and a club to defend its conquest. No doubt, among the models entered in the competition, we will prefer the one which best projects the character of a sansculotte with its figure of the people." He went on to praise David's choice of words for the statue, claiming that the Egyptians wrote

[46] Colin Lucas, "Nobles, Bourgeois and the Origins of the French Revolution," *Past and Present*, no. 60 (1973): 84–126, esp. p. 88.

[47] *Recueil complet de tout ce qui s'est passé.*

14. ENGRAVING ENTITLED "LE PEUPLE MANGEUR DE ROIS"
From the collections of the Musée Carnavalet
(Photo by Lynn Hunt)

on their public monuments because these "were the only basic
books of the multitude." The editor could not resist adding his own
suggestion: Why not have the same kind of monument in every
city and hamlet in France? Why not put a monumental statue at
every critical point along the frontier? And, because "Homer called
the kings of his time *mangeurs de peuples* [people-eaters], we will
write on the figures of the French sans-culottes these words: *Le
Peuple Mangeur de Rois* [The People, Eater of Kings]."[48] Soon after,
the paper provided its own printed image of the figure (plate 14).

Here Hercules has become a sans-culotte. The iconographic club
of the mythological hero has turned into a real instrument of popular power. In Dupré's figuration (plate 12), the classical Hercules
stood nude, resting lightly on his "symbolic" club. In the cartoon,
he actively wields the club against the figure of monarchy. He is
dressed, moreover, much like a rough-and-ready sans-culotte, in
Phrygian bonnet and rolled-up pants, ready for his work of the

---

[48] *Révolutions de Paris*, no. 217 (10–18 frimaire an II). Engravings to accompany
the text appeared later and were inserted into the bound journals.

day. The profusion of hair on his head and his face clearly distinguishes him from the clean-shaven and carefully coiffed deputies as well as from the hairless Hercules envisaged by David (plates 12 and 13). David's unclothed Hercules had no social identification. He was an entirely abstract figure, standing above class and partisan politics. In short, the cartoon figure was an even more radical image than David's; the Eater of Kings is more "transparent" because it is lifelike, nonclassical, clear in social content, and explicit in its action. It is not obscure or "aenigmatical." The image is not allegorical; the figure is the sans-culotte who is the people. As a consequence, the image comes close to the zero-point of representation, in which there is no metaphorical content. As a radical image, it is meant to be a reflection of reality and not a distorted, abstracted reinterpretation of it.

The cartoon figure clearly draws on popular sources for its appeal. In typical carnivalesque inversion, the king has become a pygmy, a helpless plaything in the hands of popular brute force. But this time the turning of the tables is not playful; the people were not kings for an hour or a day. The people now devour kings (and by implication become what they eat, the incarnation of the sovereign power). The comment by the editor also subtly reinforces the underlying emphasis on the fraternal conquest of power. The figure is supposed to carry "the liberty that it conquered and a club to defend its conquest." Liberty, that precious, fragile achievement, is now a trophy from the war on kings. The brothers captured her from the grasp of their enemies (the patriarchal rulers) and now must defend their "conquest" with all their might. There is no active role for women. It is possible that Liberty does not actually appear in the engraving because by then the issue of women's participation was no longer in contention. For both the Jacobin leaders and their sans-culotte followers, politics was a quarrel between men.[49]

Despite the endeavor to make this a transparent image of the people, the Eater of Kings still shared the fundamental ambivalence of the David figuration. Like the classical Hercules, the figure

---

[49] "Les sans-culottes, même s'ils eurent à l'occasion une attitude plus libérale, estimaient comme les Jacobins que les femmes doivent être reléguées 'dans la sphère étroite de leur ménage'" (Albert Soboul, *Les Sans-Culottes parisiens en l'an II*, 2nd ed. [Paris, 1962], p. 507).

in the cartoon embodies action rather than reason; as brute force, he acts without thought. Like David, the radical newspaperman must provide the logos, the reason behind the people's action. This figure too is "inscribed." The radicals write on the body of the people in order to reincorporate them and their power into the radical political world. Once again, the radical represents the people to themselves—"here you are violently defending our conquest of liberty." But could anyone imagine the figure writing a constitution? The figure of force is, after all, a brute.

Although David's proposed competition for the statue was put off along with many other projects, some kind of plaster version was apparently constructed.[50] One late-nineteenth-century historian claimed that a representation of Hercules was in fact set up on the Pont-Neuf, but the description he gives fits the figure of the festival of 10 August (Hercules clubbing the hydra of federalism) and not the Hercules of the statue.[51] Engravings of the Festival of the Supreme Being of 8 June 1794 show a statue of Hercules in a prominent spot next to the mountain erected on the Champ de Mars (plate 15). This statue does follow the guidelines set out by David for the Pont-Neuf colossus; it is not as big as proposed, but the classical figure holds the two tiny representations of Liberty and Equality in his hand.[52] It is apparent from this engraving that David, Robespierre, and the other radicals in the Convention had no intention of deviating from the classical Herculean model of the people. The brutality and violence of the cartoon figure are effaced in this model of grace and composure. The figure of the people makes his own offering to the Supreme Being, and his demeanor is

---

[50] A design competition for a variety of monuments, including the "figure of the French People" from the Festival of 10 August was opened but never judged. On 29 November 1794 (several months after the fall of Robespierre and David), Thibaudeau suggested that the artists themselves name a jury. As far as I can determine, though this report was adopted, it was never executed (*Procès-verbaux du Comité d'Instruction publique* 4 [1 germinal an II (21 mars 1794)–11 fructidor an II (28 août 1794)]: 253–58).

[51] M. Castonnet-Desfosses, *Paris en 1794: La Fête de l'Etre suprême* (Paris, 1883), B.N., 8° Le Senne 6790.

[52] A detailed list of expenses for the Festival of Supreme Being includes 12 days masonry work for scaffolding and the positioning of the figure on the column located to the left of the mountain. Wherever the figure came from, this accounting shows that a version of David's figure was made (A.N., F$^{\rm ic}$ I 84, *Fêtes publiques*, an II–an IV, dossier labelled II, 14 juillet [26 messidor an II]).

15. DETAIL FROM AN ENGRAVING OF THE
FESTIVAL OF SUPREME BEING, JUNE 1794
From the collections of the Musée Carnavalet
(Photo by Lynn Hunt)

not the demanding one of the fall of 1793. The people in the mean-
time have been brought under control.

The engraving of the Festival of Supreme Being prompts one
question that cannot be answered, but that nevertheless is worth
posing. Is it accidental that the Hercules in the engraving looks
very much like Michelangelo's David?[53] Was this a sign of David's

[53] In Renaissance Florence, Hercules was often associated with the Biblical David

own egotism (his name now associated with Hercules, the people, and the Biblical hero), or was this the ironic comment of an anonymous engraver? The same statue also appears in engravings of the Festival of Victory held at the end of October 1794, three months after the fall of Robespierre and the disgrace of David himself. The exactitude of such engravings is far from trustworthy, however, because, as Bronislaw Baczko argues, the festive Paris of engravings often had little to do with actual events or topography. Engravers effaced the provisional character of plaster monuments and made them look like marble or granite instead. At times, the artists included statues or monuments that never had existed![54] Engravers, too, were motivated by didactic concerns; their work was meant to reconstitute the world rather than report it.

Like many of the plaster representations used in the Jacobin festivals, the colossus was destroyed in early 1795.[55] At the end of October 1795 a deputy suggested that the Convention vote for a seal showing a beehive. This proposition was rejected after another deputy remarked that beehives were royalist, if only because they had a queen bee. The proper emblems of a republic, in this deputy's opinion, were the liberty cap and the level (the symbols of liberty and equality).[56] In other words, after the fall of the radicals, the remaining deputies turned increasingly to abstract symbols. Grégoire's report of 1796 shows this influence. He proposed the choice of three designs: a female figure without the distinctive liberty cap; a triangle to represent the union of the two legislative Councils and the Executive Directory (the liberty cap sat on top of the triangle); or three interlocking circles in the center of a shield whose border would represent the invincible chain of the united departments (with the liberty cap appearing in one of the circles).[57] The seal on the official proceedings of the Council of Five Hundred

---

(Ettlinger, "Hercules Florentinus"). Moreover, David considered himself a great admirer of Michelangelo (David Lloyd Dowd, *Pageant-Master of the Republic: Jacques-Louis David and the French Revolution* [Lincoln, Neb., 1948], p. 10).

[54] Baczko, *Lumières de l'Utopie* (Paris, 1978), pp. 361–62. According to the engravings, the decor of the Festival of Victory followed quite closely that of the Festival of Supreme Being a few months earlier. See the engraving reproduced as plate no. 34 in Marie-Louise Biver, *Fêtes révolutionnaires à Paris* (Paris, 1979).

[55] Biver, *Fêtes révolutionnaires*, p. 101.

[56] *Procès-verbaux du Comité d'Instruction publique* 6 (6 germinal an III [26 mars 1795]–4 brumaire an IV [26 octobre 1795]) (Paris, 1907): 818, 861, 869.

[57] *Rapport . . . sur les sceaux . . . 11 pluviôse an IV.*

consisted of an oval with a liberty cap, rays of the sun, and a compass and balance.[58] Like the American republicans before them, the French republicans were moving toward the abstract and enigmatic in symbolic representation. The people were no longer directly represented in imagery; the republic might be for the people, but it was neither by nor of them.

Although Hercules did not capture the seal of the Republic, he did not disappear from circulation altogether after the fall of Robespierre and his radical followers. A law passed in August 1795 divided the coins of the Republic into two types: silver pieces would bear the figure of Hercules "uniting Liberty and Equality" with the legend "Union and Force"; and the lesser bronze pieces would show the figure of Liberty with the legend "French Republic."[59] Hercules, however, had changed: he had been domesticated. (See plate 16, a sketch by Dupré that matches the guidelines of the decree.)[60] Now he appeared as a life-size brother to Liberty and Equality; he is not a giant, he no longer carries his little sisters in his mammoth hand, and he does not brandish the threatening iconographic club of popular power. Instead, he looks older, wiser, conciliatory, even somewhat paternal. Popular forces, too, had been tamed; after the last desperate uprisings of the spring of 1795, the sans-culottes withdrew from the political arena. Abstract female figures, who had little resemblance to living women, returned to the iconographic scene in numbers.

Many of the deputies would have liked to eliminate Hercules completely. In July 1798 the Council of Five Hundred proposed that "an allegorical figure representing a seated woman" replace Hercules on silver coins. The legend would read "Liberty, Prosperity."[61] Hercules–the people would give way to a tranquil, inactive figure of prospective wealth. The radical male and the radical female (even the Liberty of plate 5 was more active) were to be su-

---

[58]See, e.g., *Procès-verbal des séances du Conseil des Cinq-Cents, nivôse an IV* (Paris, n.d.). From the beginning of the Revolution, much of the most abstract symbolism had been taken, consciously or not, from masonic sources (Jules Renouvier, *Histoire de l'Art pendant la Révolution considéré principalement dans les estampes* [Paris, 1863]).

[59]Michel Hennin, *Histoire numismatique de la Révolution française*, 2 vols. (Paris, 1826) 1: 519–20.

[60]Ibid., p. 519.

[61]*Journal des débats*, report on the session of 3 floréal an VI of the Conseil des Cinq-Cents.

16. SKETCH BY DUPRÉ FOR HERCULES COIN, 1795
From the collections of the Musée Carnavalet
(Photo by Lynn Hunt)

perseded. The higher council, the Council of Ancients, agreed that such a change was "inevitable," because they considered the Hercules figuration "an allegory whose conception and execution were not fortunate." [62] But, because the Ancients felt compelled to turn back the rest of the monetary proposal, Hercules continued to circulate a while longer. [63]

---

[62] Ibid., report on the session of 27 messidor an VI of the Conseil des Anciens.
[63] Ibid. See also ibid., discussion on 12 messidor an VI. The Hercules coin circu-

After 1799 the memory of Hercules faded. Marianne, the figure of Liberty and the Republic, did not disappear, but she was soon overshadowed by representations of Bonaparte himself. When Marianne reappeared with subsequent republics, so did Hercules, but as a secondary figure: he was revived on French coins in 1848, 1870–78, and even in 1965.[64] He was never as prominent as he had been during the Terror of 1793–94. Yet, though the male figure was never supreme in republican imagery after the Revolution, it did come to play a preeminent role in socialist and proletarian iconography. Eric Hobsbawm has tried to explain why the female figure declined in importance with the transition from democratic-plebeian revolutions of the nineteenth century to the proletarian and socialist movements of the twentieth.[65] He cites the tendency of women to stop working when they married, the exclusion of women from trade unions, and the association of female figures with declining preindustrial millennialism.

Whatever the merit of these social and political explanations in themselves (and they have been contested[66]), they fail to take account of the antecedent contest between female and male figures during the Revolution. The "bare-torsoed worker" does not appear for the first time in the early nineteenth century (Hobsbawm gives no precise date); he is there already in David's representation of the people (with *travail* written on his hands), long before the rise of a proletarian-socialist movement. Indeed, as Hobsbawm inadvertently shows, Hercules is often the model for socialist iconography; who else is that figure that Hobsbawm describes as "a naked muscular figure, his loins lightly draped, kneel[ing] on a rock wrestling with a large green serpent" (on the banner of the Export Branch of the Dockers' Union in the 1890s)?[67] Already in 1818 an English

---

lated until the Year IX at least (P. Ciani, *Les Monnaies françaises de la Révolution à la fin du premier empire, 1789 à 1815* [Paris, 1931], p. 122).

[64] Barbara Ernst, *Les Monnaies Françaises depuis 1848: Die Französischen Münzen seit 1848* (Braunschweig, 1968), pp. 20, 33, 54. In these later periods, the original designs of Dupré were simply revived without major changes, except in the legend: "Union and Force" were replaced by "Liberty, Equality, Fraternity."

[65] "Man and Woman in Socialist Iconography," *History Workshop Journal* 6 (1978): 121–38.

[66] See the criticisms by Maurice Agulhon and by Sally Alexander, Anna Davin, and Eve Hostettler in *History Workshop Journal* 8 (1979): 167–82.

[67] "Man and Woman," p. 129.

syndicalist movement was referred to as the "Philanthropic Hercules." [68] And the figure had enough resonance in mid-nineteenth-century France to influence Gustave Flaubert; his one heroic character in *Sentimental Education*, the worker Dussardier, is characterized as "a sort of Hercules" when he first appears in the narrative. [69]

In his criticism of Hobsbawm, Maurice Agulhon maintains that the male figure was favored by the left in the nineteenth century because the female figure had been too closely associated with the moderate republic. [70] But it did not require the experience of the Second and Third Republics in the nineteenth century to reveal the tension between moderate and radical conceptions of republicanism; the choice between Marianne and Hercules was posed already in the 1790s. Moreover, the colossal male figure represented more than just a repudiation of the moderate, feminine civic image; it reminded its beholders that radical revolution, like industrial labor and much of socialist politics, was "man's work."

The Herculean figure incorporated the same basic tensions that continued to bedevil the self-conception of later proletarian and socialist movements. Hercules did not unambiguously represent the people. The figure chosen by David was not the people's own self-image, reflected out of the depths of popular culture. It was rather the artist-intellectual-politician's image of the people for the people's edification. The proletarian figures described by Hobsbawm conveyed the same kinds of ambivalence: rarely did they have a realistic look. More often, they were idealized, classical, usually nude or semi-nude figures of powerful masculinity, not the worn-down, undernourished, and dirty figures of Europe's coal fields or factories. Like Flaubert's Dussardier, who was a "big fellow [*le terrible garçon*] . . . so strong that it took at least four of them [police] to overpower him," the figures conveyed brute strength without much intelligence. [71] The workers, like the people of the French

[68] John Foster, *Class Struggle and the Industrial Revolution: Early Industrial Capitalism in Three English Towns* (London, 1974), p. 101.

[69] *Sentimental Education*, trans. by Robert Baldick (London, 1964), p. 41.

[70] Agulhon's criticism of Hobsbawm echoes many of his themes in *Marianne au combat*: "On Political Allegory: A Reply to Eric Hobsbawm," *History Workshop Journal* 8 (1979): 167–73.

[71] For the French version, see Gustave Flaubert, *L'Education sentimentale* (Paris, 1965), p. 49.

Revolution, proved difficult to represent, yet those who championed their cause felt compelled to do so.

Although radical images of the people were filled with tension and ambivalence, they nevertheless succeeded in opening up new fissures in the social and political terrain. The radicals called on the people to look at themselves, to recognize themselves as central figures, to make their "terrible cry" resound in the halls of the Convention as well as in the streets of Paris. The power as well as the tension in the radical representation of the people can be heard in Robespierre's momentous speech on "The Moral and Political Principles of Domestic Policy" given in February 1794:

> But when, by prodigious efforts of courage and reason, a people breaks the chains of despotism to make them into trophies of liberty; when by the force of its moral temperament it comes, as it were, out of the arms of death, to recapture all the vigor of youth; when by turns it is sensitive and proud, intrepid and docile, and can be stopped neither by impregnable ramparts nor by the innumerable armies of the tyrants armed against it, but stops of itself upon confronting the law's image; then if it does not climb rapidly to the summit of its destinies, *this can only be the fault of those who govern it.*[72]

For Robespierre, the people were the force of the Revolution, its propelling motor. Once in motion, however, the people were hard to stop. Their representatives were there to hold up the "law's image" before them, to stop the people in time, to explain how the law was their handiwork, and to guide the people in the right path, "to the summit of its destinies." Without the people, the Revolution had no motive force; without the people's representatives, the Revolution had no sense of direction.

The depth of the fissures opened up by radical appeals to the people can be measured by the determination of subsequent attempts to close them up again and pretend they never existed. After 1794 all calls to the people were squashed. The monumental Hercules disappeared from sight, and most representations of the Republic were life-size, abstract, arcanely allegorical, and often cluttered with a profusion of enigmatic symbols. Hercules had required a few words of identification, but the abstract allegories of

---

[72] Trans. in Philip Dawson, *The French Revolution*, p. 134. Italics mine.

17. OFFICIAL VIGNETTE OF THE EXECUTIVE DIRECTORY, 1798
(Photo from Cabinet des Estampes, courtesy of the Bibliothèque nationale)

the bourgeois republic came with whole pages of explication, designed for those who could read complex prose. The official vignette of the Directory (plate 17) was issued with a full-page explanation of its allegorical content. It featured a figure of Liberty
wearing her cap, but she was surrounded by many other, much
less easily recognized symbols.[73] In contrast to the Marianne of
1792 (see plate 5), this Liberty is sitting, looking contemplative
rather than ready for action. She holds no pike or lance, and leans
rather languorously on the tablet of the Constitution of the Year III.
Perhaps most important, she looks off to the side (to her right!)
rather than confronting the beholder. Liberty makes no demands
on her audience. She simply sits and waits.

In 1800 a rehabilitated David oversaw the replacement of the

[73] The explanation of the allegory can be found in the *Collection de Vinck* 4 (*Napoléon et son temps*) (Paris, 1969): 3–4.

plaster statue of Liberty. Her place on the "square of the Revolution" was taken by a national column sitting on a renamed "square of Concord" (place de la Concorde). The architect Moreau projected a 67-foot column capped by a figure of Liberty, who, as one observer reported, had "a sad and sullen attitude."[74] Liberty was now a truly distant figure, elevated far above the heads of the people. Within a few months, even this remote Liberty was torn down in favor of Napoleon's Arc de Triomphe. The imperial state based on military victory had triumphed over the Republic.

The seal of state and the other representations of revolution were more than picturesque reflections of interminable political conflicts. Like the elaborate rituals of dressing the king that captivated Louis XIV's court, the representations of revolution gave definition to the experience of power. When the "master fiction" of monarchy was undermined, republicans set out to find new ways of putting their world together. Marianne and Hercules were two central figures in their new political cosmos. In America republicans could agree on a seal once and for all, because the political class could agree on the meaning of the republic. In France the representations of power continued to arouse controversy, because the political class found it difficult to agree on where the Revolution ended. The crisis of representation was never resolved during the revolutionary decade, but, as a consequence, republicans and the radicals in particular pushed the issues to their furthest limits. By daring to represent the people, with all the ambivalence and ambiguity that that representation entailed, the radicals opened up new questions about the nature and possibilities of government. The questions had great impact, because they were not limited to treatises and tracts about politics, but rather sounded their echoes in all segments of French society. The memory of revolution was not carried forward in a book or a document. It was propagated by a few simple slogans, ribbons and caps, and memorable, lifelike figures.

[74] Biver, *Fêtes révolutionnaires*, p. 148.

II

THE SOCIOLOGY
OF POLITICS

4

The Political
Geography of Revolution

RHETORIC, rituals, and images provided a symbolic framework for revolutionary political culture. Although the political content of speeches, festivals, and representations of authority, such as seals and coins, changed over the decade, many of the principles and aspirations that shaped them remained fundamentally the same. Primary among these continuing motivations were the desire to break with deference to tradition; the belief in the possibility of a regenerated nation; the reliance on rationalism and universalism in the construction of new values; and the emphasis on the needs of the community over the interests of individuals and particular groups. Even the basic tensions within revolutionary theory and practice were recurrent: between transparency and didacticism, between the people and its representatives, and between the self-evidence of nature and reason and the opacity of symbols and costumes. In the process of working out these principles and polarities, revolutionaries explored new political terrain, including direct democracy, terror, and eventually authoritarian rule.

The symbolic framework of revolution gave the new political culture unity and continuity. The constant references to the new Nation, to the community, and to the general will helped bring into being a stronger sense of national purpose. Marianne, Hercules, the national cockade, and the festivals were conceived as appealing to all French people. Liberty trees, patriotic altars, Jacobin clubs, and electoral procedures were established in nearly identical fashion everywhere. This symbolic framework did not so much reflect already-present feelings of nationalism or the democratic strivings of the masses as it created them. The processions, the swearing of oaths, and the circulation of coins with the image of

Liberty or Hercules elicited and consolidated the new Nation that revolutionary rhetoric posited in the first place.

Most of the new practices got their official stamp of approval in Paris, and their operation often worked to increase the power of a centralizing and bureaucratizing government. Standard weights and measures, a uniform coinage, identical election procedures, and the like facilitated the task of governing from Paris. Nevertheless, the new political culture was not dominated by Paris. Revolutionary values and symbols were powerful, because so many people in so many different places began to act on them in concert with the aim of restructuring social and political life. Sometimes people far from Paris developed their own symbols and rituals, but, even when they were willing to follow the Parisian lead, they did so on their own terms and in their own way. And, after all, what was Parisian about politics at the center? Much of the local population in Paris was made up of immigrants from the provinces, and the overwhelming majority of the deputies to the national legislatures came from the provinces. The government in Paris could claim to speak for the nation because it was made up of people from different parts of France.

Making a new nation through revolution was therefore a complex process; more was involved than the incorporation of the periphery by the center into a new polity. As a consequence, mapping the spread and development of revolution is no easy task. Yet the questions are essential: where was the Revolution best received, in what places, and among which groups? To whom did the new values appeal most? Who was responsible for putting them into action? The meaning of the set of political practices that together constituted the process of revolution cannot be deduced from its intellectual and philosophical origins. The practices have to be placed in their social context. The liberty trees were planted by someone, and the festivals were more successful in some places than in others. A symbolic framework does not fall out of the sky, nor is it taken out of books. It is fashioned by people who find something attractive in the vision offered by the new political culture.

The second half of this book proceeds from the supposition that people, especially people acting together, make culture. It is not assumed that the meaning of culture or politics can be deduced from the social identity of the people involved, but it does assume that social identity provides important clues about the process of inventing and establishing new political practices. Contemporaries of the Revolution made the same assumption. In 1791 Edmund Burke claimed that "The moneyed men, merchants, principal tradesmen, and men of letters . . . are the chief actors in the French Revolution."[1] French conservatives in the 1790s saw the handiwork of Freemasons, Protestants, insensate mobs, fanatic anticlericals, Jacobins, or, more generally, men of untoward ambition. The revolutionaries themselves were loath to make such distinctions because they wanted to emphasize the generality of the process. Opponents were simply factious, selfish, aristocratic, or unpatriotic. In 1795, for instance, the conservative republican Boissy d'Anglas maintained that "the French Revolution . . . is not at all the production of a few individuals, but the result of enlightenment and of civilization."[2]

Although the revolutionaries preferred to emphasize the universality of the revolutionary process, on a day-to-day level they were themselves very concerned with the various forms of resistance they encountered. The bureaucracy expanded in large measure in order to gather information about public opinion. The government wanted regular reports and loyal servants so that it could keep abreast of local differences in response to its innovations. In response to this concern, the government of the 1790s collected massive amounts of information about the spread of revolutionary practices. While publicly proclaiming the unity of the nation, the government frantically studied the sources of disunity.

Besides the traditional police concern for public order, the chief political preoccupation of the revolutionary government was the annual ritual of elections. Although the festivals brought together larger masses of people, including women and children who were excluded from voting, elections were the most telling expression of the nation's new sovereignty. Elections had been the cornerstone of the revolutionary achievement since 1789; it was elections that

[1] From *Thoughts on French Affairs*, in Robert A. Smith, ed., *Burke on Revolution* (New York, 1968), p. 190. On Burke's views, see J. G. A. Pocock, "The Political Economy of Burke's Analysis of the French Revolution," *Historical Journal* 25 (1982): 331–49.

[2] *Projet de Constitution pour la République française et discours préliminaire* (Paris, an III), p. 7.

opened up political, judicial, ecclesiastical, and even military careers to talent.[3] Under the Old Regime, many high offices were patrimonial; judgeships passed from father to son as property, and
clerical and military positions were often open to the highest bid-
der within certain restricted family circles. Elections were consequently essential to the revolution against privilege, and no revolutionary government considered scuttling them, even after 1795.
However, the electoral system was also the weakest spot in the
precarious constitutional structure. Because most adult Frenchmen
qualified to vote in the "primary assemblies," elections provided a
regular opportunity for the mobilization of the masses and for the
expression of resistance to the political direction of the moment.
After Napoleon's coup d'état, his supporters repeatedly harped on
the dangers of the frequent elections under the Republic: according to the doctor Cabanis, for example, "annual elections put the
people in a fever state at least six months out of twelve."[4]

Elections, then, were one of the most important of the symbolic
practices of the Revolution. They offered immediate participation
in the new Nation through the performance of a civic duty, and
they opened up previously restricted access to positions of political
responsibility. Because they had such direct impact on the political structure, they attracted the attention of officials, and, as a result, they are one of the best documented revolutionary practices.
The series F[1c] III of the *Archives nationales* is largely devoted to correspondence about electoral results, and departmental and municipal archives are also rich in documentation about the government's
concerns. Moreover, unlike festivals or liberty tree plantings, elections left behind specific results: the names of those chosen to represent the voters. Hercules, Marianne, and the tricolor cockade
stood for everyone, and it is consequently difficult to read the messages of conflict and struggle embodied in them. The appeal of
such symbols was in part their lack of particularity. By contrast, the
men who were elected stood for their club, their profession, their
neighborhood, their village, their town, their department—as well
as for the general will. They were elected from a place; therefore

---

[3]Lynn Hunt, David Lansky, and Paul Hanson, "The Failure of the Liberal Republic in France, 1795–1799: The Road to Brumaire," *Journal of Modern History* 51
(1979): 734–59.
[4]Quoted in ibid., p. 737.

they almost necessarily represented something particular. Electoral results are consequently excellent tracers of the differences in reception of the Revolution.

This is not to say, however, that the interpretation of electoral results is entirely straightforward. Voters did not cast ballots for or against the Revolution; they chose men to represent them in the courts, in the municipalities, in the departments, and in the national legislature. The more removed the position, the less the voters knew about the men they were choosing. Deputies to the legislature, for example, were chosen in two stages: first the voters met in primary assemblies to choose electors, and then the electors of each department met in a central place to pick the deputies.[5] The translation from deputies to public opinion is consequently uncertain. Even on the local level where elections were direct, the difficulties of interpretation are striking. Because the rhetoric of revolution militated against party identification, the development of party labels was, to say the least, inconsistent. In addition, voting was too new to be an engrained habit, and, as a result, the proportion of voters varied enormously from election to election and from place to place, and it sometimes fell to under one in ten.[6] Voting in some places became a statement of support for the regime, not a test of differences in political opinion.

Nevertheless, election results offer possibilities of comparison, however rough, that are too interesting to be ignored. Studies of particular departments, for example, have shown that political divisions established during the Revolution of 1789 carried over, often canton by canton, to 1849 and even down to 1956.[7] For the first time, the French experimented with virtually universal, adult manhood suffrage.[8] Not surprisingly, the frequency of elections

[5] Electoral procedures are described in Jacques Godechot, *Les Institutions de la France sous la Révolution et l'Empire*, 2nd ed. (Paris, 1968). The difficulties of electoral analysis are emphasized in Jean-René Suratteau, "Heurs et malheurs de la 'sociologie électorale' pour l'époque de la Révolution française," *AESC* 28 (1968): 556–80.

[6] Various published results are compared in Melvin Edelstein, "Vers une 'sociologie électorale' de la Révolution française: Citadins et campagnards," *RHMC* 22 (1975): 508–29.

[7] See, for example, Paul Bois, *Paysans de l'Ouest: Des structures économiques et sociales aux options politiques depuis l'époque révolutionnaire dans la Sarthe* (Le Mans, 1960).

[8] The suffrage became virtually universal for adult males beginning in 1792. After 1795 property requirements were reinstituted for electors (Godechot, *Les Institutions*

fostered the development of proto-party organizations, such as the Jacobin clubs, even though parties per se were officially despised. Local studies and studies of particular elections have shown that those who did vote often did so in a politically self-conscious way. From the beginning of their formation, the Jacobin clubs engaged in active and vocal electioneering, and even under the relatively repressive Directory regime, resuscitated Jacobin clubs organized demonstrations, meetings, and public banquets to influence local voting.[9] In response royalists and moderates began to develop their own electoral organizations.[10] Newspapers from the big provincial capitals and from Paris proselytized for their various causes, and the government in power used *commissaires*, representatives-on-mission, and local administrators to sway local elections in its favor.[11] Voters, though sometimes few in number, did not make their choices in a political vacuum.

The growth of electoral politics sharpened everyone's sense of the meaning of political division. During the decade, the vocabulary of politics consequently expanded dramatically. The profusion of labels was overwhelming: there were democrats, republicans, patriots, ultra-patriots, exclusives, Jacobins, *enragés* (wild men), sans-culottes, pantheonists, the Mountain, anarchists, moderates, Girondins, Feuillants, monarchists, royalists, ultra-royalists, federalists, not to mention the scores of labels associated with particular politicians and particular epochs of the Revolution.[12] Many of these labels continued to have political significance well into the nineteenth century. But perhaps most lasting of all was the division of the National Assembly into "right" and "left," the two sides of the hall divided by the president's chair. Mirabeau called it "the geography of the Assembly." Like the country as a whole, the national

---

de la France). Even with property requirements for electors, indeed even under the regime of 1790–91 when eligibility to vote was limited to those paying a certain level of taxes, the suffrage was much broader under the Revolution than it was during the subsequent period, 1800–1847.

[9] Michael L. Kennedy, *The Jacobin Clubs in the French Revolution: The First Years* (Princeton, 1982), esp. pp. 210–23. Isser Woloch, *Jacobin Legacy: The Democratic Movement under the Directory* (Princeton, 1970), pp. 241–71.

[10] W. R. Fryer, *Republic or Restoration in France? 1794–97* (Manchester, 1965).

[11] For the government's own efforts, see Jean-René Suratteau, *Les Elections de l'an VI et le "coup d'état du 22 floréal" [11 mai 1798]* (Paris, 1971).

[12] Max Frey, *Les Transformations du vocabulaire français à l'époque de la Révolution (1789–1800)* (Paris, 1925), pp. 138–67.

legislature had its spatial differentiations; deputies who thought alike sat together on the same side of the center aisle.[13] During the National Convention, the topography became more subtle yet: the most radical deputies became known as the Mountain (or as the mountain men, the *montagnards*) because they preferred the highest rows of benches. Their opponents were known as Girondins because some of their leaders came from the Gironde department headquartered in Bordeaux. The large uncommitted center was known as the Plain or the Swamp, terms that referred to the lower seats occupied by these deputies. Newspapers and clubs taught the voters about the new categories.

Even as political sensibilities developed, the politically engaged continued to use the rhetoric of transparency, virtue, and community. This uneasy combination can be found in a typical pro-Jacobin election pamphlet from Amiens in 1798:

> Already the Royalists in their sinister haunts are preparing lists of candidates for the electors, for the legislative councils, the administrations, and the courts. They want to resuscitate those who were crushed by the republican club on 18 Fructidor [the date of an antiroyalist coup in the legislature]. What should therefore be your task at the opening of the primary assemblies? Here it is: from the first session, weed out, if I can use this term, the voters; examine with attention those who wish to exercise this honorable function. . . . Read on the brow of those who present themselves as voters, and you will see the men who are unfaithful to their engagements pale. . . . It is essential to name energetic men who profess our principles and share our sentiments. We need pronounced characters, strong souls, muscular and athletic spirits.[14]

The author could suggest political maneuvers, but the only party directly in reference was the opposition, the royalists. He knew that some men were on his side, and others were not, but he could only publicly advocate the most vague qualities: energy, firmness, strong character. Before long, however, the same printer issued a much more forthright pamphlet, this time on behalf of a new Con-

[13] Ferdinand Brunot, *Histoire de la langue française* 9 (*La Révolution et l'Empire*): 769–70; and Frey, *Les Transformations du vocabulaire*, p. 46.

[14] A.N., F¹ᶜ III Somme 9, Correspondance et divers, 1789–an IX, election pamphlet entitled "Aux Amis de la République" and signed Caron-Berquier, Printer of the Department of the Somme.

stitutional Circle, the name commonly given to the reconstituted Jacobin clubs: "What are you waiting for, then, before organizing Constitutional Circles? Hurry up! It is there that you will find the arms for crushing the 'reactors' [*les réacteurs*]: unite, be useful, support each other."[15] Continuing political conflict taught militants the virtues of concerted action.

Although there were men with these convictions all over France, they were successful in influencing elections only in some places. With the aid of a statistical technique known as discriminant analysis, it is possible to map the results of parliamentary elections (map 1).[16] Previous studies of the election of deputies in 1792 to the National Convention and in 1795–98 to the Directorial Councils have established the existence of distinct political groupings among the deputies elected.[17] Those elected in 1792 subsequently divided into Montagnards, Girondins, and the uncommitted center or Plain. Even more fundamental was the division of the deputies on the question of the appropriate punishment for the king. Just over half of them voted for the death sentence without reprieve or appeal. Those elected in 1795, 1797, and 1798 were identified by the government's agents in the departments as royalists (counterrevolutionaries), Jacobins (terrorists or anarchists), or Directorials (supporters of the government). Using information gathered about the political leanings of deputies, the Directory government arrested, expelled, or refused seats to scores of deputies in purges directed against presumed royalists in 1797 and against supposed Jacobins in 1798. The statitistical procedure takes all this information about the deputies and combines it into a function or functions that lo-

[15] Ibid., pamphlet from the Constitutional Circle of Amiens, dated 26 pluviôse an VI, signed Caron-Berquier, Printer of the Constitutional Circle.

[16] The map published with the earlier version of this chapter in *The Journal of Interdisciplinary History* (14 [1984]: 535–59) included only those departments classified with a high degree of probability. Twenty-one departments were excluded because of missing information on one of the variables in the discriminant analysis. Here the departments are classified in their category of highest probability, regardless of missing values; the lowest probability was .63. For the purpose of further analysis, however, the departments with missing values or low probabilities of classification (<.99) were excluded. See tables 1–3. Readers interested in the technical aspects of the analysis should refer to the article.

[17] Alison Patrick, *The Men of the First French Republic: Political Alignments in the National Convention of 1792* (Baltimore, 1972); and Surrateau, *Les Elections de l'an VI*, which includes maps of election results in 1795 and 1797 as well as 1798 (pp. 298–300).

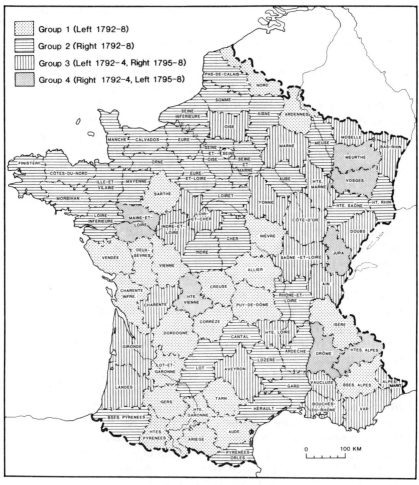

Group 1 (Left 1792–8)
Group 2 (Right 1792–8)
Group 3 (Left 1792–4, Right 1795–8)
Group 4 (Right 1792–4, Left 1795–8)

Map 1.
The Political Geography of Revolutionary France

cate individual departments along a continuum, so that they can be separated into distinct groups. In other words, the department's national delegation serves as an indicator of the department's political complexion.

For the purpose of tracing political allegiances, three questions were asked: (1) which departments were on the right and on the

left at the time of the Convention (1792–94)? (2) which departments were on the right and left during the Directory regime
(1795–99)? and (3) what was the continuity or discontinuity of political allegiance from the first period to the second? "Left" and
"right" were used, because the Revolution made them into the
classic political categories of division. Although there was an identifiable "center" in the legislature, most critical decisions forced the
deputies to choose one side or another. In addition most elections
pitted one side against the other on the local level. In 1797, for instance, voters opted for or against the right challenge; in 1798 they
voted for or against the Jacobin revival.[18] The political structure
seemed to divide most naturally in two.

The discriminant analysis shows that left and right were not artificial categories, because the discriminant functions derived by
this method were statistically significant.[19] If the voters were making random or entirely personal decisions, then it is unlikely that
there would have been distinct patterns in departmental choices.
Not only were the patterns distinct; they were also relatively per-
sistent. More departments stayed in the same camp than changed
(54 as opposed to 29). There was continuity within the Directorial
period, 1795–98, and also within the entire republican era, 1792–98.
Through the frequent upheavals and turnabouts of national politics, voters maintained their sense of political categories.

Map 1 shows that national elections produced definite regional
patterns. The parliamentary right was strongest in the Paris Basin
(the Seine department itself moved from left to right), the Rhône
valley, and the northwest. The parliamentary left was strongest in
the center-west and southwest. Many of the departments that
moved from left to right were part of the region around a major
city: Paris, Bordeaux, Lyon, Marseille, and Strasbourg. Most of the
departments that moved from right to left were in the mountains
close to the frontier. In general the left was strongest on the periphery (except in the southeast). This geographical pattern is telling: it
shows that the Jacobin deputies got most support from the periph-

[18]Suratteau, *Les Elections de l'an VI.*
[19]The Statistical Package for the Social Sciences, in which discriminant analysis is
a subprogram, generates many significance tests. A standard significance level of
.05 was used. See also William R. Klecka, *Discriminant Analysis,* in Sage University
Papers, no. 19 (Beverly Hills, 1980).

ery, not from the center of the country.[20] Paris itself was fickle in its allegiance to the left, and the regions closest to Paris were usually staunchly right wing. The deputies who rallied most enthusiastically around the new rhetoric, rituals, and images came out of places far removed from Parisian sophistication.

The significance of this map extended far beyond the First Republic. Many regions have continued to vote similarly to this day. In the 1970s, for example, when the left was not in power, the bastions of socialist (not communist) strength were still located in the far north and the center-southwest.[21] In the legislative elections of June 1981, the noncommunist left had its best showing in the southwest and in parts of the center and the northeast. The parties of the "former majority" (Gaullists and Giscardiens) did best in the northern half of the country and in a string of departments extending down the Rhône River.[22] No one has yet studied the continuity of political allegiances over the past two centuries in systematic fashion, but the division between a conservative north and a much more radical south seems almost "traditional."[23] The discriminant analysis demonstrates that it dates back to the First Republic.

[20] A map of Jacobin Club foundations shows that the clubs were numerous in the Nord department and the southwest (and to some extent in the southeast) (Michel de Certeau, Dominique Julia, and Jacques Revel, *Une politique de la langue: La Révolution française et les patois: L'Enquête de Grégoire* [Paris, 1975], p. 37). The map of parliamentary tendencies should be compared as well to Richard Cobb's characterization of the geography of "'ultra-racism' and revolutionary extremism" as extending in a vast half-moon from Perpignan and Toulouse to the Nièvre and then down the valley of the Rhône. Cobb was characterizing the Terror, and, as a consequence, his picture does not entirely coincide with mine. However, both the map of Jacobinism and Cobb's geography of extremism emphasize the radicalism of the Midi (*The Police and the People: French Popular Protest, 1789–1820* [Oxford, 1970], pp. 127–28).
[21] Hervé Le Bras and Emmanuel Todd, *L'Invention de la France: Atlas anthropologique et politique* (Paris, 1981), map p. 348.
[22] See the election results published in *Le Monde*, 16 June 1981, pp. 6–7.
[23] The classic study is François Goguel, *Géographie des élections françaises de 1870 à 1951* (Paris, 1951). The provocative analysis of Le Bras and Todd (n. 21) does not include the First Republic. However, they do argue that political divisions in France have long-term origins in regional family structures. They discern three types: regions of nuclear structures (Normandy, near west, Champagne, Lorraine, Burgundy, Franche-Comté, Orléanais); regions of complex structures with little control over marriage (southwest, Provence, Nord department); regions of complex structures with controlled marriages (Brittany, Basque country, south of the Massif central, Savoy, Alsace). Each corresponds to a political structure: nuclear families correspond to desires for independence and isolation; complex with little marriage control corresponds to desires for community and dependence; complex with

Under the Second Republic (elections of 1849), departments that had been consistently on the right in the 1790s continued to vote right.[24] The departments shifting from the left to the right during the First Republic also tended to be right wing in 1849. Many of the exceptions to this pattern were located in the southeast. In his investigation of the Var, Maurice Agulhon found that the department turned to the right during the Revolution, was staunchly Legitimist during the first half of the nineteenth century, but then was won over to radical republicanism during the Second Republic of 1848.[25] A similar process was evidently going on in nearby departments.

With the important exception of those of the far north and the center-southwest, departments voting for the left during the First Republic were less consistent in their political allegiance than were the departments voting for the right. More departments shifted from left to right than from right to left. In the long run, moreover, the south, which was generally more receptive to the left, proved much more volatile than the north. Not only did a number of departments in the southeast shift from left to right and then back to left again by 1849; a number of departments in the west shifted from left to right by 1849. The Vendée, Deux-Sèvres, and Charente-

_____

strong control corresponds to authoritarianism. Although there are many problems with this schematic and sometimes superficial analysis, it also suggests some interesting directions for research. It seems likely, for instance, that the backward west (Brittany) was distinguished from the backward southwest by significant cultural differences that did have political consequences. Family structures may have been only one of them. Replacing a monocausal interpretation, such as Marxism (class struggle), with another (family structure) is stimulating but unsatisfactory for the same reasons, e.g., map 1 shows that the southwest and Provence did not develop in identical fashion politically despite their similarities in family structure.

[24] See the map on p. 174 of Maurice Agulhon, *1848 ou l'apprentissage de la République, 1848–1852* (Paris, 1973). This comparison is discussed in greater detail in Hunt, "The Political Geography." The comparison with 1849 is central because the elections of the Second Republic were most like those of the First in their wide suffrage. The same regional patterns do not seem to hold in the 1820s and 1830s (Thomas D. Beck, *French Legislators, 1800–1834* [Berkeley, 1974]; and Patrick-Bernard Higonnet, "La Composition de la Chambre des Députés de 1827 à 1831," *Revue historique* 239 [1968]: 351–78). However, comparison with the interim period between the two republics is difficult because the suffrage was much more restrictively defined than during the republican eras. As a consequence, the republican left was probably not represented; the opposition then was much more like the republican *right*.

[25] Agulhon does not discuss the revolutionary period in any detail, so the reasons for this shift in the Var remain unclear (*La Vie sociale en Provence intérieure au lendemain de la Révolution* [Paris, 1970] and *La République au village* [Paris, 1970]).

Inférieure departments all gave less than 20 percent of their votes to the left in 1849.

The dramatic shift of the Vendée departments illustrates the limitations of studying elections to the legislature. These departments were in the notorious Vendée region, which was beset by popular counterrevolutionary movements during the First Republic. In response to the threat, local republican notables were able to galvanize limited but determined electoral support for a radical republic (i.e., deputies on the left). The rebels did not vote and hence left the field open to the Jacobins. In this region, even the government of the Directory encouraged Jacobin organizations as a counterweight to the rebels; they did not repress the left with the same determination they showed elsewhere because they could not afford to alienate the supporters of a republic, however radical they might be.[26] Thus, even though the masses of the region were far from enthusiastic about the republic, those men who voted were able to express support for the left. After the 1790s, this situation did not endure, and the Vendée region, except the Sarthe and the Maine-et-Loire, moved to the right in the nineteenth century.

The geographical pattern of voting under the First Republic had social meaning. In fact, the social differences between the regions voting left and right were more significant than the differences in their experience of the upheavals of the Revolution.[27] The choice between left and right was not associated with the department's rates of emigration, rates of executions during the Terror, or the

[26] Marcel Reinhard, *Le Département de la Sarthe sous le régime directorial* (St. Brieuc, 1935).

[27] An interesting attempt to explain regional differences for the modern period can be found in William Brustein, "A Regional Mode-of-Production Analysis of Political Behavior: The Cases of Western and Mediterranean France," *Politics and Society* 10 (1981): 355–98. He uses the results of national elections in 1849, 1885, 1936, and 1978 and focuses in particular on right voting in the west and left voting in the Mediterranean departments. This choice diminishes the usefulness of comparisons with the revolutionary period because the left was strongest precisely in the area in between those regions! As Brustein himself admits, his model of the effects of mode of production works best for the 1936 and 1978 elections (p. 396). Brustein's emphasis on rational calculation of material interests contrasts sharply with Yves-Marie Bercé's insistence on the long-term persistence of regional rebelliousness in the southwest (*Croquants et Nu-pieds: Les Soulèvements paysans en France du XVIe au XIXe siècle* [Paris, 1974]). The map of peasant uprisings in the seventeenth century does overlap to a considerable extent with the map of left voting during the Revolution. Bercé himself says little about the revolutionary period.

TABLE 1

Political Divisions and Experience of the Revolution (means)

Political Divisions	Clerical Oath (Percent)	Emigration (per 100,000 pop.)	Terror Deaths (per 100,000 pop.)
Left (N = 16)[a]	50	337	50
Right (N = 21)	50	310	75
Shift right (N = 15)	61	793	49
Shift left (N = 5)	62	304	2

Sources: See OATH, EMIPER, and TERPER in Appendix A.

[a]For the purpose of comparison, only those departments classified with a high degree of confidence are included. See n. 16, chap. 4.

attitudes of the local clergy toward the Revolution (see table 1). Given the nineteenth- and twentieth-century association between religious sentiment and political conviction (areas of consistent religious practice voted for the right), some relationship might be expected during the First Republic.[28] Table 1 shows that there is no difference between left and right on this score. Moreover, the more volatile departments (those that shifted in allegiance) had especially compliant clergymen. The attitude of the clergy had no obvious political effect. The only noteworthy differences registered by table 1 are the high rates of emigration in the shifting right departments and the low rates of Terror-related deaths in the shifting left departments. However, it is difficult to draw much significance from these figures; high rates of emigration may have contributed to an especially unstable political atmosphere in the shifting right departments, but there seems to be no reason why low rates of Terror-related deaths would have pushed some departments leftward rather than leaving them content with the government in power.

A correlation analysis based on all departments regardless of political categories likewise shows little relationship between the particular experiences of the Revolution, such as emigration, and

[28]Religion clearly was a factor in some areas, however (Timothy Tackett, "The West in France in 1789: The Religious Factor in the Origins of the Counterrevolution," *Journal of Modern History* 54 [1982]: 715–45).

TABLE 2

Social Differences in Politically Grouped Departments (means)

Political Divisions	Distance from Paris (lieus)	Literacy (Percent)	Urban (Percent)	Land Tax (francs per capita × 1000)
Left (N = 16)	129	22	14	80
Right (N = 21)	68	41	17	91
Shift right (N = 15)	95	31	26	91
Shift left (N = 5)	126	51	14	13

Sources: See DISTPAR, TOTLIT, URB1806, and PCFONC in Appendix A.

most voting choices (see Appendix A). The correlation between the departmental delegations' votes in the trial of the king and the departmental clerical oath rates, for example, was close to completely random ($r = -.04$). Not surprisingly, however, rates of emigration and of executions were negatively correlated with rates of clerical oath-taking ($r = -.26$ and $-.23$, respectively); the less compliant the clergy, the more likely the department was to have high rates of emigration and of deaths during the Terror. Nevertheless these traumatic experiences did not have much influence on voting in national elections.

By contrast, the economic and social differences between right and left were important (table 2). The left was most successful far from Paris, where the population was less urban (mean urbanization for France as a whole was 18.8 percent),[29] less well-off, and less literate than average (33.3 percent for all departments).[30] Not much can be made of the shifting left departments because there were so few of them, but the presence of departments in the mountains is evident in the high average literacy, low urbanization, and low per capita land tax.[31] The mountains of the east, in particular, were

[29] The mean reported is taken from René Le Mée (Appendix A, entry for URB1806). The mean for the 83 departments considered here was 17 percent.
[30] An average of male and female literacy was used rather than just male literacy alone. In any case, the correlation between male literacy and "total literacy" is .98, and the correlation between female literacy and total literacy is .96.
[31] In addition, the shifting left departments had less acreage devoted to agricul-

known for their high rates of literacy under the Old Regime, but their terrain was not congenial to the development of big towns or intensive agriculture.

The right had two distinct socioeconomic components; the persistently right-wing departments were rich, agricultural, literate, and close to Paris, whereas the shifting right departments were farther away, more urban, and less literate than the persistently right departments. The socioeconomic characteristics of the shifting right departments reflect the pivotal importance of certain big peripheral cities (Marseille, Bordeaux, and Strasbourg, most notably) in the shift away from the left after 1794. Paris and its department, the Seine, were also in this group. The greatest volatility, especially rightward moving volatility, was to be found in the more urbanized departments. The most consistent political divisions (right or left without shifts) were to be found in the agricultural hinterland. Rather than Edward Whiting Fox's two Frances, then, there seem to have been at least four or five Frances; rather than dividing France between towns of the hinterland and cities of the periphery, this analysis demonstrates that the hinterland itself was deeply divided between right and left. The big commercial cities of the periphery did indeed occupy a pivotal position, but rather than drawing their departments to support of the Gironde, they pushed them—after the Terror—into the ranks of the Gironde's successors, the parliamentary right.[32] In this respect, the peripheral cities were not at odds with Paris, but rather right in line.

The importance of socioeconomic factors is highlighted if a more restricted comparison is made between right and left departments (table 3). For this comparison the departments chosen were among those classified with the highest probability. Eleven departments were singled out from the consistently right-wing group in the north; Brittany and the few isolated departments in the south were excluded, leaving Aube, Calvados, Eure, Loiret, Manche, Orne, Pas-de-Calais, Seine-et-Marne, Seine-et-Oise, Seine-Inférieure, and Somme. Nine departments from the consistently left-wing group were included, all of them from the center and southwest regions

---

ture. The means were 42,000 hectares for shifting left departments; 55,000 hectares for left departments; 61,000 hectares for right departments; and 53,000 hectares for shifting right departments (Appendix A, under AGPROD).

[32] Fox, *History in Geographical Perspective: The Other France* (New York, 1971).

TABLE 3

Socioeconomic and Political Statistics for Sample Departments (means)

Sample Group	Literacy (Percent)	Urban (Percent)	Land Tax (francs per capita × 1000)	Clerical Oath (Percent)	Terror Deaths (per 100,000 pop.)	Emigration (per 100,000 pop.)
Left (N = 9)	19	11	75	50	4	263
Right (N = 11)	54	18	118	57	12	330
All departments (N = 83)	33	17	84	53	45	452

Sources: See tables 1 and 2.

(excluding the Vendée departments on the grounds that their situation was peculiar). The left's lower rates of emigration and executions are here dramatically overshadowed by the fact that both left and right were far below average on these counts; the consistently politically committed departments had few traumatic experiences during the Terror. Neither the core of the parliamentary left nor the core of the right was formed in reaction to the most dramatic experiences of the decade. But the socioeconomic differences are striking: the right-wing regions were rich and literate; the left regions were relatively poor, distinctly unurbanized, and woefully illiterate. These were two distinct agricultural hinterlands: one modern, wealthy, and near Paris, the other backward and far removed from the cultural and commercial mainstream.

Given the inadequacies of statistical measurements in the eighteenth century, it is difficult to be precise about the working of socioeconomic factors, even when taken in isolation. It is impossible, for example, to test Charles Tilly's hypothesis that counter-revolution was fostered by uneven rates of urbanization, because the information available for the departments describes levels of urbanization, not rates of urban growth.[33] Moreover, socioeconomic

[33] Tilly, The Vendée (Cambridge, Mass., 1964).

factors cannot be treated adequately in isolation, because their effects vary depending on the context. Urbanization is an illuminating example.[34] Tables 2 and 3 show that the departments that consistently voted for the right and those that shifted to the right were both more likely to be highly urbanized. But the partial correlations for all departments taken together (correlation matrix in Appendix A) indicate that the level of urbanization fostered various, even contradictory kinds of political involvement. Urbanization was positively correlated with support for the right in 1797 ($r = .64$), support for the left in 1798 ($r = .41$), and support of Bonaparte's coup in 1799 ($r = .41$). In other words, highly urbanized departments sometimes changed their political allegiances from year to year, and rates of urbanization taken alone cannot predict how departments made their political choices.

Here what is offered is a set of hypotheses concerning the development of different regional political cultures. The hypotheses are consistent with the information presented in tables 1 to 3, but they are not testable by quantitative methods. Regional political cultures developed within the confines set by social and economic factors, but they were more than simple translations of such factors into politics. The government's agents in the field quickly discovered that the key to local and regional politics was the development of concentric circles of personal relationships. The government depended on personal contacts for its information, and the competing political organizations depended on such contacts for electoral success. As one departmental agent wrote to the Minister of the Interior in 1798, "there are in every canton a certain number of energetic and virtuous men who are sincerely attached to the Republic. They retain all the influence necessary to neutralize the efforts of the malicious and to direct choices in the sense of the Revolution."[35] Jacobinism and royalism were propagated by pamphlets, brochures, and newspapers, but they only took root when their message was carried from one person to another, from one village to another, from one club to another. In some places the Jacobin

[34] The importance of urbanization is emphasized in ibid. and in various studies reviewed in Gilbert Shapiro, John Markoff, and Sasha R. Weitman, "Quantitative Studies of the French Revolution," *History and Theory* 12 (1973): 163–91.

[35] A.N., F^{ic} III Vendée 7, Correspondance et divers, 1789–1815, letter from the Directory's agent to the departmental administration, 19 ventôse an VI.

message traveled farther and faster, while in others resistance to innovation and clandestine support for a restoration won the day. The variability has to be sought in the local patterns of reception to different forms of political relationships.

In addition to the many rural paramilitary bands that operated against the Republic, popular royalism built a base in the biggest cities, using clientage relationships. In some places federalist networks may have first established the pattern.[36] Popular royalism had solid bases in Paris and Lyon after 1794, and officials feared that it might spread outward from other big cities as well.[37] In 1799, for instance, one hysterical police report claimed that supporters of Louis XVIII had an enormous paramilitary organization inside of Bordeaux.[38] An official report in April 1799 concluded that only eight departments could be considered reliably republican: Creuse, Meurthe, Haute-Saône, Hautes-Pyrénées, Finistère, Jura, Haute-Garonne, and Pyrénées-Orientales. Significantly, there were only two big cities (Nancy and Toulouse) in these areas; by then all of the others were suspect.[39]

Studies of such cities as Lyon and Marseille have shown that the big cities had huge, floating populations of frequently unemployed day laborers and wageworkers who were not much like the more stable and militant sans-culottes described by Soboul.[40] In times of food shortage and political uncertainty, they were readily recruited into right-wing groups organized around clientage relationships. For example, in Bordeaux in September 1796 the police reported that anti-Jacobin riots attracted many workers and artisans from the workshops and warehouses of the Chartrons district, which

[36] Some suggestive comments on clientage relations in the federalist movement can be found in Paul Richard Hanson, "The Federalist Revolt of 1793: A Comparative Study of Caen and Limoges," Ph.D. diss., University of California, Berkeley, 1981, esp. pp. 337–423.

[37] On Lyon, see A.N., F⁷ 6759, Police générale: Troubles à Lyon.

[38] A.N., F⁷ 6216, Affaires politiques, an V–1830, no. 3963, "Conspiration de la Gironde," report from the Police Ministry to the Directory.

[39] "Résumé des comptes-rendus au Ministre de l'Intérieur par les Commissaires du Directoire éxécutif près les administrations centrales des départements, pendant le mois de floréal an VII," reprinted in Félix Rocquain, *L'Etat de la France au 18 brumaire* (Paris, 1874), p. 380.

[40] Albert Soboul, *Les Sans-culottes parisiens en l'an II*, 2nd ed. (Paris, 1962). Michel Vovelle only touches on this issue briefly in his "Le Prolétariat flottant à Marseille sous la Révolution française," *Annales de démographie historique*, 1968, pp. 111–38.

was dominated by the city's rich merchants and shippers.[41] Paris seems an exception in this regard only if we limit our consideration to the period of the Terror, when the Jacobins succeeded in mobilizing some segments of the artisanal and wageworking population. After 1794 the republican right established its control in Paris too. Rapid urban growth in the decades before the Revolution, economic dislocation caused by bad harvests and war-related shortages, popular apathy after the dismantling of local clubs, bitter divisions provoked by the Terror (there were more executions in highly urbanized departments), even religious conflicts between Protestants and Catholics—all contributed to the confusions and upheavals of politics in the big cities.[42]

The left departments of the southwest and center-west clustered around a few "old" cities (what some have called "villes-villes") as opposed to new industrial or commercial centers. "Red" Toulouse was the biggest and most worrisome of them for the Directorial regime, but the Jacobins and neo-Jacobins there had counterparts in many similar towns of the southwest: in his study of the 1798 elections, for instance, Woloch found important Jacobin strongholds in Brive, Tulle (both in the Corrèze), Perigueux (Dordogne), Auch (Gers), Clermont, and Issoire (Puy-de-Dôme).[43] All of them traditionally enjoyed great influence and prestige in their relatively backward regions, and, though none of them were particularly fast-growing industrial or manufacturing centers (many, if not all, of them could be characterized as relatively stagnant), they did stand out as the commercial and cultural centers of their often poor and nearly always illiterate hinterlands.

These modest cities of the southwest became the centers of a lasting left-wing tradition, because their Jacobins were able to establish influence not only in town, but also in the surrounding rural areas. Bois' study of the Sarthe department shows, for example, that the Jacobins of 1792–93 were headquartered in the towns (especially Le Mans) and bourgs and that they were able to dominate the eastern half of the department and the departmental elec-

[41] Gaston Ducaunnès-Duval, *Ville de Bordeaux: Inventaire-Sommaire des Archives municipales: Période révolutionnaire (1789–an VIII),* 4 vols. (Bordeaux, 1896–1929) 3: 37 (reprint of document dated 8 vendémiaire an V).

[42] See, e.g., Gwynne Lewis, *The Second Vendée: The Continuity of Counterrevolution in the Department of the Gard, 1789–1815* (Oxford, 1978).

[43] *Jacobin Legacy,* p. 283.

tions. Their domination was made possible by the poverty of peasants in the eastern half of the department, which in turn made the peasants dependent on the relationships built up by supplemental textile weaving organized in the towns. Just as city merchants were able to penetrate the countryside with commercial relationships, so too the Jacobins were able to penetrate the countryside with their new political relationships. Where they were resisted by a more prosperous and independent peasantry, as in the western half of the department, the Revolution failed, and counterrevolutionary movements were able to establish a base.[44]

Marcel Reinhard demonstrated how this kind of penetration continued in the Sarthe department after 1794. During the Jacobin revival of 1798, the Jacobins in Le Mans established a Constitutional Circle that soon spread its influence. Almost every *décadi* (the day of rest in the revolutionary calendar), the circle organized a procession to a nearby town or village, where the participants planted a liberty tree and offered a "civic soup," which would culminate in the establishment of a new Constitutional Circle. Before long, other circles were organizing the same processions. Their greatest success was in the eastern half of the department, the same half that had been won over by the Jacobins earlier. At general meetings, the circles drew up lists of candidates for the elections and then circulated them.[45]

In the departments of the center and southwest that voted left, the same story was repeated again and again. The Jacobins had not necessarily won the enthusiasm of the masses; as the departmental administration claimed in the Vienne in 1798, "the mass of the people counts for absolutely nothing in the Revolution."[46] But they had won determined converts who worked actively for electoral successes. In Poitiers, the capital of the Vienne department, the Constitutional Circle had 600 members by the spring of 1798, and it was affiliated with smaller societies in the other towns of the department. The successes of 1798 usually reflected the gains made in the early years of the Revolution. In the Gers, for instance, there were fourteen Jacobin clubs associated with the Paris club in March

[44] *Paysans de l'Ouest.*
[45] Reinhard, *Le Département de la Sarthe.*
[46] As quoted in Roger Doucet, *L'Esprit public dans le département de la Vienne pendant la Révolution* (Paris, 1910), p. 263.

1791. The club of Auch was the primary one, and it was closely related to the bigger club in Toulouse.[47] In the Ariège department,
the influence of the Toulouse Jacobin Club was so great that the
departmental administration complained to the Minister of the Interior in 1792.[48] Small village clubs were affiliated to the bigger city
clubs; the bigger clubs were affiliated with each other and with
Paris.

The merchants, lawyers, shopkeepers and artisans of the Jacobin
clubs were able to exercise such influence, in part because they had
few rivals in these departments. Other than Toulouse, Grenoble,
and Douai, there were no cities in the consistently left departments
with *parlements* and their accompanying noble dynasties of magistrates. Moreover, the clergy had not shown much sympathy for the
Revolution. Consequently the smaller fry of the towns and market
centers found themselves with an unparalleled opportunity to exercise new kinds of power. In the center and southwest, these urban groups were among the relatively few literate people. The
south of France as a whole was less literate than the north, and the
gap between literacy in the towns and in the countryside was usually much greater in the south than in the north, where newer industrial towns often had quite low rates of literacy.[49] The illiterate
and non–French speaking peasants in the Corrèze, for example,
were likely to follow the lead of Brive and Tulle, whereas the literate, prosperous peasants in Calvados were less dependent on the
intellectual and political leadership of Caen.

Just as the rule of republican notables was unchallenged in the
left departments from above, so too it was unthreatened from below. Because none of the left departments (except the generally ex-
ceptional Nord) had large cities with enormous working-class communities (compared to Rouen in the north or Marseille in the
south, for instance), bourgeois and petit bourgeois leaders in these
areas were not faced with the problems created by mobilization
of unskilled, often unemployed and hungry, lower-class people.

[47]G. Brégail, "Le Gers pendant la Révolution," *Bulletin de la Société d'histoire et
d'archéologie du Gers* 30 (1929): 89–120, 224–59, 354–77.
[48]G. Arnaud, *Histoire de la Révolution dans le département de l'Ariège (1789–1795)*
(Toulouse, 1904), p. 309.
[49]For the urban-rural differential, see François Furet and Jacques Ozouf, *Lire et
écrire: L'Alphabétisation des français de Calvin à Jules Ferry* (Paris, 1977), pp. 229–45.

Spared the tensions of the large cities with their workers, resident nobles, refractory clergymen, and divided bourgeoisie (there were also no large and rich communities of merchants in the left departments, outside of the Nord, at least none that could compare to Bordeaux or Nantes, for example), the more modest bourgeoisie of the left departments were able to pursue their apprenticeship of republicanism unhindered.

Thus, paradoxically, the political culture of the left—the party of movement—took root best in a context of relative social stability, perhaps even of economic stagnation. In the midst of a rapidly changing political world, those who had the least painful experience of social and economic modernization had the most to look forward to in the coming of the new political order.

Conversely, right-wing republicanism and royalism appealed to the political notables who lived in regions in which the potential for social conflict was great. For example, textile weaving in a rural department like the Sarthe gave poor peasants extra income and cemented clientage relationships favorable to a republican bourgeoisie, but textile weaving in the more urban departments had drawn peasants off the land into the cities, where their potential menace to bourgeois control was all the greater. In the face of masses of unemployed and restive workers, notables in these departments turned to the right; democracy and equality had a different and more ominous ring to them. The Revolution had revealed the dangers of political mobilization. Similarly, the landlords, old and new, of the large farms and cereal-producing regions of the north saw no virtue in the mobilization of the landless or the small farmers. The experience of rapid modernization and economic growth fostered a political culture that was favorable to the development of right-wing politics. Support for Bonaparte's coup, for instance, was positively correlated with urbanization, literacy, wealth, and previous support for the right (Appendix A).[50]

[50] See also Hunt, Lansky, and Hanson, "The Failure of the Liberal Republic." Too little is known about socioeconomic structures to make a more refined judgment. A systematic comparison of sales of national lands might prove informative. Bois has shown that this was one of the critical differences between the eastern and western districts of the Sarthe: in the western and counterrevolutionary districts, there were more clerical lands and more of them were bought up by nonresident townsmen. Georges Lefebvre found that the peasants were able to purchase considerable

In contrast, the more contained popular mobilization in the relatively undeveloped areas of the southwest and center-west favored the Jacobins. Jacobins from the few cities and small towns were able to control not only most of the clubs, but also many of the new local offices, and clubs and officeholding in these areas integrated the upper ranks of the sans-culottes and the republican bourgeoisie (see chapter 5 on this process in Toulouse). In the regions far from Paris, removed from the tensions of rapid economic development, and without major religious divisions, local republicanism flourished. The emphasis on speaking from the heart, the virtues of simple folk, and the politics of didacticism all had a ready audience in such places.

A nationally based, quantitative analysis cannot reveal the workings of political culture on the local level. Rather, it serves to suggest the kinds of contexts in which different political options were worked out. The numbers do rule out certain kinds of explanations, however. The analysis demonstrates, for example, that Paris was not the model for national politics, at least not a model for enduring left-wing politics, despite the importance of the Jacobin–sans-culottes alliance of 1793–94. At the same time, the statistical analysis shows that revolutionary France was not characterized by extreme particularism; France was not an utterly random patch-

amounts of land in the Nord, though he does not examine the sales in tandem with voting patterns (*Les Paysans du Nord pendant la Révolution française* [Bari, 1959], esp. pp. 514–23). Unfortunately, most of the studies of sales have focused on northern France, and the impact on the peasants has been shown to be very variable. For an overview, see Michel Vovelle, *La Chute de la monarchie, 1787–1792* (Paris, 1972), p. 195.

Since the work of André Siegfried, commentators have drawn attention to the impact of land-tenure arrangements, but overall patterns have proved difficult to establish. See the review in Theodore Zeldin, *France, 1848–1945: Politics and Anger* (Oxford, 1979), pp. 1–28. Brustein tries to systematically explore this variable in nineteenth- and twentieth-century French politics (n. 27 above). On a more local level, this factor is emphasized by T. J. A. Le Goff, *Vannes and its Region: A Study of Town and Country in Eighteenth-Century France* (Oxford, 1981). No one has succeeded in generalizing this factor to the national level.

A recent study of prices during the Revolution by Dominique Margairaz shows an interesting regional overlap with the political map described here: the agricultural north had low grain prices but high beef prices; the southeast had high grain prices but low meat prices; and the southwest had low meat prices and variable grain prices. Margairaz attributes these differences to developmental variations ("Dénivellations des prix et inégalités de développement régional dans la France de 1790: Essai de cartographie," *AHRF* 53 [1981]: 262–78).

work of neighborhoods, villages, towns, and departments. True, France did not divide neatly down the middle, between classes, between regions, or between modernity and backwardness. The bourgeoisie in the north chose different options than the bourgeoisie in the south. Parts of the north went left, and parts of the south right; some backward areas were right wing, others left wing. But the divisions were not haphazard: the left won elections where the Jacobins of the towns and villages were able to develop relationships and organizations favorable to the rhetoric of liberty, equality, and fraternity; and the right won elections where royalists and/or partisans of a republic of order were able to galvanize their clients into movements against the innovating Republic.

Some elements in the difference between left and right are suggested here, but others remain mysterious. Little is known, for instance, about the way regional cultural factors impinged on political development. A recent study of Freemasonry in the eighteenth century shows that the diffusion of lodges did not correspond to population density, patterns of regional wealth, or literacy, yet the map of towns of less than 2,000 population with lodges suggests some interesting parallels with the success of the left in the 1790s; the density of such towns was highest in the southwest quadrant of the nation and lowest in the northern half of the country.[51] It is possible then that, though the lodges did not turn automatically into Jacobin clubs,[52] both Freemasonry and Jacobinism reflected social and cultural proclivities that had distinct political consequences. The small-town sociability of the southwest may have made residents more receptive to the promises of the Republic.

Even with the limitations of such an analysis, the political geography of revolution suggests some new directions for research. Why did politics have a regional base? If there were four or five distinct regions (the counterrevolutionary west, the right-wing north, the left-wing southwest, and the volatile and often violent southeast), then what accounts for their distinctiveness? How were political cultures shaped in each region? Although such questions are still without complete answers, the map itself tells many interest-

---

[51] See the map on p. 84 of Ran Yedid-Halévi, "La Sociabilité maçonnique et les origines de la pratique démocratique," *Thèse de 3e cycle* (Paris: Ecole des hautes études en sciences sociales, 1981).

[52] Kennedy, *The Jacobin Clubs*, pp. 5–7.

ing tales. The rhetoric of revolution appealed to the peripheries of the nation, to people who lived in the economic, social, and cultural backwaters. Yet these were people who were in the forefront of joining and belonging, who believed that politics could change daily life and with it the character of men. In the next chapters, attention will turn away from the places to the people in order to determine which groups took the lead in this process.

$\approx 5 \ll$

The New
Political Class

MOST RECENT WORK on the social identity of the revolutionaries divides into two sharply antagonistic camps. On the one side, the late Albert Soboul and his Marxist followers emphasize the organized and ideologically engaged activities of the Jacobins and sans-culottes.[1] In their writings, revolutionaries appear as committed militants, who share a certain social outlook (egalitarianism) but are knit together most tightly, even if only temporarily, by common political goals (e.g., defense of the Republic, belief in democracy, or hostility to the Old Regime). In this view, the revolutionary coalition between bourgeois Jacobins and petit-bourgeois sans-culottes served the interests of the bourgeoisie in the long run.

On the other side, revisionists draw attention to the less lofty interests of a variety of groups that do not fit into any kind of predictable social class framework. Alfred Cobban argued that the revolutionary bourgeoisie was composed of "declining" professionals and royal officials rather than "rising" capitalist merchants and manufacturers.[2] In a more extreme revisionist vein, Richard Cobb concentrates on the personal and psychological underpinnings of militancy. In his view, the sans-culotte, for example, was "a freak of nature, more a state of mind than a social, political, or economic entity."[3] In the works of Cobb and his followers, revolutionaries seem truly marginal to normal society; they are the creatures of social and political breakdown rather than the architects of an enduring new order.

Most of the controversy about the social interpretation has been

[1] See esp. Soboul, *Les Sans-culottes parisiens en l'an II,* 2nd ed. (Paris, 1962).
[2] *The Social Interpretation of the French Revolution* (Cambridge, 1964), esp. pp. 54–67.
[3] *The Police and the People: French Popular Protest, 1789–1820* (Oxford, 1970), p. 200.

based on remarkably limited evidence, for example, the social composition of the sans-culotte movement in one city, the occupational
identities of deputies in one or two national assemblies, or just the
differences between factions in one legislature.[4] In my view, there
were three defining elements in the social context of revolutionary
political action: geographical place, social identity, and cultural ties
and values. In chapter 4, political action was shown to have a distinct regional pattern; the most revolutionary departments were
geographically peripheral and relatively disadvantaged economically, socially, and culturally. In this chapter, the social identity of
the revolutionary elite is examined in systematic fashion. The review of evidence will suggest that the new political class was defined as much by its cultural positions and relationships as by its
membership in occupationally defined social groups.

On the basis of an occupational analysis of the Constituent Assembly (the delegates from the Third Estate to the Estates General)
and the National Convention, Alfred Cobban insisted that "the *officiers* [royal officials, who for the most part held hereditary offices]
and the men of the liberal professions prepared and directed the
revolution."[5] Not only is it dubious whether the direction of the
Revolution can be attributed solely to a few national leaders, but
Cobban's assertion is also not entirely correct. If he had continued
his investigations into the Directory period, he would have found
that the proportion of *officiers* declined, even in the national legislature, from nearly one-half of the deputies to the Third Estate, to
only one-quarter of the *conventionnels*, to only one in eight of the
Directorial deputies.[6] Officials of the Old Regime did not direct the
Revolution; they participated in large numbers at the beginning
but steadily dropped out thereafter.

Still, the other half of Cobban's assessment of the national deputies remains true: the majority of them were lawyers or profes-

[4]For example, an extended controversy was provoked by Elizabeth Eisenstein's
article on "Who Intervened in 1788? A Commentary on *The Coming of the French Revolution*," *American Historical Review* 71 (1965): 77–103. The limitations of evidence
were inherent in early stages of debate over the Marxist or social interpretation.

[5]*The Social Interpretation*, p. 61; and Cobban, *Aspects of the French Revolution* (New
York, 1970), pp. 109–11.

[6]Lynn Hunt, David Lansky, and Paul Hanson, "The Failure of the Liberal Republic, 1795–1799: The Road to Brumaire," *Journal of Modern History* 51 (1979):
734–59, esp. p. 746.

sionals by training, even if they were not former royal officials. Merchants never comprised more than 14 percent of the legislature, and the number of merchants constantly declined during the decade, to 4 percent in the Directory councils.[7] The steady decline in the number of merchant deputies suggests that the legislature was becoming professionalized; voters increasingly preferred professional politicians to venerable local notables. One indication of this preference is the age of national deputies: they were no older than local officials, that is, they were chosen for their political skills rather than for their seniority or notability on the local level. The average age of Directorial deputies in 1795, for instance, was 43 years. In 1789, 32 percent of the deputies to the Constituent Assembly had been under 40 years old; in 1793, 46 percent of the deputies to the National Convention were under 40; and in 1795, 40 percent of the Directorial deputies were under 40.[8] Leaders on the local level were about the same age. In Nancy, for example, the average age of city councillors was 43 years under the constitutional monarchy, 43 under the Terror, and 47 under the Directory.[9] In other words, the national deputies were selected from the same pool of men as local officials.

Deputies usually came to national office with some political experience behind them, but the nature of that experience changed over the years. Not only did the number of former royal officials decline; so too did the proportion of former deputies. Only 37 percent of the deputies to the Convention had served as deputies before, and, even though the rump of the Convention decreed that

[7] For the Constituent Assembly, see Edna-Hindie Lemay, "La Composition de l'Assemblée nationale constituante: Les Hommes de la continuité?" *RHMC* 24 (1977): 341–63, esp. p. 345. For the Convention, see Alison Patrick, *The Men of the First French Republic: Political Alignments in the National Convention of 1792* (Baltimore, 1972), p. 260 ("business" deputies = 9 percent). The figure for the Directorial Councils (3 percent, and 4 percent if unknowns are excluded) is based on a random sample of 100 deputies taken from Auguste Kuscinski, *Les Députés au Corps législatif, Conseil des Cinq Cents, Conseil des Anciens, de l'an IV a l'an VIII* (Paris, 1905).

[8] A summary of age distributions for three legislatures can be found in Hunt, Lansky, and Hanson, "The Failure of the Liberal Republic," p. 745.

[9] See Appendix B for sources. Ages were found for 71 percent of the city councillors, 1790–99. Ages given are for all officeholders in the specified periods, for 1790, 1793, and 1795, respectively. The city councillors were no older than the rank-and-file militants. Martyn Lyons found, e.g., that the average age of revolutionary *commissaires* in Toulouse was 45 years in 1793 (*Revolution in Toulouse: An Essay on Provincial Terrorism* [Berne, 1978], p. 188).

the first Directorial Councils must have two-thirds of their members taken from the outgoing Convention, the proportion of *conventionnels* dropped dramatically in every election, from 67 percent in the Year IV to 12 percent in the Year VII. The number of deputies who had served in previous legislatures (including all the legislative bodies, 1789–94) dropped from 77 percent in the Year IV to 16 percent in the Year VII. By the Year VII only 4 percent of the deputies had served in the original Constituent (or National) Assembly.[10] The deputies were constantly being overwhelmed by waves of men who were new to their positions. This situation prompted a disenchanted observer to declare, "one is forced to see the principal [cause of the troubles of the Revolution] in the flood of new men called all at once to posts as new as them . . . these new men would become the playthings of the factious."[11] Professionalization did not entail permanence in office.

Although many deputies were new to national office, they had had considerable experience in local affairs. Almost all of the deputies to the National Convention (86 percent) had held some kind of revolutionary office, and even in the Year VII three-fourths of the deputies to the Directorial Councils had served in local offices.[12] Thus, though new, relatively young men kept appearing on the political scene in Paris, they entered their new roles with political experience as well as professional formation behind them. In addition, deputies kept coming to Paris by the same routes. One of the most obvious places for preparation was the departmental administrations. Four of the eleven executive officers (*procureur général-syndic*, then *commissaire du pouvoir exécutif*) of the Allier department, for example, went on to serve as national deputies, and ten of the other departmental councillors were similarly promoted. In the Marne, three of the nine executive officers served in the na-

---

[10] For the National Convention, see Patrick, *The Men of the First French Republic*, p. 204. For the Directorial deputies, see Hunt, Lansky, and Hanson, "The Failure of the Liberal Republic," p. 750.

[11] Quatremère de Quincy, *La Véritable liste des candidats, précédée d'observations sur la nature de l'institution des candidats, et son application au gouvernement représentatif*, 2nd ed. (Paris, 1797), pp. 37, 39.

[12] Alison Patrick does not give a specific figure for local officeholders among the *conventionnels*; the figure of 86 percent was calculated from her table, *The Men of the First French Republic*, p. 203 (adding those with no experience to those who were only club members or journalists and subtracting the sum from the total number of deputies). The figure for Directorial deputies comes from Hunt, Lansky, and Hanson, "The Failure of the Liberal Republic," p. 747.

tional legislature; in the Haute-Saône ten councillors became deputies.[13] Conversely, the men who served in the earlier assemblies of the Revolution usually returned home and held local offices. Etienne Douyet, for instance, was a 36-year-old notary when he was elected to the Allier departmental council in 1790. After serving in the Legislative Assembly, he returned home to sit out the Terror. He was picked as an administrator of his district in the Year III and then was promoted to the department again in the Year IV. He was appointed mayor of his hometown by Napoleon.[14]

The career of Douyet points to one of the stabilizing features of revolutionary politics: though officials usually did not hold particular offices for long periods, they often left one office to take on another. The circulation of officials facilitated the formation of a new political class by familiarizing politicians with each other and with the problems encountered at different levels of administration. The departmental administrations were the critical links in this interlocking political system, because the men who had the time, money, and skills needed to pursue national political interests were usually found at some point in the departmental administrations.

As might be expected, the departmental administrations were manned for the most part by lawyers, notaries, and, increasingly, men who were making careers as revolutionary officials. In the Haut-Rhin, according to Roland Marx, the departmental administration included few merchants, virtually no artisans, a strong proportion of lawyers, and a mixture of "bourgeois professions," such as professors, functionaries, and doctors. In both the Haut- and Bas-Rhin departments, electors showed a preference for men with political experience: mayors, outgoing administrators, district officials, and the like. Most of the administrators in these two departments were city dwellers, and only a handful were farmers (*laboureurs* or *cultivateurs*).[15]

In the Allier department in central France, the lawyers were

---

[13] The numbers for the Allier are based on the lists given in G. Rougeron, *Les Administrations départementales de l'Allier (1790–an VIII)* (Montluçon, 1957). For the Marne, see the names given in Raymond Nicolas, *L'Esprit public et les élections dans le département de la Marne de 1790 à l'an VIII* (Châlons-sur-Marne, 1909). For the Haute-Saône, see Jean Girardot, *Le Département de la Haute-Saône pendant la Révolution*, 3 vols. (Vesoul, 1973).

[14] Rougeron, *Les Administrations départementales de l'Allier*.

[15] *Recherches sur la vie politique de l'Alsace pré-révolutionnaire et révolutionnaire* (Strasbourg, 1966), pp. 165–67.

even more prominent: 59 percent of those administrators who listed occupations were either lawyers or officeholders in Old Regime jurisdictions. In this less urbanized area, the landowners were influential: 23 percent of the administrators called themselves *propriétaires*. The others were doctors, merchants, clergymen, or retired military officers. The administrators who listed no occupation often referred instead to their positions as mayors or district officials. In the Allier, as in the Alsatian departments, political experience was essential: 43 percent of the departmental administrators chosen after August 1792 had been district officials, and in all, nearly three-fourths of the administrators under the Republic had held local revolutionary offices before being named to the departmental council.[16]

Although rural landowners had some influence in the Allier department, they do not seem to have dominated the departmental councils anywhere in France. In the Marne in 1790 lawyers and professionals outnumbered rural proprietors (those who made their living solely in this fashion) more than two to one; in 1792 there were even more merchants on the departmental council (ten) than landowners (six). The Haute-Saône councils resembled those of Alsace: in 1790–91, 60 percent of the departmental councillors were lawyers or Old Regime officials, 18 percent were merchants, and only 4 percent rural proprietors; in 1792–94, 50 percent were lawyers or Old Regime officials, 12 percent were merchants, and 6 percent rural proprietors. In the Meurthe, the weakness of merchant representation was extreme: in 1790 no merchants or shopkeepers were elected to the departmental council, which included 58 percent lawyers and 11 percent rural proprietors.[17]

Despite the variation in occupational mix from department to department, the general pattern is evident: the new official class on the regional level was comprised overwhelmingly of townsmen

---

[16]The figures given here are based on the lists in Rougeron, *Les Administrations départementales de l'Allier*. This is one of the few studies that includes the whole decade and that provides considerable biographical information on each departmental administrator. Most studies give general characterizations rather than quantitative data or information susceptible to quantification.

[17]Nicolas, *L'Esprit public . . . département de la Marne*, annex III; and Girardot, *Le Département de la Haute-Saône* 2: annex V, and 3: annex I. After 1790 in the Meurthe, administrators only identified themselves by their revolutionary offices (Henry Poulet, "L'Administration centrale du département de la Meurthe de l'établissement des départements à la création des préfectures (1790–1800)," *La Révolution française* 51 and 52 [1906–1907], esp. 51: 446–47).

who identified themselves primarily by their urban occupations. In this respect, too, the departmental officials were much like the national deputies. About one-half of the deputies came from towns with over five thousand people, as compared to less than 20 percent of the population as a whole.[18] The regional domination of urban elites continued even into the last years of Napoleon's reign: 40 percent of the notables of 1810 had been either professionals, officials, or merchants before the Revolution as compared to 34 percent landowners.[19] No doubt land was an important element of local prestige for most of these men, revolutionary officials and Napoleonic notables alike. Nevertheless, it was not a rural class of English-style gentlemen who gained political prominence on either the national or the regional level, but rather thousands of city professionals who seized the opportunity to develop political careers.

As in the national legislature, in the departments former royal officials had most influence at the beginning of the Revolution. In the Meurthe and the Cher, the number of royal officials was high at 39 percent (1790 elections), but elsewhere their presence was more limited: 19 percent in the Indre, 14 percent in the Haute-Saône, and a mere 8 percent in the Ain in 1790. Although the sources do not permit thoroughgoing comparisons, it appears that the exclusion of royal officials grew more pronounced everywhere under the Republic. In the Allier, for example, only 1 administrator elected in 1792 had been a royal official, as compared to 11 in 1790.[20]

The decline of the royal officials did not benefit the commercial classes on the regional and national levels, but evidence suggests that the merchants may have held their own in the cities. In Marseille, over half of the city officers elected in 1790 were identified as merchants or manufacturers [*négociants* or *fabricants*], and no one

---

[18] A summary of residential distributions can be found in Hunt, Lansky, and Hanson, "The Failure of the Liberal Republic," p. 744.

[19] Louis Bergeron and Guy Chaussinand-Nogaret, Les *"Masses de granit"*: Cent mille notables du Premier Empire (Paris, 1979), p. 29.

[20] Calculations of numbers of royal officials were based on Poulet, "L'Administration centrale du département de la Meurthe"; Marcel Bruneau, Les *Débuts de la Révolution dans les départements du Cher et de l'Indre (1789–1791)* (Paris, 1902), pp. 143–49; Girardot, Le *Département de la Haute-Saône* 2: annex V; Eugène Dubois, *Histoire de la Révolution dans l'Ain*, 6 vols. (Bourg, 1931–1935), esp. 1: 204–5; and Rougeron, Les *Administrations départementales de l'Allier*, pp. 8–10, 39–40. The rejection of royal officials apparently continued throughout the Napoleonic era; only 7 percent of the notables of 1810 had occupied positions in the civil administration of the crown (Bergeron and Chaussinand-Nogaret, Les *"Masses de granit,"* p. 29).

claimed the law as a profession. Even in the smaller, inland city of Angers, merchants were the single largest group on the town councils between 1790 and 1795, and between 1796 and 1799 the proportion of merchants increased from 35 percent of the known occupations to 65 percent; lawyers were in second place.[21]

For the most part, however, the evidence about the big city elite is fragmentary; it usually concerns one city for only a limited period during the Revolution. This gap in our knowledge deserves attention, because locally elected officials were unusually important during the Revolution. They were delegated considerable authority by the various constitutions, and they often widened their purview during the all-too-frequent crises. At the beginning of the Revolution in particular, offices were keenly sought after; anyone with an interest in the shape of the new order tried to get a position of influence and authority, and these were all up for grabs in elections. In a sense, there was no gap between the "reputational" and "positional" elite on the local level; because there was no politics as usual, influence required position.[22] The nature of the new order was too uncertain to permit regular behind-the-scenes manipulation. Even after the turmoil of the Terror and its accompaniment of interference from Paris, local notables had to garner offices for themselves if they were to have the upper hand in local affairs. On the local level, office meant power.

If there was one place where merchants might be expected to have a voice in political affairs, it was in the big cities. In order to systematically compare the fortunes of different social groups on the local level, I have chosen four big cities for examination. Amiens, Bordeaux, Nancy, and Toulouse were geographically and politically heterogeneous. Although they were all major centers for administration, marketing, services, and culture, they were located in four different corners of the nation and served as the capitals in four departments that had different political colorings.

[21] Louis Méry and F. Guindon, eds., *Histoire analytique et chronologique des actes et des délibérations du corps et du conseil de la municipalité de Marseille*, 8 vols. (Marseille, 1841–1873) 5: 37. If unknowns are not excluded from the totals in Angers, the increase was from 29 to 37 percent. Calculations are based on the lists given in F. Uzureau, "La Municipalité d'Angers pendant la Révolution," *Andegaviana* 13 (1913): 272–84.

[22] A review of these issues as applied to American cities can be found in David C. Hammack, "Problems in the Historical Study of Power in the Cities and Towns of the United States, 1800–1960," *American Historical Review* 83 (1978): 323–49.

Amiens was the chief city and administrative headquarters of the Somme department, located north of Paris (map 1). The city was known for its great Gothic cathedral and its woolen manufactures, which employed a large segment of its 40 thousand inhabitants.[23] Amiens never became solidly republican. In November 1795 a deputy on mission from the Council of Five Hundred reported that "the Ninth of Thermidor [fall of Robespierre] which ought to have reassured the citizens again of their personal tranquillity has on the contrary aroused all of their royalist hopes."[24] Two years later both the departmental and municipal administrations were revoked as suspected royalists. In the summer of 1799 the government's renewed conscription efforts provoked massive demonstrations led by the cries, "Down with the Jacobins, down with the Administration, down with the beggars, long live the King, long live Louis XVIII."[25] Amiens, then, was representative of northern, right-wing, manufacturing cities.

Nancy, with 33 thousand inhabitants, was the capital of Lorraine and cultural center of the east. Like Bordeaux and Toulouse, Nancy was the seat of a high court or *parlement* and of a major university. It is not easy to characterize the political complexion of the city during the Revolution. According to the analysis presented in chapter 4, the department of the Meurthe (map 1) was one of those few departments moving from right to left during the decade, and government sources considered it one of the few reliably republican departments in 1799. However, the major historian of the department calls it "a good example of those peaceful departments where indifference to the [Directory] regime contributed to its failure."[26] The behavior of the departmental deputies at the end of the decade

[23]Roger Agache et al., *Histoire de la Picardie* (Toulouse, 1974), esp. chap. 12, "Forces et faiblesses de l'Ancien Régime," by Pierre Deyon, pp. 313–28. See also Charles Engrand, "Pauperisme et condition ouvrière au XVIIIe siècle: L'Exemple amiénois," *RHMC* 29 (1982): 376–410.

[24]A.N., F¹ᶜ III Somme 9, Correspondance et divers, 1789–an IX, letter from Scellier, member of the Council of Five Hundred, to the Minister of the Interior, 30 brumaire an IV.

[25]A. Dubois, *Notes historiques sur Amiens, 1789–1803* (Amiens, 1883); Albéric de Calonne, *Histoire de la ville d'Amiens*, 3 vols. (Amiens, 1899–1900), esp. vol. 2; and F.I. Darsy, *Amiens et le département de la Somme pendant la Révolution: Épisodes historiques*, 2 vols. (Amiens, 1878–1883) 1: 181.

[26]Pierre Clémendot, *Le Département de la Meurthe à l'époque du Directoire* (Raôn-l'Etape, 1966), p. 502. On the earlier period, see Albert Troux, *La Vie politique dans le département de la Meurthe d'août 1792 à octobre 1795*, 2 vols. (Nancy, 1936).

indicates that Bonapartism found considerable support there; half of the delegation took a leading role in preparing the way for the Consulate government.[27] The Directory's commissioner to the departmental administration readily accepted the Napoleonic coup in November 1799 and eagerly announced to the Minister of Interior that "at the first news of the results of these days, the generality of the citizens of the capital [Nancy] gave evidence only of sentiments of confidence and joy."[28] In short, the department shifted its allegiances on more than one occasion without ever becoming a hotbed of opposition to the regime in power. The city of Nancy itself was also divided, but neither the Terror nor the anti-Terrorist reaction provoked the kinds of turmoil experienced by other big cities. Nancy is of interest here precisely because it was not identified with any one political faction.

Bordeaux was the largest of the four cities; with over 100 thousand people, it was nearly twice the size of Toulouse. It was also the most economically vibrant. Winegrowers (often local *parlementaires*) and shippers dominated the local and regional economy.[29] In 1793 the department of the Gironde gave its name to the federalist revolt, even though all of its deputies were not political "Girondins." The city of Bordeaux, however, was a leading center of the revolt. After the defeat of federalism, scores of prominent Bordelais were sent to the guillotine by a military commission manned by local radicals.[30] Later the pendulum swung hard to the right. Local officials complained of "brigandage" by counterrevolutionaries, and in 1797 local and departmental elections were annulled as royalist.[31] Nevertheless, Bordeaux did not suffer the devastations of

[27] Regnier, Jacqueminot, and Boulay sat on the commission that headed the transition to the Consulate; all three were named counts under the Empire. Another deputy, Mallarmé, sat in the Tribunate and became a baron (Christian Pfister, "Les Députés du département de la Meurthe sous la Révolution (1791–1799)," *Mémoires de la Société d'Archéologie de Lorraine*, 4th ser., 11 [1911]: 309–425).

[28] A.N., F^{1c} III Meurthe 15, Correspondance et divers, 1789–an V, letter from Saulnier, which he signed "Commissaire du Pouvoir Exécutif" (having crossed out "Directoire" on the official form), 25 brumaire an VIII.

[29] William Doyle, *The Parlement of Bordeaux and the End of the Old Regime, 1771–1790* (New York, 1974).

[30] Alan Forrest, *Society and Politics in Revolutionary Bordeaux* (Oxford, 1975). Between October 1793 and July 1794, 302 people were sentenced to death by the Commission (Pierre Bécamps, *La Révolution à Bordeaux [1789–1794]: J.-B.-M. Lacombe, président de la Commission militaire* [Bordeaux, 1953], p. 384).

[31] See, e.g., the speech by the Directory's commissioner to the department de-

outright civil war (such as that suffered by Lyon), and in many ways its experience of the Revolution resembled those of the other big ports.

Of the four cities, Toulouse was without doubt the most paradoxical. Under the Old Regime, an exceptionally wealthy group of *parlementaires* dominated social and political life in the city of some 58 thousand people. During the early years of the Revolution, Toulouse attracted little attention; the revolutionary authorities tried to steer a moderate course in the face of noble and *parlementaire* protests against institutional innovations. Despite the sympathies of some town leaders, federalism echoed only faintly in Toulouse.[32] After 1794, however, the city gained increasing notoriety as a Jacobin stronghold. When the right began to dominate national politics in 1797, for example, the municipal administration of Toulouse was forced to write a memoir defending itself against the charge of "terrorism": "it is not true," they insisted, "that the officials elected by the people in the communal assemblies of the Year IV had been the craven tools of the regime of the Terror."[33] Toulouse alone among the big cities in France was consistently left wing, and, as a consequence, it was the center for Jacobin politics in the larger southwest region (map 1, Haute-Garonne).

The focus of comparison here is the city councils of the four cities. They were not the only local political bodies, nor were they always the most powerful ones. Jacobin clubs often enjoyed a strong, albeit informal, influence on local affairs, and a variety of revolutionary committees and commissions came and went with the tides of political sentiment. Between 1793 and 1795 representatives-on-mission from the National Convention frequently intervened in local disputes; an entire municipal government might be thrown out, only to be reinstated several months later when the political winds shifted. Yet, despite alterations in their size and method of selec-

---

nouncing "the hordes of brigands" organized in the Gironde (reprinted in Gaston Ducaunnès-Duval, *Ville de Bordeaux. Inventaire-Sommaire des Archives municipales: Période révolutionnaire [1789–an VIII]*, 4 vols. [Bordeaux, 1896–1929] 3: 45–46 [his inventory of A.M., Bordeaux, D 155, 28 brumaire an V]).

[32] Lyons, *Revolution in Toulouse*.

[33] A.M., Toulouse, 2D 4, Correspondance de l'administration municipale, 17 fructidor an V, "Observations analitiques [*sic*] de l'administration municipale de la commune de Toulouse sur les points du rapport du citoyen Saladin qui la concerne."

TABLE 4

Occupational Representation on City Councils in Amiens, Bordeaux,
Nancy, and Toulouse, 1790–1799 (percentages)

Occupation	Amiens (N = 84)	Bordeaux (N = 195)	Nancy (N = 129)	Toulouse (N = 112)
Clergy	0	1	2	1
Law	17	13	35	21
Other liberal professions	4	16	11	15
Commerce and manufacturing	46	41	18	36
Artisans and shopkeepers	22	23	24	18
Military	0	4	5	0
Agriculture	2	1	2	5
Bourgeois [a]	9	1	3	5
Occupation unknown	2	28	12	12

Note: Percentages given are of known occupations. The figures for Bordeaux are the least reliable, because the percentage of unknown occupations is largest for that city.

[a] "Bourgeois" includes *rentiers* and *propriétaires*, i.e., those who had incomes provided by investment in various forms of property and did not exercise any profession.

tion, the councils were the most regular, continuous feature of local political life during the Revolution.[34]

Despite the social and political differences between the cities, the occupational representation on the revolutionary councils was remarkably similar overall (table 4); in all but Nancy, the merchants and manufacturers predominated, and more often than not the artisans and shopkeepers were in second place (see Appendix B for a discussion of methods used in establishing the tables). In the big cities, Burke's characterization of 1791 was remarkably accurate: his

[34] A brief account of changes in local government can be found in Cobban, "Local Government during the French Revolution," *Aspects of the French Revolution*, pp. 112–30. The standard account of institutional questions is Jacques Godechot, *Les Institutions de la France sous la Révolution et l'Empire* (Paris, 1968).

"moneyed men, merchants, principal tradesmen, and men of letters" were indeed "the chief actors in the French Revolution."[35]
City elites differed dramatically in social composition from those on
the regional and national levels: merchants, rather than lawyers,
were the single largest group on the councils in three of the cities.
Royal officials had even less prominence on the local level than
they did higher up the ladder. In Amiens only three Old Regime
officiers sat on the revolutionary councils; one of them was a *bailliage*
court magistrate (the regional court under the jurisdiction of a *parlement*). In Nancy, a city crowded with officials of the crown, there
were ten (8 percent); five were either in the *bailliage* or *parlement*.
Most former royal officials either actively opposed the Revolution
or dropped out of public life altogether.[36]

The rise of the merchants to local power marked a significant
shift in politics in the cities. In his study of Old Regime city alma-
nacs, Daniel Roche found that the overwhelming majority of men
listed as local notables in the four cities were clergymen, military
officers, magistrates, or officials in the civil administration of the
crown. Men of commerce counted for only between 1.2 percent
(Amiens) and 5.5 percent (Bordeaux) of the Old Regime urban
notables.[37] Merchants came at the tail end of local notability under
the Old Regime; rarely did anyone below them on the social scale
appear in the lists. In Bordeaux and Amiens, the merchant communities were relatively large and consequently hard to ignore entirely. The merchant-shippers of Bordeaux were frequently overshadowed by the rich and noble magistrates of the local *parlement*,
but in Amiens the merchants were particularly well-represented
on the city council before the Revolution. Even though the positions of mayor and deputy mayor were almost always held by
nobles, between 1782 and 1789 one-third of the aldermen (*échevins*)

[35] From *Thoughts on French Affairs*, in Robert A. Smith, ed., *Burke on Revolution*
(New York, 1968), p. 190.

[36] Information on officeholding comes from the sources cited in Appendix B.
Philip Dawson concluded similarly that "the majority of *bailliage* magistrates revealed, during the revolutionary years, inaptitude for democratic politics, reluctance to engage in factional controversy, and inability to set aside their commitment
to some familiar conception of legality" (*Provincial Magistrates and Revolutionary Politics in France, 1789–1795* [Cambridge, Mass., 1972], p. 329).

[37] *Le Siècle des lumières en province: Académies et académiciens provinciaux, 1680–
1789*, 2 vols. (Paris, 1978) 2: 347–56. The percentages are based on Roche's figures.

on the Amiens council identified themselves as merchants.[38] Even in Amiens, however, the merchants fell far short of dominating the local political scene.

In Nancy and Toulouse, by contrast, the merchants were of relatively little weight before 1789; they were largely ignored by the large and aggressive communities of magistrates and lawyers, many of whom were noble and much wealthier than the merchants. According to Jean Sentou, the average *parlementaire* of Toulouse left a fortune evaluated at eight times that of the average merchant or manufacturer. Even the number of merchants in Toulouse appears to have actually declined by the end of the eighteenth century.[39] A crude quantitative index of the Old Regime ratio of merchants to officials and members of the liberal professions shows the relative weakness of merchants in Nancy and Toulouse: 1.2 for Amiens (i.e., 1.2 merchants for every member of the liberal professions or official, according to the 1776 *capitation* roll); 1.5 for Bordeaux (1777 *capitation* roll); 0.5 for Nancy (1789 evaluation); and 0.5 for Toulouse (1788 marriage contracts).[40] Although nobles, clergymen, royal officials, and members of the liberal professions dominated local politics in all four cities under the Old Regime, the merchants in Amiens and Bordeaux enjoyed more potential power in numbers than their counterparts in Nancy and Toulouse.

As a result, it is not surprising that the merchants and manufacturers of Amiens and Bordeaux benefited immediately from the revolutionary situation (see tables 5 and 6, social composition for 1790–91). During the Terror, however, merchants declined in number on the councils, while the representation of artisans and shopkeepers doubled. The reaction of the Year III brought the merchants back in force, but their preponderance was never again as absolute as it had been in 1790–91. In Toulouse and especially in Nancy, merchants were overshadowed at the beginning of the Rev-

[38] Marie-Yvonne Dessaux, "La Vie municipale à Amiens de 1782 à 1789," U.E.R. de Sciences historiques et géographiques (Amiens, 1978).

[39] *Fortunes et groupes sociaux à Toulouse sous la Révolution (1789–1799): Essai d'histoire statistique* (Toulouse, 1969), pp. 84, 153. On the number of merchants, see Georges Marinière, "Les Marchands d'étoffe de Toulouse à la fin du XVIIIe siècle," D.E.S. (Toulouse, 1958).

[40] Based on figures given in Roche, *Le Siècle des lumières* 2: 363–72. Each of the sources used by Roche has its defects, but the ratios derived from them do indicate the order of magnitude of differences between the cities.

TABLE 5

Amiens: Changes in Occupational Representation on the City Council,
1790–1799 (percentages)

Occupation	1790–91 (N = 32)	1793– Year II[a] (N = 28)	Year III (N = 34)	Years IV–VII (N = 19)
Law	25	12	18	5
Other liberal professions	3	12	0	5
Commerce	56	23	47	42
Artisans and shopkeepers	16	38	26	32
Others	0	15	9	16
Occupation unknown	0	7	0	0

[a] Amiens did not complete the elections ordered by decree in October 1792 until the beginning of 1793.

TABLE 6

Bordeaux: Changes in Occupational Representation on the City Council,
1790–1799 (percentages)

Occupation	1790–91 (N = 45)	1793– Year II[a] (N = 92)	Year III (N = 44)	Years IV–VII (N = 64)
Law	21	8	9	10
Other liberal professions	5	21	20	24
Commerce	55	33	40	37
Artisans and shopkeepers	17	32	20	20
Others	2	6	12	9
Occupation unknown	7	32	20	36

[a] Bordeaux did not complete the elections ordered by decree in October 1792 until the beginning of 1793.

TABLE 7

Nancy: Changes in Occupational Representation on the City Council,
1790–1799 (percentages)

Occupation	1790–91 (N = 44)	1792– Year II (N = 55)	Year III (N = 30)	Years IV–VII (N = 30)
Law	53	26	24	25
Other liberal professions	7	15	8	21
Commerce	16	15	32	29
Artisans and shopkeepers	12	36	32	11
Others	11	8	4	14
Occupation unknown	2	15	17	7

olution by men of the law and liberal professions (see tables 7 and
8). Under the Republic, however, the two *parlementaire* cities seemed
to follow different paths. Merchants in Toulouse increased their
representation over the decade, while lawyers faded into insignifi-
cance. In Nancy, merchants improved their position over time but
never came to enjoy the prominence that merchants had elsewhere.

In a small manufacturing town such as Elbeuf, the preponderance of merchants and manufacturers during the Revolution is
not surprising: the commercial classes dominated social and political life in the town before the Revolution and continued to do so,
despite a brief challenge from below, through the end of the decade and then during the Consulate and Empire as well.[41] In Elbeuf,
men of commerce simply faced no serious competition. In the big
cities, however, the mercantile elite did not enjoy the same superiority under the Old Regime. Nevertheless, the Revolution brought
them new opportunities for public prominence. Most surprising is
the ability of merchants to make their presence felt even in places
like Toulouse and Nancy, where their numbers and wealth were
relatively unimpressive. Merchants were not simply acceding to

[41] Jeffrey Kaplow, *Elbeuf during the Revolutionary Period: History and Social Structure*
(Baltimore, 1964), esp. the tables on pp. 86, 87, 162, 167, 169, 170, 171.

TABLE 8

Toulouse: Changes in Occupational Representation on the City Council, 1790–1799 (percentages)

Occupation	1790–91 (N = 41)	1792– Year II (N = 40)	Year III (N = 35)	Years IV–VII (N = 26)
Law	35	9	18	9
Other liberal professions	5	29	15	9
Commerce	32	21	47	52
Artisans and shopkeepers	11	26	9	26
Others	16	15	12	4
Occupation unknown	10	15	3	12

their "natural" slot in local affairs; they were making a bid for leadership of the Revolution on the local level. Lawyers, notaries, and former magistrates had most weight in the cities at the beginning of the Revolution, but their numbers declined everywhere after 1791. Other professionals, such as doctors, schoolteachers, and minor functionaries, often became more important than the lawyers.

In the smaller administrative towns, the merchants were often less well represented than in the big cities. The pattern in Nancy, the smallest of the cities examined, suggests this to be true. The revolutionary elite in Aix-en-Provence, a royal administrative capital of some 28 thousand inhabitants, seems similar. Overall the merchants of Aix came in behind the lawyers (12 percent as opposed to 21 percent).[42] In nearby Arles, merchants barely outnumbered lawyers overall (10 percent to 9 percent), yet merchants continually improved their standing from 3 percent of the council in February 1790, to 13 percent in December 1792, to a high of 38 percent in May 1797. In both of these southern towns without large-scale manufacturing, the merchants and lawyers were outnumbered by artisans and shopkeepers, who comprised 31 percent of

[42] Christiane Derobert-Ratel, *Institutions et vie municipale à Aix-en-Provence sous la Révolution (1789–an VIII)* (Millau, 1981), pp. 602–3, 590.

the revolutionary councillors in Aix-en-Provence and 37 percent of the councillors in Arles.[43]

Even in a tiny town such as Vence in Provence (pop. 2,600), where peasants made up 61 percent of the households, men of commerce were active in revolutionary politics: 3 of the 10 municipal officers elected in 1790 were merchants or shopkeepers (3 others were trained in the law), and 8 of the town's 29 *commerçants* sat in some capacity on the first revolutionary town council. Merchants and shopkeepers, like the lawyers, doctors, and so-called "bourgeois" (men who lived off their investments), were actively interested in revolutionary politics. These groups had much higher levels of participation in the voting of 1790 than did the artisans, workers, or peasants: around 40 percent voted as opposed to 20 percent for the peasants, 14 percent for artisans, and even less for wageworkers.[44]

In sharp contrast to the turbulent history of city and national politics, most village studies have emphasized the continuity of leadership between old regime and new, and in particular the continuing hegemony of the same local notables. Patrice Higonnet, for example, asserted that in Pont-de-Montvert (Lozère department, pop. 1,350) "jobs, titles and distinctions went to the local notables," and he was struck by "the apparent ease with which notables used the population to their own end."[45] The author of a study of Ormoy (Haute-Saône, pop. 747) concluded that there, as "in the great majority of our rural areas, if the regime changes, the ruling classes stay the same. It is in effect the well-to-do classes which take over the most important functions of the commune."[46]

The tiny, prosperous peasant village of Bénesse-Maremne (Landes department, pop. 380, four-fifths peasant) exemplified this pattern. A small group of rich farmers faced little opposition in village politics. The mayor there until 1795 was Jean Destribats, a

---

[43] For the social composition of the Arles municipality, see Fabio Sampoli, "Politics and Society in Revolutionary Arles: Chiffonistes and Monnaidiers," Ph.D. diss., Yale University, 1982, pp. 331, 326–27. For artisans and shopkeepers in Aix-en-Provence, see Derobert-Ratel, *Institutions et vie municipale*, p. 590.

[44] Georges Castellan, *Une Cité provençale dans la Révolution: Chronique de la ville de Vence en 1790* (Paris, 1978), pp. 47–51. At the time of the February vote, there was no list of "active" citizens, hence all heads of households who paid taxes were eligible.

[45] *Pont-de-Montvert: Social Structure and Politics in a French Village, 1700–1914* (Cambridge, Mass., 1971), pp. 85, 87.

[46] R. Rondot, *A Ormoy pendant la Révolution* (Besançon, 1958), p. 41.

40-year-old farmer and sixth highest taxpayer in the village. He lost his post to Pierre Destribats (a relative?), the village's second highest taxpayer, and Pierre in turn was replaced by François Desclaux, the richest landowner of them all. Almost all of the village posts during the Revolution were held by farmers.[47]

Nevertheless, many villages experienced the same process of democratization going on in the big towns and cities. In Pont-l'Abbé (Finistère department, pop. 1,885), for instance, the first municipality was run by the village's leading lawyers: the mayor and the city attorney (*procureur*) were both *avocats*, and two of the five other officers were lawyers too (in addition to a shoemaker, baker, and merchant). After the declaration of the Republic in 1792, however, the balance of power shifted dramatically, and the new council was filled with artisans and shopkeepers. Included among the seven top officials were two butchers, one shoemaker, one merchant, and two shopkeepers (*marchands détaillants*).[48] A similar change took place in Les Authieux-sur-le-Port-Saint-Ouen (Seine-Inférieure, pop. 395). The first municipalities were dominated by the same rich farmers who controlled local affairs before 1789, but in December 1792 the sans-culottes pushed them aside. A journeyman bargeman became mayor, and among the three municipal officers was a boatman and a carter. They kept their places until the Year IV.[49] In most villages, the years 1793–94 saw the appearance of artisans and poor peasants on the village councils, while in the cities the same years marked the emergence of artisans and shopkeepers in urban politics.[50]

Taken as a whole, then, the new political class was not socially homogeneous. Lawyers dominated national and regional politics; merchants, artisans, and shopkeepers were prominent in the cities; and a mixture of peasants, artisans, and small merchants ran the villages. There were significant patterns behind this apparent di-

[47] Francis Hirigoyen, "Bénesse-Maremne pendant la Révolution française," *Bulletin de la Société de Borda* 103 (1978): 51–70.

[48] Alain Signor, *La Révolution à Pont-l'Abbé* (Paris, 1969), pp. 132–35 and 216–17.

[49] Albert Soboul, "Une Commune rurale pendant la Révolution: Les Authieux-sur-le-Port-Saint-Ouen (Seine-Inférieure), 1789–1795," *AHRF* 25 (1953): 140–60.

[50] In Lourmarin, artisans and *travailleurs* appeared on the councils in 1793 and 1794 (Thomas F. Sheppard, *Lourmarin in the Eighteenth Century: A Study of a French Village* [Baltimore, 1971], p. 204). Sheppard is at pains to minimize the social significance of this changeover, but similar developments occurred in most villages at this time.

versity, however. The most important of them was the social and
political break with the Old Regime. Nobles virtually disappeared
from politics after 1792. In Toulouse, there were eight nobles on the
councils (7 percent of the total), and only three of them held office
after 1792. In both Amiens and Nancy, there were only three nobles on the councils.[51] At a slower pace but just as surely, the royal
officials also dropped out of revolutionary politics. City councillors
from the Old Regime were also few in numbers in the councils of
the new regime. In Toulouse 13 former councillors from the large
"general council" of the 1780s sat on various revolutionary municipalities; 7 of them had places in the first new councils of 1790–91.[52]
In more tradition-minded Aix-en-Provence, 63 percent of the councillors chosen in February 1790 had been Old Regime councillors,
but by the time of the Directory the number had fallen to 4 percent.[53] The new times were for new men.

The newness of the revolutionary political class took several
forms. On the local level, the most dramatic novelty was the appearance of previously excluded social groups in the corridors of
power. At the beginning of the revolution in the cities, merchants
and non-noble lawyers seized the opportunity to turn the tables on
haughty *parlementaires* and oligarchic officials of the crown.[54] In the
next wave were the artisans and shopkeepers, merchants of more
modest means, and professionals of lesser standing: cutlers and
carpenters, clothiers with a few employees, merchants for a limited
regional market, barber-surgeons, and schoolteachers as opposed

[51] The figures for nobles are probably overestimates. Included are two men in
Amiens who styled themselves *écuyers*, but who did not attend the meetings of the
nobility for the *bailliage* of Amiens in 1789. Both were rich merchants. Names of
nobles are taken from Louis de la Roque and Edouard de Barthelemy, *Catalogue des
gentilshommes en 1789 et des familles anoblies ou titrées depuis le premier empire jusqu'à nos
jours*, 2 vols. (Paris, 1866). In Aix-en-Provence, another parlementary town, the
number of nobles on the revolutionary councils was 7 percent (Derobert-Ratel, *Institutions et vie municipale*, p. 590).
[52] The file of revolutionary city councillors was checked against lists given in the
Almanach historique de la province de Languedoc, 1780–90.
[53] Derobert-Ratel, *Institutions et vie municipale*, p. 601.
[54] This point is made in detail in Lynn Hunt, *Revolution and Urban Politics in Provincial France: Troyes and Reims, 1786–1790* (Stanford, 1978). On the local level, lawyers were not as active as their numbers would have indicated. Lenard R. Berlan-
stein found only 54 *avocats* out of 276 who held public office at any level during the
Revolution in Toulouse, and most of them dropped out during or just after the Terror (*The Barristers of Toulouse in the Eighteenth Century [1740–1793]* [Baltimore, 1975],
esp. pp. 165, 176).

to doctors and law professors (see tables 5–8). Crane Brinton found the same shift downward taking place in Jacobin Club membership in the cities.[55] In the villages, the process was similar, even though the social groups in question were not identical to those in the cities.

The democratization of local government can be seen in the relative wealth of councillors at different moments of the Revolution. In Toulouse, where the evidence is most complete, the average tax assessment for municipal officials went from 962 francs in 1790–91, to 706 francs under the Terror, and back up to 1,093 francs under the Thermidorian reaction. Local officials were less wealthy during the period of greatest openness to lower ranking social groups. When Toulouse came under the influence of the Jacobins once again during the Directory regime (1795–99), the average tax assessment of councillors went back down, this time even further to 448 francs.[56] The process of social opening can be traced even within a single social group, such as the merchants. Five of the six merchants who sat on the Toulouse councils during the Directory regime (when Toulouse was a Jacobin stronghold) were assessed at under 700 francs property revenue; by contrast, five of the merchants elected in 1790–91 and seven of those chosen during the Year III were assessed at over 700 francs.[57]

To a surprising extent, the democratization of local politics occurred even in places controlled by right-wing coalitions. Under the Directory regime, for example, the city councils in right-wing Bordeaux and Amiens had just about the same social composition as the notoriously left-wing councils of Toulouse. In part, however, the similarity in social composition simply reflects the vagueness of social categories based on profession. The merchants on the Toulouse councils during the Directory were probably less well-off than the merchants in Amiens or Bordeaux. Only one of the seven

[55] *The Jacobins: An Essay in the New History* (New York, 1930), p. 60.

[56] A.M., Toulouse, 1G 38–53, Contribution foncière, 1791. Assessments were found for 44 percent of the councillors. Data were no worse for the Terror councillors: 40 percent were found. In his comparison of members of the revolutionary committees, Lyons found that "the thermidoreans tended to have higher incomes, more property and capital than their Jacobin counterparts," yet he nevertheless insists that social distinctions were "blurred" (*Revolution in Toulouse*, pp. 172–74). Given the differences in city councillors, it seems more appropriate to argue that social differences were real but not overwhelming.

[57] A.M., Toulouse, 1G 38–53.

Toulouse merchants on the Directory councils was assessed at over 1,000 francs property revenue, but two of the three merchants on the Amiens councils at the same time were assessed at over 2,000 francs.[58] Unfortunately, the tax rolls are too incomplete for trustworthy comparison, and the assessments are not necessarily comparable from town to town. Yet, other evidence also indicates that councillors in Amiens were exceptionally well-off. In the Year IX two-thirds of the men who had been councillors under the Directory in Amiens were listed as Napoleonic "notables" for the Somme department, including two men who had begun as shopkeepers.[59] Only the cream of local society made it onto the Napoleonic lists. Despite the uncertainties inherent in the documents, two conclusions seem valid: the Revolution opened political access to groups that previously had been excluded for social reasons, and the more left local government became (in 1793–94 everywhere, and in Jacobin strongholds more than elsewhere), the more likely it was to include modest merchants, artisans and shopkeepers, and minor professionals.

The new political class was not just new in comparison to the men who had ruled under the Old Regime; it was repeatedly renewed during the decade of revolution itself. One of the most dramatic facts of local politics was nearly constant upheaval. Amiens, for example, had no less than fifteen different municipalities in nine years and four different ones just in the turbulent Year III. Sometimes the social complexion of city hall changed almost overnight. The "federalist" council elected in Bordeaux in January 1793, for instance, included 61 percent merchants and 22 percent artisans and shopkeepers. The radical provisional municipality picked in September to replace it had only 13 percent merchants and more than 44 percent artisans and shopkeepers.[60] Even more striking,

[58] The figures given are for those merchants whose assessments were located. Amiens tax assessments can be found in A.M., Amiens, 1G 2.11, Contribution foncière, 1791.

[59] A.D., Somme, Mb 107529 bis, Liste de Notabilité du département de la Somme, an IX.

[60] Percentages given are of known occupations. For the January 1793 council only officers were counted, not *notables*; 2 of 20 occupations were not ascertained. The unknowns are much higher in the case of the September 1793 municipality; 18 of 50 were undetermined. Forrest apparently included *notables* in his figures for the January 1793 council: he mentions 46 men of commerce, 12 members of the liberal professions (including 5 lawyers), and 7 artisans or small businessmen (*Revolutionary Bordeaux*, pp. 122–23).

TABLE 9

City Councillors During the Terror:
Continuity with Other Revolutionary Municipalities (percentages)[a]

City	Councillors Who Also Held Places in Municipalities of				
	1790–Jan. 1793	Year III	Both	Directory	Both Year III and Directory
Amiens (N = 16)	75	56	25	13	13
Nancy (N = 39)	26	41	10	13	10
Toulouse (N = 25)	48	28	12	16	8

[a] I have counted councillors who sat either as *notables* or as *officiers* in other revolutionary municipalities.

TABLE 10

City Councillors During the Directory:
Continuity with Previous Revolutionary Municipalities (percentages)[a]

City	Councillors Who Also Held Places in Municipalities of		
	1790–Jan. 1793	1793–Year II	Year III
Amiens (N = 19)	37	11	53
Nancy (N = 30)	37	27	33
Toulouse (N = 26)	15	23	8
Bordeaux (N = 64)	25	8	20

[a] I have counted councillors who sat either as *notables* or as *officiers* in previous municipalities.

however, was the massive turnover in personnel. None of the councillors chosen in September 1793 had been on a city council before.

Bordeaux in 1793 was only the extreme example of a more general process of displacement and reshuffling (tables 9 and 10). Of the men elected in the four cities during 1790–91, about three-fifths went on to serve in subsequent revolutionary regimes, while two-fifths of them dropped out of local politics altogether. The regime of reaction in the Year III rehabilitated many of the men who had served under the constitutional monarchy; in Nancy 73 percent and in Toulouse 67 percent of the municipal officials of the Year III had served in some capacity before, from national deputy to neighborhood police official. But few of them continued to serve after the Year III: in Nancy only 27 percent and in Jacobin Toulouse only 14 percent held office of any kind under the Directory.

With the exception of the brief Year III, when reaction meant restoring officials purged during the Terror, every change in regime opened the doors again to new men. Even in Jacobin Toulouse, the continuity between the councils of the Terror and the councils of the Directory was minimal; only four men sat as officers in both (table 9). Each turn in local political fortunes required new men. As a consequence, the merchants, lawyers, or shopkeepers who sat in 1798 were rarely the same ones who sat in 1790. The constant shifting of personnel had an enormously important result everywhere: large numbers of men gained some political experience during the revolutionary decade.

The spread of active political responsibility was most apparent in the villages. Even where the rich dominated the top positions, scores of villagers gained firsthand experience in local affairs. In Bénesse-Maremne 52 voters had to pick 10 men for the municipality in 1790, and that was only the *first* of many elections. In poorer Ormoy only 22 men voted in the first mayoral elections, and that afternoon they had to choose 5 other municipal officers and 12 *notables*! In nine years, seven different men acted as mayor there, including a miller, a "bourgeois," a merchant, a lawyer, and a farmer.[61] Meximieux, in the Ain department, had just over 300 households, only 119 men eligible to vote in 1790, and 62 men eligible for office. The voters had to select 19 of their number for the new municipality. In the first five years of the Revolution, Meximieux had four different mayors, and, despite the recurrence of certain family names, the number of men holding municipal office was high: 42 men between 1790 and 1795 or one representative for every seven households.[62] Whether their memories were bitter or

[61] Hirigoyen, "Bénesse-Maremne," and Rondot, *Ormoy*, pp. 14–16, 41.
[62] Like many village studies in French, this one was written by the local parish priest (F. Page, *Meximieux: Une commune pendant la Révolution* [Belley, 1903]).

sweet, thousands of men had tested the political waters in revolutionary France. Ironically, therefore, the very discontinuities of revolutionary experience contributed to the force of the revolutionary tradition. The collective memory of revolution was so sharp, because so many had participated in shaping it.

During the process of constant renewal and enlargement of the political class, certain characteristics remained constant. One of them was age. Whether Jacobin or federalist, republican or royalist, the political elite, both nationally and locally, was of the same generation. They had been born in the 1740s and 1750s, too young to have experienced firsthand the major battles of the Enlightenment, but just old enough to have witnessed the struggles between a modernizing monarchy and the old elite in the early 1770s. The councillors of the democratic opening of 1793–94 were perhaps a bit younger than the others: in Nancy, 68 percent of them had been under 40 years old in 1789 as opposed to 44 percent of those sitting in 1790–91. But the new elite did not continue to get younger after 1795: only 46 percent of the councillors in Nancy after 1795 had been under 40 in 1789.[63]

The new political class was also distinguished by its special relationship to the urban world. Urban-based professionals dominated national and regional politics, and even in the villages leadership roles were most often taken by men with connections to urban markets or urban culture. In the small towns and villages, the level of political involvement was not necessarily lower than in the cities; indeed, it might have been higher, at least in certain regions. Jacobin Club membership for the nation as a whole, for example, ran about 4 percent of the total population, but, in the small towns and villages of Provence, the rate might be 18, 20, or even as high as 39 percent.[64] Every village social group was not equally active, however, and peasants in particular were underrepresented. In Pacy (Eure department) a few vinegrowers [*vignerons*] and gardeners sat on the village council at the beginning of the Revolution, but they were overshadowed by former tax and court officials and artisans and shopkeepers. In the Year III the mayor was a woodworker, and included among the officers were two grocers, a

[63] See n. 9 above.
[64] Michael L. Kennedy reviews the available data in *The Jacobin Club of Marseilles, 1790–1794* (Ithaca, N.Y., 1973), p. 151.

tailor, and an innkeeper.[65] Similarly, in Meximieux the landowner mayor was outnumbered by two innkeepers, a doctor, a tailor, a notary, and a saddler on the 1794 council.[66]

Even in the towns themselves, this pattern was evident. Most eighteenth-century towns had numerous residents working in agriculture; in Arles, for example, 37 percent of the taxpayers were either farmers or agricultural workers, but only 10 percent of the municipal councillors during the Revolution came from the agricultural sector.[67] Likewise, though 35 percent of the population of Aix-en-Provence was employed in agriculture, only 6 percent of the revolutionary councillors came from the peasantry.[68] In a population that was 80 percent rural and employed in agriculture in overwhelming numbers, the participation of the peasantry was essential to the success of the Revolution and the Republic. Yet, other than the peasant uprisings of 1789 and periodic disturbances afterward, peasants were distinctly underrepresented in the ranks of revolutionary militancy. In some villages, they took charge, but more often they looked to artisans, shopkeepers, and professionals for leadership.

The French Revolution was made in various ways by thousands of people. Some of them rioted to protest high prices; others demonstrated for political causes they held dear. Regularly, however, tens of thousands voted in elections, and thousands of men became officials of various sorts. The Revolution was not made by a few cranks and crackpots who got their scripts from brilliant strategists in the capital. The militants of the notorious Year II were only one part of the new political class brought to prominence in the decade of revolution. The tobacco seller, former concièrge, wine vendor, bookseller, shoemaker, gardener, and dance master who appeared in the "second class" of terrorists denounced in Nancy, for instance, could not have succeeded in "terrorizing" the former elite if they did not have at least tacit support in higher places.[69]

[65] The only list of officials that includes all occupations is the one for 4 Germinal, Year III (Edouard Isambard, *Histoire de la Révolution à Pacy-sur-Eure*, 2 vols. [Pacy, 1894] 2: 279).

[66] This is the most complete list for Meximieux (Page, *Meximieux*, p. 228).

[67] Sampoli, "Politics and Society in Revolutionary Arles," pp. 58, 331.

[68] Derobert-Ratel, *Institutions et vie municipale*, pp. 29, 590.

[69] The list appears in A.M., Nancy, D 14, Delibérations municipales, 15 prairial an III.

Most of the artisans and shopkeepers who sat on the revolutionary councils were hardly the *hommes de sang* (bloodthirsty men)
their opponents made them out to be, but there is no denying the
fact that their entry into the political arena frightened and outraged
the *honnêtes hommes* (decent men). Many officials from the Year II
were later prosecuted as *prévaricateurs* (betrayers of the public trust)
or as *terroristes*. A few, like Toulouse's mayor of the Year II, were
murdered by counterrevolutionary death squads during the White
Terror after 1794. The more fortunate were simply denounced as
the followers of "Clubocracy."[70]

The men who gave their good names and support to local government were, overwhelmingly, respectable sorts. As might be expected, the city and village councillors were in general more respectable than the most vociferous local militants and members of
local revolutionary committees and popular societies. Surprisingly
few of the city councillors, even among those who held office in the
Year II, were officially denounced as terrorists after 1794.[71] The repression was directed more at those men whose stars had risen in
spectacular fashion in the space of a few turbulent months (see
chapter 6). As a consequence of the social difference between elected officials and rank-and-file militants, merchants and successful
lawyers were more likely to be found in numbers in the former
group than in the latter. Crane Brinton claimed, for example, that
less than 10 percent of the Jacobin Club members that he studied
were merchants. Using Brinton's categories, Michael Kennedy
showed that the proportion of businessmen in the Marseille Club
declined from 17 percent in 1790–91 to 0.6 percent in 1793–94.
Similarly, Martyn Lyons found only two or three merchants and

[70] Bernadau of Bordeaux called them "ces atroupements [*sic*] de Bavards, dont on
n'a plus besoin" ("Tablètes contemporaines, historiques et cryptografiques, de
l'Ecouteur bordelais," vol. 3 (21 septembre 1793 au 22 septembre 1802) in *Oeuvres
complètes de Bernadau*, B.M., Bordeaux, ms. 713, vol. 7, entry for 14 pluviôse an III.
[71] Few city councillors appeared on the lists of "terrorists" compiled in 1794–95.
For the four cities, see A.M., Nancy, D 14, 15 prairial an III; A.M., Amiens, 2I 19,
"Liste des citoyens dénoncés au représentant du peuple Blaux," 13 prairial an III;
A.M., Toulouse, 2I 26, "Liste des terroristes bien reconnus pour tels"; A.M., Bordeaux, I 69, Police: list of 109 citizens to be disarmed, 14 prairial an III. The social
characteristics of the men listed in all four cities are much the same: many occupations were not given, but those that were consisted largely of a variety of clerks,
artisans, and shopkeepers. The most common occupations on the Bordeaux list, for
instance, were shoemakers, wigmakers, and tailors.

even fewer lawyers among some 30 members of the "terrorist" *comité de surveillance révolutionnaire* (the local arm of the Terror) in Toulouse.[72] Yet, in the important local offices and in positions of regional and national power, lawyers, notaries, merchants, and doctors came forward again and again to take up the challenge. In 1790 Gouverneur Morris called such men "new in Power, wild in Theory, raw in Practise."[73] But what he bemoaned as the "Pursuit of metaphisical [*sic*] Whimsies" was undertaken by respectable, urban professionals and tradesmen.

Was the new political class "bourgeois" in a Marxist sense? If Marxist is interpreted somewhat loosely, the answer is Yes. There are two distinct parts to the answer, because there are two analytically separate parts in the Marxist concept of class: social position in the relations of production and class consciousness. Marx himself emphasized the former in his theoretical works (e.g., *Capital*), but he gave considerable emphasis to the latter in his historical works (especially his various writings on the 1848 revolutions in France and Germany).[74] Marx's classic statement of their interrelation can be found in *The 18th Brumaire of Louis Bonaparte*: "In so far as millions of famillies live under economic conditions of existence that separate their mode of life, their interests, and their culture from those of the other classes, and put them in hostile opposition to the latter, they form a class. In so far as there is merely a local interconnection among [them], and the identity of their interests

---

[72] Brinton, *The Jacobins*, p. 51. He counted only *négoçiants* (the big wholesalers) and lumped together cities of various sizes. His figures for Le Havre (1791) show 22 percent merchants (of known professions), with merchants outnumbering professionals two to one. Similarly, the merchants of Strasbourg made up 40 percent of the members of the club in 1791 and outnumbered the professionals two to one. See Brinton, tables, pp. 302–3. In the big cities, then, the participation of the merchants in the Jacobin clubs was far from inconsequential, though it probably declined as the Revolution became more radical. See, in addition, the figures given in Michel de Certeau, Dominique Julia, and Jacques Revel, *Une politique de la langue: La Révolution française et les patois: L'Enquête de Grégoire* (Paris, 1975), p. 44; Kennedy, *The Jacobin Club of Marseilles*, p. 156; and Lyons, *Revolution in Toulouse*, pp. 182–83.

[73] Morris was referring to the members of the National Assembly (Beatrix Cary Davenport, ed., *A Diary of the French Revolution by Gouverneur Morris [1752–1816], Minister to France during the Terror* [Boston, 1939], p. 68, 22 November 1790).

[74] This is not the place for a full rehearsal of either different interpretations of Marx or of Marxism more generally. Some recent literature on the question is critically reviewed in Frank Parkin, *Marxism and Class Theory: A Bourgeois Critique* (New York, 1979).

begets no community, no national bond, and no political organization among them, they do not form a class."[75] For Marx, class formation depended on both economic condition and culture, social category and consciousness. In this particular passage, Marx was concerned to explain the general passivity of peasants during the 1848 revolution in France; peasants failed to act together because they did not form a class. Marx's analysis can also be taken as an explanation of the peasantry's relative underrepresentation in the 1789 revolution; peasants were usually isolated from the mainstream of political life, and they depended on others (innkeepers, tailors, shopkeepers, etc.) for information and representation of their interests.

The revolutionary political class can be termed "bourgeois" both in terms of social position and of class consciousness. The revolutionary officials were the owners of the means of production; they were either merchants with capital, professionals with skills, artisans with their own shops, or, more rarely, peasants with land. The unskilled, the wageworkers, and the landless peasants were not found in positions of leadership or even in large numbers among the rank and file.[76] The "consciousness" of the revolutionary elite can be labeled bourgeois in so far as it was distinctly antifeudal, anti-aristocratic, and anti-absolutist. In their language and imagery, revolutionaries rejected all reminders of the past, and they included in their ranks very few nobles or Old Regime officials. The revolutionary elite was made up of new men dedicated to fashioning a new France.

Unfortunately, these distinctions are at the same time too loose —too general—to be of much use. As a social category, "bourgeois" does not distinguish the militant revolutionaries and republicans from much of their opposition; the moderates of Bordeaux and the royalists of Amiens were just as or even more "bourgeois" than the republicans of Toulouse or Meximieux or Les Authieux. Moreover, the most advanced (most capitalist) regions of France were often right wing, while republicanism flourished in the areas

[75](New York, 1963), p. 124.

[76]When describing the membership in Jacobin clubs, Brinton claimed that they "give a complete cross-section of French society, with the old court aristocracy, and the recent industrial proletariat, left out" (*The Jacobins*, p. 68). Even the sans-culottes in Paris were dominated by shopkeepers and artisans of some independent means (Soboul, *Les Sans-culottes parisiens*, pp. 439–55).

least affected by the development of capitalism. Similarly, the common cultural ground of anti-absolutism and anti-feudalism does not mark off the militant republicans from their predecessors of 1790–91 or separate the Jacobins of Amiens, for instance, from their wealthy merchant opponents. The Marxist version of the social interpretation is not so much wrong in its particulars, therefore, as it is insufficiently discriminating. It cannot explain the difference in regional responses, the divisions within the bourgeoisie, or the failure of the Revolution to stop in 1791, when the capitalist and commercial sectors had made their greatest gains.

The revisionist interpretations have other faults. The primary defect of the revisionist accounts has been their failure to offer a plausible alternative to the Marxist version. In their concern to combat the Marxist interpretation, many critics argue against the thesis of "bourgeois" revolution without offering anything convincing in its place. Alfred Cobban, for example, was much more successful in arguing against the view that the Revolution benefited capitalism than he was in arguing that it was made by declining royal officials and members of the liberal professions. Royal officials dropped out of the movement after 1790, and lawyers, like the bourgeoisie more generally, could be found on all sides in the political conflict. The more extreme revisionist position of Cobb and his followers claims that the Revolution had little or no social significance. In this view, the Revolution becomes a hodgepodge of particularities and peculiar, individual foibles. Every place has its own individual reaction, and the decade of upheaval is defined as the sum of "thousands of individual bitternesses, ambitions and longings" that "expressed the desperation of countless unfulfilled lives, seeking an outlet in naked greed, or utopian hopes."[77]

The village gardeners and innkeepers, the small town grocers and doctors, the big city lawyers and merchants had too many divergent economic and social interests to justify lumping them together in a single economic or social category. Revolutionary intention and meaning therefore cannot be deduced from the social composition of the new political class; at the same time, they cannot be reduced to a random collection of individual states of mind. The members of the new political class shared certain values that

[77]Lyons, *Revolution in Toulouse*, p. 174.

were shaped in large measure by common cultural positions, for example, their experiences as a younger generation and their relationship to the urban world. The abstract elements in that culture have been shown in operation in previous chapters: secularism, rationalism, an emphasis on the Nation over all particularisms, and, in the case of republicans, what Isser Woloch calls a "democratic persuasion," a belief in the inherent virtue of widespread political participation.[78] In chapter 6, those values will be traced more precisely to the local structures of the new political culture. Family networks, organizational experiences, and common cultural relationships all helped form the new political class.

[78] *Jacobin Legacy: The Democratic Movement under the Directory* (Princeton, 1970), esp. pp. 149–86.

∞6∞

Outsiders,
Culture Brokers,
and Political Networks

REVOLUTION was like a rite of passage in which the end point was unknown. Society turned upside down, and the old structures fell into disrepute. The revolutionaries believed that they would emerge from their time of troubles with a new community based on reason and nature, but they found it difficult to move quickly across the threshold of a new social and political order. In the terms of anthropologists, the French seemed stuck in a "liminal" phase, a period of transition, in which the nation appeared to hover on the margins between what had been declared old and what was hoped for as the new.[1] The new values had been announced, but they had not yet taken hold. Uncertainty about the future prevailed.

In this anxious liminal period of social and political uncertainty, the new political class played a critical role. The new officials were to constitute the political and cultural vanguard of the crossing over into the new order. Just before the outbreak of the Vendée revolt, one republican wrote confidently about his expectations: "I have the misfortune of inhabiting a place that is extremely hostile to our Revolution . . . but I have seen with pleasure that [the people] is naturally good and has only strayed. If we succeed in instructing them, they will easily realize their mistakes."[2] It was not long before the realities of counterrevolution showed just how much "instruction" was needed, yet, despite the disappointments and dangers of governing, the revolutionary political class continued to

[1] I am using liminal in the sense given the term by Victor Turner, *The Ritual Process: Structure and Anti-Structure* (Ithaca, N.Y., 1969), esp. pp. 94–130.

[2] A.N., F^{1c} III Vendée 4, Comptes rendus administratifs, 1791–an VIII, letter from St. Christophe-du-Ligueron, 1 January 1793.

find new recruits. Many different factors might motivate men to take on the new positions of responsibility. But implicit in the thousands of individual choices were more general cultural patterns that decisively shaped the workings of revolutionary politics.

One of the most subtle and pervasive patterns was the relationship between revolution and mobility. The traumatic upheavals of revolution set the French population in motion. Thousands of people were uprooted from their customary residences and work habits. The requirements of the army, the lure of new official positions, service in the national guard, and even emigration for political reasons disrupted old habits and forcibly redistributed the population. Thousands of refugees flooded into the cities of the Vendée in their desperation to avoid the ravages of civil war, and many thousands of others fled cities caught in the turmoil of invasion or federalist agitation. The population of Bordeaux, for instance, declined from 110,000 in 1790 to 88,394 in the Year IV.[3] In quiet Chartres, twice as many newlyweds were out-of-towners in the revolutionary decade as in the 1780s, and only about one-half of the outsiders now came from the immediate region (as compared to three-quarters of them a decade earlier).[4]

With its emphasis on equality of citizenship, universalistic values, and the destruction of regional and local privileges, the new political culture appealed to the newly arrived, gave them a sense of belonging to one nation, and in turn depended on them for its further propagation. In his pathbreaking study of the Jacobin clubs, Crane Brinton found that 38 percent of the members he studied were immigrants to the towns and cities where they were living. A smaller, but very telling, number (13 percent) had moved into their cities of residence after 1789. In the big cities, the figures were even higher: 54 percent of the Jacobin Club members in Marseille were immigrants, and in time the number rose to 70 percent.[5] The coupling of migration and revolution did not escape the notice of contemporaries. During the debate on the constitution of 1795, one

---

[3] Alan Forrest, *Society and Politics in Revolutionary Bordeaux* (Oxford, 1975), p. 243.
[4] Michel Vovelle, *Ville et campagne au 18e siècle: Chartres et la Beauce* (Paris, 1980), p. 115.
[5] *The Jacobins: An Essay in the New History* (New York, 1930), pp. 56–57. On Marseille, see Michael Kennedy, *The Jacobin Club of Marseilles, 1790–1794* (Ithaca, N.Y., 1973), p. 153.

deputy complained that "all of the men who are most useful to the arts and sciences will abandon the hamlets of their fathers . . . in order to throw themselves into the midst of a great population and play there the necessary role for obtaining positions."[6]

Migration had begun long before the Revolution. In a small town, such as Chartres (13 thousand inhabitants), one-quarter of the newlyweds in the 1780s had come from outside the town. In a big port city, such as Bordeaux, the proportion of non-natives might reach as high as one-half the marrying population.[7] Yet, despite the influx of newcomers to towns and cities in the eighteenth century, local politics before 1789 remained the last bastion of every city's old families. In many towns, recent arrivals were legally prohibited from holding office, and as late as 1789 town councils still fought to retain the prohibition against newcomers.[8] The Revolution opened the floodgates to a stream of new arrivals. All the provisions against recent arrivals were eliminated along with restrictions on religious minorities and electoral stipulations that ensured the dominance of particular groups. Before 1789 most towns had some kind of regulation providing for a specified number of clergymen, lawyers, nobles, merchants, or even artisans on the council.[9] With the disappearance of such restrictions, new social groups, new families, and even new religious groups worked their way into city politics.

The Revolution offered unparalleled opportunities to religious minorities, and they did not ignore the occasion. Protestant and Jewish merchants appeared on the city councils in Bordeaux from the beginning of the Revolution. The Protestant Pierre Sers, for example, was the first president of the Jacobin Club in Bordeaux. He

[6] From a speech by Bordas as reported in *Le Moniteur universel*, no. 302 (2 thermidor an III [20 July 1795]), p. 1217.

[7] Vovelle, *Ville et campagne au 18e siècle*, p. 113. The literature on migration is reviewed in Jean-Pierre Poussou, "Les Mouvements migratoires en France et à partir de la France de la fin du XVe siècle au début du XIXe siècle: Approches pour une synthèse," *Annales de démographie historique*, 1970, pp. 11–78.

[8] In Reims, the town's *cahier de doléances* for the Estates General repeated the demand of many corporations for modification of the restriction of town office to natives of the city; it suggested that 15-year residents be eligible. The town council put its rejection of this position in writing (Lynn Hunt, *Revolution and Urban Politics: Troyes and Reims, 1786–1790* [Stanford, 1978], p. 60).

[9] Ibid., p. 23. For Amiens, see Marie-Yvonne Dessaux, "La Vie municipale à Amiens de 1782 à 1789," U.E.R. de Sciences historiques et géographiques (Amiens, 1978).

was elected to the city council in 1790 and then was chosen as deputy to the Legislative Assembly. He became president of the federalist Popular Commission of Public Safety in 1793, was outlawed, but survived to become an official of the Reformed Church under Napoleon.[10] The Vaysse family of Protestants in Toulouse took the Jacobin side. Jacques and Paul Vaysse (they were cousins) were elected to municipal office under the Directory. Both were Jacobins but relative political unknowns before 1796. Jacques was a well-to-do merchant and a Freemason; Paul had been a police official in the Year IV and then was elected president of the municipal administration in the Year VI, after having accumulated considerable property by buying *biens nationaux* (lands confiscated from the Catholic church to secure the national debt).[11] Unlike the Vaysse cousins, however, most members of religious minorities shied away from the radical extremes. In Bordeaux most Protestants and Jews gravitated toward federalism and the support of the Girondins. On a departmental level, however, the presence of religious minorities did not seem to affect voting patterns; the number of Protestants, for example, was negatively correlated with voting in the trial of the king, but otherwise there was no correlation between the proportion of Protestants in a department's population and voting for either the left or the right (see correlation matrix, Appendix A, under PROTPOP).

Members of religious minorities shared the attitudes of the new political class. The London-born, Jewish merchant Furtado, for example, was an early Jacobin Club member and a supporter of the Bordeaux federalist movement. He survived the Terror and was elected again in the Year IV to local office, but flatly refused the honor. In his view, the republic was "premature." Yet, despite his disenchantment, Furtado remained fundamentally attached to the revolutionary promise:

> I believe that every government is good or bad according to the morality of the men who direct it. What is worse than despotism, more revolting than aristocracy, more turbulent than democracy? . . .

[10] Forrest, *Revolutionary Bordeaux*, pp. 243–45.

[11] Jean Beyssi, "Le Parti jacobin à Toulouse sous le Directoire," *AHRF* 22 (1950): 28–54, 109–33, esp. p. 37; Martyn Lyons, *Revolution in Toulouse: An Essay on Provincial Terrorism* (Berne, 1978), pp. 186–87; and Georges Marinière, "Les Marchands d'étoffe de Toulouse à la fin du XVIII siècle," D.E.S. (Toulouse, 1958), pp. 154–88.

> [Yet], imagine a democracy composed of serious, virtuous men, who
> are filled with a profound respect for the laws, and you will have the
> highest degree of liberty possible with the most constant order and
> peace.

Like the other new officials, Furtado believed in the difference between private interests and the public good. Speaking of Madame
de Staël, with whom he had dinner in 1799 in Paris, he said: "I cannot understand either the spirit or the supposed patriotism of
those people. They love public affairs, rather than the public good
[*la chose publique*]. Love of the public good does not often lead to
places, pensions, business interests; only intrigue leads to all of
those." [12]

The new social groups, new families, and men of different religious faiths can be subsumed under the more general phenomenon of the appearance and even prominence of the outsider in
local politics. In Paris, the importance of visiting and migrant pro-
vincials is well known and hardly surprising. In the provinces, the
influence of deputies-on-mission from Paris has often been noted,
especially during the period of the Terror and subsequent reaction.
Even more striking, however, is the role of "marginal" men within
local circles. These men were the natural collaborators of the visiting deputies, but they were much more than puppet figures manipulated by an invasive external force. A political activist might be
an outsider by virtue of his social station, his geographical provenance, his religion, or some combination of these. In the revolutionary decade of uncertain authority, the outsider served as a vital
link between the national government and local people. Deputies-
on-mission turned to them precisely because they were outsiders,
that is, they were not tainted by dubious local connections; and local people also looked to them, no doubt for a variety of motives.
For those who were suspicious of impending changes, the outsider
provided a convenient displacement of responsibility, and it was
much easier to turn against him once a crisis had passed. To local
militants the outsider conveyed a sense of belonging to a larger
movement, and his presence enabled locals in opposition to separate themselves more sharply from previous rulers.

The outsider was particularly important during those periods

[12] "Souvenirs d'Abraham Furtado," *La Révolution française* 69 (1916): 543–51,
quotes pp. 549, 547, entry for 14 messidor an VII.

and in those places where local conflicts were most intense. Take, for example, the mayor's office in the big cities. In 1790 the voters chose symbolic figures who represented a possible rapprochement between the liberal elements of the Old Regime and the revolutionary movement. The mayor of Bordeaux in that year was the Count Joseph de Fumel, the 70-year-old commander-in-chief of the armies in Guyenne. Mayor Rigaud of Toulouse, a law professor, was also in his seventies. The mayor of Nancy was the illustrious Count Custine d'Auflance, and the mayor of Amiens was the rich merchant Degand-Cannet, who had recently bought an ennobling office. After the insurrection of 10 August 1792, the voters of Amiens picked Louis Lescouvé, a prosperous 58-year-old wigmaker. Neither he nor his wife were natives of Amiens, and they had no family or social ties to the all-important community of merchant-manufacturers. The occupations of their relatives demonstrate the couple's modest social standing: cited in their marriage contract were farmers (*laboureurs*), a master saddler, and a barber-surgeon (the professional poor cousin to the medical doctors).[13]

In 1793–94 the mayor's offices of the other big cities were rocked by frequent upheavals. Bordeaux's new mayor, Joseph Bertrand, was a watchmaker who had come to the city from Avignon in 1779 or 1780. His stepping stone to the political limelight was one of the local radical clubs, over which he presided in the critical summer of 1793. In the Year III Bertrand was sentenced by the departmental criminal court to 12 years in prison for illegally confiscating the property of victims of the Terror, including the belongings of François Saige, his predecessor. He was released in the Year V and moved to Paris.[14] His successor was another, somewhat more respectable outsider, Pierre Thomas. Thomas was a Protestant minister in Sainte-Foy-la-Grande, a small town on the Dordogne. When

[13] Lescouvé was assessed at 1,295 francs revenue for the *contribution foncière*; the mean for all councillors was 1,164 francs (assessments were found for 42 percent of the councillors) (A.M., Amiens, 1G 2.11, Contribution foncière, 1791). When he married a farmer's daughter in 1757, he made a modest marriage contract evaluated at only 2,000 livres (A.D., Somme, 2C Etude Morel, 28 May 1757). This can be contrasted with the marriage contract of the merchant Pierre Guérard, who married in 1764; his contract was evaluated at 131,000 livres (A.D., Somme, 2C 705). Guérard was elected to the city council in 1790.

[14] Renée Dubos, "Une Société populaire bordelaise: Les Surveillants de la Constitution," *Revue historique de Bordeaux* 25 (1932), 26 (1933), 27 (1934), and 29 (1936). According to Dubos, the club was composed primarily of artisans and small shopkeepers.

he was named to the mayor's office in 1794, he was only 34 years old. He came to the attention of the deputy-on-mission because he was a reliable departmental official. Although he was denounced as a terrorist, Thomas was chosen by the Directory to be its commissioner to the departmental administration in the summer of 1799.[15] The Directory's motives in 1799 were much the same as those animating the deputies-on-mission in the Year II; Bordeaux's native leaders could not be counted on to forcefully resist the encroachments of the right.

Nancy too had outsiders as mayors in 1793 and 1794. The first, Nicolas Géhin, was a 40-year-old clergyman from Toul; he was succeeded by the 42-year-old actor Emmanuel Glasson-Brisse, who was in turn succeeded by Joseph Wulliez from Sarrebourg. Two of them were not residents, and the third had what most considered a less-than-respectable occupation (acting). No doubt locals recognized that the tempest had passed when they saw Claude Mallarmé installed as mayor in December 1794. The 35-year-old lawyer and ex-*parlementaire* was a native of Nancy who had held various revolutionary offices since 1790. In the spring of 1795, both Glasson-Brisse and Wulliez were listed by the new municipality as "first-class terrorists," that is, among "the principal authors or accomplices of oppression." This distinguished them from the second class—"those who were perhaps equally evil but whose activities were less deadly because they did not enjoy the same influence"—and the third class—"those who only fell in behind the banners of the agents of tyranny out of cowardice, weakness, or vanity."[16]

Mayors had an obvious importance in local politics, but the phenomenon of the outsider was not limited to that august position. Quite often the critical ramparts of revolutionary militancy were manned by outsiders too. Pierre Philip, the president of the popular society in Nancy, exemplifies the peripatetic politician. He was born in Bordeaux in 1750, the son of a ship's captain. He himself was a sailor in his youth, then a clerk in Paris and would-be author of poetry and plays. By 1792 he had obtained an official position as a director of supply storage in the war ministry. He first appeared

[15] R. Brouillard, "Un Maire de Bordeaux inconnu: Pierre Thomas," *Revue historique de Bordeaux* 11 (1918) and 12 (1919).
[16] A.M., Nancy, D 14, Delibérations municipales, 15 prairial an III.

in Nancy in September 1793 on an official mission to establish a clothing supply depot. His brief political career in Nancy was punctuated and finally foreclosed by arrest and imprisonment for conspiracy. Needless to say, he joined the former mayors on the list of first-class terrorists.[17]

No one was more locally notorious, however, than J.-B. Lacombe, the president of the Military Commission established to punish federalists in Bordeaux. He was born in Toulouse, the second son of a humble tailor. A local priest first noticed his intelligence and offered to tutor him, and in 1784 at the age of 24 Lacombe became a schoolteacher. Three years later he moved to Bordeaux with his wife and two children. Like many of the other militants, Lacombe migrated from one big city to another in search of his fortune. No doubt it seemed easier to move up far away from the reminders of humiliating social origins. Like Marat, Lacombe found the doors to success closed against him; he was denied admission to the *Société littéraire du Musée*, where the cream of Bordeaux's intellectual elite came together. The federalist mayor of Bordeaux, later a victim of Lacombe's commission, was one of the *Musée*'s founding members. Lacombe was admitted to a masonic lodge, and in 1790 he joined the *Club National*. After yet another disappointment—he hoped to be named provisional mayor or *procureur* (city attorney)—he was named president of the Military Commission in the fall of 1793. In August 1794, a few days after the fall of Robespierre, Lacombe himself was executed for extortion, corruption of morals, and treason.[18] Men like Lacombe and Mayor Bertrand were especially quick to absorb the main themes of revolutionary rhetoric; both made their way up through the more radical clubs where political influence depended primarily on persuasive public speaking. The success of such men prompted one horrified Bordelais to observe, "it is by *words* that they accomplished their ends: *words* did everything."[19]

The outsider might be defined in a variety of ways. There were

[17] Henry Poulet, "Le Sans-culotte Philip, président de la Société populaire de Nancy," *Annales de l'Est et du Nord* 2 (1906): 248–83, 321–66, 501–29.

[18] Pierre Bécamps, *La Révolution à Bordeaux (1789–1794): J.-B.-M. Lacombe, président de la Commission militaire* (Bordeaux, 1953).

[19] Sainte-Luce-Oudaille, *Histoire de Bordeaux pendant dix-huit mois ou depuis l'arrivée des représentants Tallien et Ysabeau, Beaudot et Chaudron-Rousseau, jusqu'à la fin de leur mission* (Paris, n.d.), p. 3.

religious outsiders, such as Protestants and Jews. There were social outsiders, such as the much maligned actors and struggling lay schoolteachers. There were geographical outsiders, too, such as the immigrants from other cities and sometimes other countries. Even the rich merchants and prosperous tradesmen had had reason to feel like outsiders under the Old Regime, when nobles, judges, and a few high-ranking clergymen had dominated political and social affairs. Nevertheless, "outsider" is not a category like occupation or profession. It did not define a social station in revolutionary or Old Regime society. It was, rather, a relationship, the relationship defined by being left out in some fashion. Lacombe, the schoolteacher and militant, did not fit into the same social or political category as Furtado, the Jewish merchant. Indeed, Lacombe's commission specialized in condemning such men as Furtado and his friends. Yet Lacombe and Furtado were each outsiders in their own way, and the fact of being marginal gave them a reason to join the new political class.

The common element of marginality did not turn the new political class into a bunch of itinerant troublemakers, that much-feared but rarely seen breed of professional revolutionary.[20] The remarkable stories of such men as Lacombe and Philip should not lead us to the hasty conclusion that the Revolution was simply the sum of "thousands of individual bitternesses," that is, of personal frustrations and resentments. For some, no doubt, frustration and resentment were involved. But for others the motives were entirely different. Individual motives cannot be summed to provide a measure of the new class's intentions, because the political class was not defined by individual psychologies. It was defined, rather, by common opportunities and shared roles. "Marginality"—taken in a structural sense rather than as a term of invidious social comparison—gave the new officials an affinity for the role of culture and power brokers. Just as certain peripheral or marginal regions of the country proved more amenable to the penetration of revolutionary political culture, so too certain kinds of marginal men proved most eager to take on the role of political and cultural middlemen. Such roles were critical since the Revolution was, in essence, the multiplication and diffusion of culture and power.

[20] Brinton makes a similar point (*The Jacobins*, p. 57).

Immigrants, Protestants, Jews, schoolteachers, actors, and merchants had ties to the world outside the city, and in particular to national networks of culture, knowledge, commerce, or religion. In the villages, too, there were similar kinds of men, albeit on a smaller scale. A prime candidate in many villages was the local schoolmaster. In little Pacy-sur-Eure, it was one Taillard, who arrived from Paris in 1791 at the age of 36 with his father and his wife to take up a post as *maître de pension et d'éducation*. After a short stint as a minor official landed him in jail, Taillard got himself named to the departmental administration by three visiting deputies and, through his relations with them, oversaw the promotion of his friends and allies to the newly reconstituted village council.[21]

There are many such stories. A schoolmaster arrived in town (a village like Pacy or even a big city like Bordeaux, where the teacher Lacombe terrorized the rich, indifferent, or hostile from his post on the Military Commission) and readily embraced the revolutionary cause, which either freed him from clerical control or actually created a new job for him. His bit of learning and knowledge of the ways of the outside world gained him a local audience, influence, enmity from some quarters, and all of these traits made him attractive to delegates from Paris or the nearest big city who were desperately looking for reliable collaborators.

The culture and power brokers were not always outsiders like Taillard, but they were men whose professions and interests naturally facilitated contact with the outside world. In the commune of Foncines-et-les-Planches in the Jura department, Jean-Baptiste Rousseau was chosen to become *agent national* in 1792. His textile business not only put him in touch with much of the local population but also gave him the financial wherewithal to consider public service and even to loan money to the commune in time of need.[22] In Les Authieux, the key figure was Nicolas Hubert, an innkeeper. *Procureur* in the first revolutionary municipality, by the spring of 1794 he had become a member of the local *comité de surveillance* (watch committee) and president of the popular society. He was seconded by another local militant in the same mold, Augustin

[21] Edouard Isambard, *Histoire de la Révolution à Pacy-sur-Eure*, 2 vols. (Pacy, 1894) 2: 25, 182–83.
[22] Pierre Doudier, *Villages comtois sous la Révolution et l'Empire* (Dôle, 1975), pp. 138–39.

Marguerite, a 30-year-old gardener who could read and write and who in addition to serving as secretary of the council also organized civic banquets and processions. In the spring of 1794 he opened a republican school.[23] In Bénesse-Maremne, the *agent national* was one of the few nonpeasants on the council, Darrigrand, a former court bailiff (*huissier*). Faced with a recalcitrant council dominated by rich peasants, he reminded his fellow villagers that if they did not toe the line, "I will be obliged to inform the superior administrations."[24] Local power brokers recognized that their influence depended on their connections to the outside.

The most successful and enduring intermediaries were not simply collaborators with outside forces, but mediators between outside and local interests. Jean-Jacques Roquette of tiny Saint-Amans (100 households, Aveyron department) is a telling example. He went to school in nearby Rodez and completed his law studies in Toulouse. Afterward he returned home to take up a not very demanding position as seigneurial judge, which left him time to read Rousseau and Voltaire. In 1790 at age 30, he was first elected *procureur* of his village and then promoted to the departmental administration. He was elected judge of the district tribunal in 1791 and named mayor of Saint-Amans in 1793. Alone among his fellow villagers, he sought affiliation with the Jacobins as early as July 1790. With several friends, he finally organized a popular society in 1793, and not surprisingly he was named president of it. Soon after he became president of the new watch committee (*comité de surveillance révolutionnaire*) as well.

In November 1793 a visiting *commissaire* named Lagarde came to Saint-Amans to organize a festival in honor of poverty. Although Roquette came from one of the richest families in the village, he duly presided over the festivities, which took place at a local inn. The official record of the proceedings made no mention of article 8 in Lagarde's remarkable decree: "Every person under arrest, every rich man, egoist, or suspect will come to the place designated for the festival; he will stay standing by the poor man and serve him;

[23] Albert Soboul, "Une Commune rurale pendant la Révolution: Les Authieux-sur-le-Port-Saint-Ouen (Seine-Inférieure), 1789–1795," *AHRF* 25 (1953): 140–60, esp. 153–56.

[24] Francis Hirigoyen, "Bénesse-Maremne pendant la Révolution française," *Bulletin de la société de Borda* 103 (1978): 51–70, esp. pp. 66–67.

he will not touch any of the dishes he carries, since the etiquette of former times requires that the Valet not sit at the table of the Master."[25] Roquette apparently managed to maintain both his dignity and his credibility during this strange episode, because after the fall of Robespierre he was named as a commissioner by the district to investigate abuses during the Terror. Later he refused higher offices and insisted on serving as a simple justice of the peace in his village.

The active involvement of such men as Roquette kept the line between urban and rural from becoming too sharp. He brought the values he had learned in the cities and in his reading to the village. Rather than moving away to Rodez, Toulouse, or Paris like the Saint-Justs and Babeufs, Roquette preferred to stay close to home, while eagerly following national developments. His decision meant that the Revolution would not be viewed simply as a foreign importation, though the connection to the cities was not lost on anyone. Although many peasants resented the food requisitions and the constant attempts to draft more young men into the interminable war effort, those of Saint-Amans found that they could count on Roquette when they voted overwhelmingly against dividing the common lands. Not only did he defend their decision to the district council, but he also sent along a long memoir analyzing the problems faced by the peasants of his region.[26]

The enthusiasm of a schoolteacher, innkeeper, or young notable was especially important in rural areas. Often revolutionary officials found the peasantry hard to reach, if not impenetrable. In the Loire department, for example, rural communes were characterized as "mountains which the lever of public opinion cannot lift up."[27] If there was a successful lever in operation, it was the subtle force applied by the power brokers and cultural intermediaries like Roquette. In some regions, they were obviously successful (see chapter 4). One former mayor explained the need for patience in 1796: "The minutes of the election are not perhaps drawn up according

[25] Antoine Roquette, *Jean-Jacques Roquette ou la Révolution à Saint-Amans-des-Cots* (Paris, 1978), pp. 118–22.

[26] Ibid., pp. 145–48.

[27] Colin Lucas, *The Structure of the Terror: The Example of Javogues and the Loire* (Oxford, 1973), quote on p. 235. Lucas gives extensive detail on the use of *commissaires* to bring the revolutionary message to the villages (esp. pp. 189–219).

to the forms required by the law, but you know that the people of the countryside do not have much education and they carry out their affairs as best they can; we can tell you that the two citizens who were chosen are the best educated and most intelligent of our commune."[28] He might have said, the most open and receptive to the new culture brought to us by city folk.

The political middlemen were able to exercise influence because they worked within the linkages and organizations of the new political culture. Roquette used his family connections, his relations with officials outside the village, his affiliation to the Jacobin Club network, and the new links forged to villagers who joined the local popular society or attended the local republican festivals. In the cities, the same kinds of relationships operated on a bigger scale. The strongest informal, social network within the new political class was that of family. In Toulouse at least three families had two members each on the city council: the Vaysses cousins and the father-son combinations of the Garys and the Maries. Family ties could work in any political direction. Gary *père* (the father) was a former *capitoul* (leading city official under the Old Regime) and a lawyer who held municipal office in 1790; his son, also a lawyer, held office during the reaction of the Year III. In the opposite camp, Marie *père* was a merchant, Freemason, and Jacobin; he held office in 1790 and again under the Directory when his son joined him on the council. In the Year IX Marie *père* appeared on the town's list of 100 highest taxpayers.[29] In Nancy, the Boulay brothers, the Nicolas brothers, and the Rollins (father and son?) were all prominent in city affairs.

In Amiens family relationships are even more impressive because more fully documented by the marriage contracts of elected officials. Two father-son combinations sat on the city council: the Anselins and the Lerouxs. But they were only the most visible relatives within an incredibly densely knit network of merchant families. At least six of the city councillors elected in 1790 were related by marriage, and all of them were merchants or dyers. From then on, family connections continued to draw new men into official positions. In 1791 Anselin *fils* (the son) and Delamorlière were elected to the council. Jean-Baptiste Delamorlière, a dyer, was the

[28] J. Brélot, *La Vie politique en Côte-d'Or sous le Directoire* (Dijon, 1932), p. 42.

[29] A.N., F[ib] II Garonne (Haute) 25, "Proclamation de la liste des cent plus imposés de la commune de Toulouse, an IX."

brother-in-law by his first marriage of Pierre Flesselles, a merchant elected to the council in January 1790, and he was related through his mother to Antoine Clément, another merchant elected in 1790. Delamorlière compromised his position by signing a petition in favor of the king in June 1792, but he was chosen again to sit on the council in the Year III. Later he became a prominent supporter of Bonaparte. By his second marriage he was related to another merchant on the 1790 council, Antoine Gensse-Duminy, and to the grocer Nicolas Dargent, who sat with him on two councils during the Year III and on several councils under Bonaparte (from the Consulate into the Empire).[30]

Anselin *fils* was followed by his father, a *chirurgien* (barber-surgeon), who sat briefly on the council of the Year II in Amiens. A sister had married the merchant Pierre Massey, who along with his father-in-law had been elected as one of the town deputies to the regional or *bailliage* meetings preliminary to the Estates General.[31] Massey was elected to the Legislative Assembly in 1791. He sat on the city council in the Year III, on the commercial court between 1798 and 1801, and then again on the council under the Consulate. Through his wife he was also related to the dyer Louis Dupont who sat on the council in 1790 and again during the Year II.[32] Dupont in turn was related through his brother-in-law to the merchant Clément on the 1790 council, who was related to Delamorlière, and so on.

Family linkage of this sort ensured a subterranean continuity of administration in Amiens. One of the strongest links was Charles-François-Bastard Delaroche, a middle-aged merchant who sat continuously on the council from 1790 into the Consulate (he was demoted briefly to *notable* in 1793). Delaroche was related on his mother's side to Charles Dely, a merchant who was elected as *notable* in 1793 and then sat as a councillor on the municipalities of the Year II and the Year III. One of Delaroche's brothers-in-law and a maternal uncle both came from the Lefebvre family of merchants, one

---

[30] For Delamorlière's first marriage, see A.D., Somme, 2C Etude Scribe, 15 July 1764. For his second marriage, see Etude St. Germain, 21 October 1788. The contracts include lists of witnesses with their relationship to the marrying couple.

[31] Albéric de Calonne, *Histoire de la ville d'Amiens*, 3 vols. (Amiens, 1899–1900) 2: 415–16 (list of 36 deputies from the city).

[32] For Massey, see A.D., Somme, 2C Etude Machart, 8 December 1779; for Dupont, see Etude Delattre, 22 January 1792.

of whom sat on the council in 1790–91. Delaroche's brother-in-law was also the paternal uncle of Louis Lefebvre, who was chosen for the council in the Year III. Louis Lefebvre in turn was related to Alexandre Poullain-Cotte, a merchant and councilman in 1790 and again in the Year III.[33] Through another brother-in-law Delaroche was related to Clément and Dupont, two other members of the 1790 council. Through a maternal cousin he was related as well to Delamorlière, with whom he sat on the first council under the Consulate.[34] Within the merchant community, at least, intermarriage bound the revolutionary officials closely together. Under Napoleon, the same men continued to dominate the city: both Lefebvres, Anselin *père*, Dargent, Delamorlière, Delaroche, Flesselles, Gensse-Duminy, Dupont, Poullain, Leroux, and Massey were all on either the lists of notables or highest taxpayers for the Year IX, the Year X, or 1810.[35]

It seems likely that the conservatism of Amiens politics was, if not caused by, at least reinforced by, the continuity and density of marriage ties between the big merchant and manufacturing families in the city. Once they had established a dominant position after 1790, they were loath to give it up. Yet pressure from Paris and the shock of new democratic ideas challenged their control for a time. In his discourse after the elections of January 1793, Doctor Rigollot (a municipal official since 1790) was probably *not* expressing the manufacturer's point of view when he proclaimed that "the honest and industrious worker is no longer rejected with disdain just because he is of mediocre fortune; he has finally recovered all his dignity and the most beautiful of his rights, the inalienable right to name his Magistrates."[36] The participation of "the honest workers" cut sharply into the representation of the merchants and manufacturers (see table 5, chapter 5). But then Rigollot, though a successful and supple politician (he became mayor in the Year IV, thus demonstrating that he could serve in governments of various political hues), was not a native himself.[37]

Unfortunately, few cities have marriage contracts that are as ac-

[33] For Louis Lefebvre, see A.D., Somme, 2C Etude Baudelocque, 5 November 1775. The notary Baudelocque was himself a city councillor in 1790, a *notable* in the Year III, and a councillor again after Bonaparte's coup.

[34] For Delaroche, see A.D., Somme, 2C Etude Turbert, 19 April 1756.

[35] A.D., Somme, Mb 107529 bis, Mb 107547, and Mb 107574.

[36] *Affiches du Département de la Somme*, 26 January 1793.

[37] Marc Edme Rigollot was born in Boegevin (Haute-Marne) (Calonne, *Histoire de la ville d'Amiens* 2: 475).

cessible as those of Amiens, so comparisons of kinship networks are difficult to establish. Was the chief difference between right-wing Amiens and left-wing Toulouse one of kinship systems? The notion is tantalizing but impossible to substantiate. The evidence from Amiens does suggest, however, that merchants there had a separate kinship network from the artisans and shopkeepers. Although marriage contracts for artisans and shopkeepers are more scarce, those located suggest that artisans and shopkeepers had their own separate pattern of social relations. The wigmaker Louis Lescouvé, for example, was related to the Baudelot family, which means that it is likely that he was related to Nicolas Baudelot, the shoemaker who was elected to the council in 1793 with him.[38] The retired shoemaker Philippe Demailly was also elected to the council in January 1793. When he had remarried in 1783, his witnesses included a retired master baker and a weaver; the latter was the brother of his new young wife.[39] Neither Demailly nor Lescouvé was related to merchant families; their kinship system was petit bourgeois (perhaps with some connection to the textile workers, since Demailly's brother-in-law was an *ouvrier saiteur* [woolworker]).

Neighborhood reinforced the sense of community within each family system and heightened their sense of separateness from each other. Most of the artisan or shopkeeper councillors in Amiens whose addresses were listed lived near the central market located a few steps from the Cathedral (see map 2). A cooper, a brewer, a goldsmith, a soapmaker, and a grocer all lived on streets leading directly into the market. The merchants and manufacturers lived either north of the cathedral or west and southwest of it; over half of the merchants on the council whose addresses were found lived on the adjoining rue des Vergeaux, rue des Sergents, rue St. Martin, and rue de Beau Puits, which were between city hall and the cathedral. Pierre Deyon found the same kind of social segregation in his study of the eighteenth-century *capitation* rolls of Amiens: the royal officials and nobles lived south and southeast of the cathedral; the industrial magnates lived north and west of it; and the center city was inhabited by middling bourgeois and artisans.[40]

In most respects, however, the artisans and shopkeepers were

[38] A.D., Somme, 2C Etude Morel, 28 May 1757.
[39] A.D., Somme, 2C Etude Baudelocque, 28 June 1783.
[40] "Les Registres de capitation d'Amiens au XVIIIe siècle," *Revue du Nord* 42 (1960): 19–26, esp. pp. 20–21.

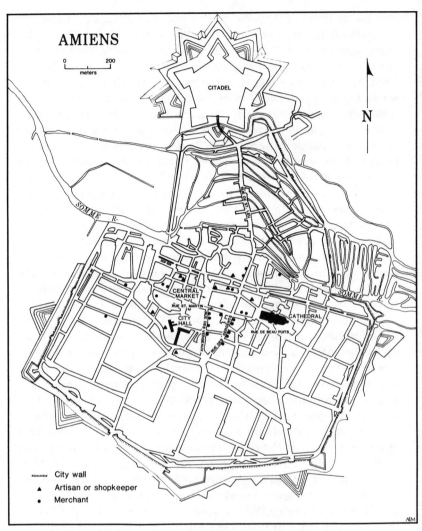

Map 2.
Residences of Revolutionary Officials in Amiens

more diverse and less inclined to stick together than the merchants and manufacturers. Much of this lack of cohesion stemmed from the economic diversity of the small trades.[41] Few trades sent more than one representative to the councils. The one exception in Amiens was the *épiciers* (grocers), who had four representatives on the councils. Two of the three grocers listed on the property tax rolls were assessed at about the same level as the average merchant on the councils, which indicates that these *épiciers* were more like the textile merchants and manufacturers than like the brewers, coopers, or shoemakers on the various councils.[42] The other artisans and shopkeepers on the councils came from a variety of different trades, each of which had their own, sometimes contradictory interests.

The artisans and shopkeepers may have been chosen for their sympathy with the city's lower classes, but it is noteworthy that the thousands of textile workers had no representatives of their own on the councils. Much of the pressure for radical change came from the city's poor sections; the parish of St. Leu in the northeast was the home of sans-culottism in Amiens, and it was inhabited largely by unemployed textile workers.[43] The July festival of woolworkers (*fête des sayeteurs*) was often the occasion for riots and demonstrations over the price of bread, and the agitation frequently spilled over into political demands for more responsive local government. In July and August 1792, for instance, large assemblies of "citizens" meeting in the St. Leu church demanded that city hall take steps to arm the National Guard, close convent churches, fire refractory priests from the hospitals, and take down the portrait of Louis XVI from its meeting room wall.[44] In elections shortly afterward, the voters chose the wigmaker Lescouvé, the doctor Rigollot, and a soapmaker to head up the new municipality. The textile workers

[41] This point is explored in detail by Antonino de Francesco, "Le Quartier lyonnais de la Croisette pendant les premières années de la Révolution (1790–1793)," *Bulletin du Centre d'histoire économique et sociale de la région lyonnaise*, no. 4 (1979): 21–64.

[42] Eight merchants on the councils were assessed more and five less than the two wealthy grocers (A.M., Amiens, 1G 2.11, Contribution foncière, 1791).

[43] Calonne, *Histoire de la ville d'Amiens* 2: 462–63.

[44] An invaluable source for the history of Amiens in the early years of the Revolution is *Documents pour servir à l'histoire de la Révolution française dans la ville d'Amiens*, 5 vols. (Paris, 1894–1902). On the *fête des sayeteurs* and the demonstrations of July-August 1792, see vol. 5: 189–298.

had provided the popular pressure, but they looked elsewhere for
leadership.

The reliance of the workers on higher-ranking social groups was
evident even during the Terror. Heading the list of "terrorists" denounced in Amiens in the spring of 1795 were a locksmith, two
musicians, two clerks, a mason, an ex-priest, and a woodworker
(the last was accused of keeping a guillotine in his woodshed!).[45]
These rank-and-file militants had less social standing than the municipal officials chosen in Amiens after August 1792, but they still
were not from the masses of textile workers. Workers in the other
cities depended on the same kinds of leadership, which was provided by artisans and shopkeepers and minor professionals of
various types. The tradesmen who sat on the Toulouse councils,
for instance, came from at least two distinct economic milieus. In
one group were those who had catered to the huge aristocratic cli-
entele provided by the *parlement*; in this category were a jeweller, a
master hatter, a leather merchant, a cutler, a pewterer, and a goldsmith. Most of them lived in the central city near the institutions
and residences of the former elite, and they tended to serve in the
early years of the Revolution. The shoemakers and carpenters and
other more modest craftsmen who sat on the Jacobin municipalities
did not seem to congregate in any special part of town, and a fair
number of them lived in the crowded suburbs, including a few
who lived across the river in the crime-infested St. Cyprien quar-
ter. Again, no particular trade stands out as a political vanguard.
Artisans and shopkeepers were elected to the councils as mediators, not as representatives of particular trades and crafts. Their
diffusion throughout a city, town, or village and their constant contact and interaction with various social groups put them in a position to "represent" all the lower ranks of local society.

In addition to family, neighborhood, and professional networks,
the new political class was also shaped by common organizational
experience. Before the Revolution, many future officials had joined
masonic lodges, which grew dramatically in numbers during the
eighteenth century. The city lodges reflected the weight of various
non-noble social groups within urban society. In Amiens, 96 per-

[45] A.M., Amiens, 2I 19, "Liste des citoyens dénoncés au représentant du peuple Blaux, comme ayant participé aux horreurs commises avant le 9 thermidor à
Amiens," 13 prairial an III. The list had only 16 names.

cent of the Freemasons came from the Third Estate: of these 46 percent were merchants or manufacturers, 31 percent came from the
judiciary or the liberal professions, and 13 percent from the petite
bourgeoisie. Bordeaux had even more merchants in the lodges;
Nancy and Toulouse many less. In Nancy, for instance, only 79 percent of the Freemasons came from the Third Estate; of these 51 percent came from the legal and other liberal professions, 21 percent
were merchants, and 15 percent were artisans or shopkeepers.[46]

Not all Freemasons became revolutionaries, and there is no evidence to suggest that the lodges plotted out the course of the Revolution from behind closed doors.[47] Relatively detailed lists of members make it possible to trace the influence of the lodges in Nancy
and Toulouse. In Nancy, Freemasons could be found in every revolutionary municipality: in 1790–91, 20 percent of the councillors
were Freemasons; during the Terror this dropped to 8 percent; during the Year III, 10 percent had belonged; and finally under the Directory their numbers grew to 20 percent again.[48] One lodge in
Nancy stands out as a reservoir of municipal officials, the lodge of
Saint-Jean de Jérusalem, which was established in 1771. Seven of
the nine Masons sitting in 1790–91 belonged to this lodge as did
five of the six Freemasons elected during the Directory. Since only
one Freemason sat on the council during both periods, the role of
the lodge itself is suggested. Even more intriguing is the fact that
more than one-half of the members of the lodge who sat during the
Directory had actually joined *after* the beginning of the Revolution.[49] In contrast, most of the lodge members who sat during
1790–91 had joined some time before 1789, including two who had

[46] The figures on the social composition of the lodges come from Daniel Roche, *Le
Siècle des lumiéres en province: Académies et académiciens provinciaux, 1680–1789*, 2 vols.
(Paris, 1978) 2: 419–24.
[47] On the relationship between Freemasonry and Jacobinism, see Michael L. Kennedy, *The Jacobin Clubs in the French Revolution: The First Years* (Princeton, 1982),
pp. 5–7.
[48] The file of councillors was checked against the names listed in Charles Ber-
nadin, *Notes pour servir à l'histoire de la Franc-maçonnerie à Nancy jusqu'en 1805* (Nancy,
1910). These figures are quite similar to those for Aix-en-Provence: 37 percent in
February 1790; 4 percent in September 1793; 15 percent under the late Directory
(Christiane Derobert-Ratel, *Institutions et vie municipale à Aix-en-Provence sous la Révolution [1789–an VIII]* [Millau, 1981], p. 602).
[49] Some masonic lodges continued to meet after 1789 in both Nancy and Toulouse. This continuity contrasts with the disappearance of lodges in Provence (Maurice Agulhon, *Pénitents et Francs-Maçons de l'ancienne Provence* [Paris, 1968]).

joined back in the 1770s. Thus it seems that aspiring politicians in Nancy recognized the advantages of affiliation with the Saint-Jean lodge. The lodge admitted members from various social stations: military officers, clergymen, merchants and manufacturers, lawyers, officials, and a good number of artisans and shopkeepers. In this sense, the lodge prefigured the intricate social balance on the revolutionary councils. Most of the Freemasons chosen for city office were merchants (36 percent), lawyers (41 percent), or professionals; none was an artisan or shopkeeper.

In Toulouse, no one lodge dominated in the same way, perhaps because Freemasonry was so broadly planted in the south of France. On the eve of the Revolution, there were between 500 and 600 Freemasons in Toulouse.[50] There were more lodges in Toulouse than in Nancy (12 in 1789 as opposed to 7 in Nancy), and several of them produced city councillors. Overall the proportion of Freemasons on the councils went from one-fifth in 1790–91 to one-third under the Directory (with only 1 Mason sitting during the Terror).[51] If any one lodge stood out, it was the lodge Encyclopédique; 3 of 8 Freemasons sitting in 1790–91 and 2 of 8 sitting during the Directory came from this lodge, which had been founded just before the Revolution. Within a year of its foundation, the Encyclopédique lodge claimed 120 members from various social groups. Artisans and shopkeepers joined in large numbers, and, unlike their counterparts in Nancy, a few of them did go on to become elected city officials: though 60 percent of the Masons on the councils were merchants, the second biggest group was the artisans and shopkeepers with 16 percent. Thus Freemasonry helped secure the merchant/artisans-shopkeepers alliance in Toulouse just as it helped shape the merchant-lawyer-professional combination in Nancy.

[50] J. Gros, "Les Loges maçonniques de Toulouse (de 1740 à 1870)," *La Révolution française* 40 (1901): 234–70, 297–318.

[51] The file of councillors was compared to the membership lists available in the B.N., Fonds Maçonniques (F.M.)[2] 443, 444, 451, 454, 455, 458, 462, 464, 471, 478, 479. No doubt some Freemasons in Toulouse went undetected because the lists are not complete for all lodges. For the Encyclopédique lodge, the list for 1786 was used. The lists for Bordeaux in the Fonds were even less complete; hence Bordeaux has been omitted here. There were 12 lodges in Bordeaux in 1789 (G. Hubrecht, "Notes pour servir à l'histoire de la Franc-maçonnerie à Bordeaux," *Revue historique de Bordeaux et du département de la Gironde*, n.s. 3 [1954]: 143–50). Some isolated biographical information was also obtained from Johel Coutura, *La Franc-Maçonnerie à Bordeaux (XVIIIe–XIXe siècles)* (Marseille, 1978).

Freemasonry spun a web of personal and sometimes even ideological ties that gave significant support to the revolutionary movement.[52] But it would be a mistake to identify this elusive network
with radical politics, because the influence of the Masons was least
apparent during the Terror. In Toulouse, for example, the last
council elected before the Terror included six Masons, whereas
those of the Terror had only one. Moreover, the lodges were not
very active during the Revolution, and there was often competition
and conflict between Masonry and Jacobinism, even though nearly
one-third of the Toulouse Jacobins were also Freemasons.[53] The
lodges of Toulouse were briefly disbanded in the Year III by the
deputy-on-mission Mallarmé, who acted on the complaint of
several Jacobins. Like intermarriage, however, lodge membership
brought a measure of continuity to city politics over the revolutionary decade, and, though they faded away during the Terror, the
lodges did not disappear entirely between 1789 and 1799. In Toulouse the lodges were eventually permitted to regroup, and in 1797 a
number of former Jacobins joined the rejuvenated Encyclopédique
lodge.[54] The lodges as organizations did not make the Revolution,
but membership in them facilitated the access to power of many
revolutionary officials.

The most obvious recruitment centers for local officials were the
Jacobin clubs. By virtue of its early appearance and its customary
affiliation with the parent club in Paris, the Jacobin Club was the
preeminent political organization in every city.[55] Yet the club did
not stand for the same principles and program in each place. In
Bordeaux the *Amis de la Constitution*, as they were usually called in
their first years, were moderate in politics and generally supportive
of the federalist movement. Socially the *Amis* "remained the un-
sullied preserve of the rich and the propertied."[56] One-half of the
city councillors of 1790–91 appear on the only extant membership

[52] Agulhon, *Pénitents et Francs-Maçons*, p. 186.
[53] Michel Taillefer, "La Franc-maçonnerie toulousaine et la Révolution française,"
AHRF 52 (1980): 59–90, esp. p. 72. Taillefer argues that the Freemasons of Toulouse
were associated with various political options: 38 percent of the Girondins were
Freemasons, 32 percent of the Jacobins, and 30 percent of the royalists. According to
my information on the city councillors, 25 percent of those who were Jacobins were
also Freemasons.
[54] Gros, "Les Loges maçonniques," p. 264; Taillefer, "La Franc-maçonnerie toulousaine," pp. 83–89.
[55] Brinton, *The Jacobins*; Kennedy, *The Jacobin Clubs*.
[56] Forrest, *Revolutionary Bordeaux*, p. 68.

list of the club.[57] More than one-half (60 percent) of the officials in the "federalist" municipality of 1793 were on the list as compared to only 11 percent of the "terrorist" (by national standards, true Jacobin) councillors. Almost one-fourth of the councillors of the Year III had been Jacobins, and 44 percent of the councillors of the Directory era had been members. The more radical officials of the Terror regime (those sitting between September 1793 and the end of the Year II) were recruited from other clubs, such as the *Club National*, an organization of modest merchants, tradesmen, and members of the liberal professions.[58]

The Toulousain Jacobins, by contrast, represented what one historian calls a "popular front" of the *petite, moyenne,* and *grande bourgeoisie*.[59] In the absence of a great commercial elite, such as that which controlled the Jacobins in Bordeaux, the modest merchants and small tradesmen proved able to work together in maintaining a more typically Jacobin presence (favoring the Montagnards or left in the Convention) in local politics. The proportion of Jacobins on the councils grew from 46 percent in 1790–91 to 65 percent in 1792–Year II, then fell briefly in the Year III to 43 percent, and finally rose to 58 percent under the Directory regime.[60] In a real sense, Toulouse was a Jacobin stronghold; even though there was just as much turnover in official personnel as in other big cities, the Jacobin Club provided a large measure of continuity.

The trajectory of Jacobin influence in Amiens followed the most typical path: the highest proportion of Jacobin councillors sat in the Year II (56 percent), and only one-half as many councillors were Jacobins before and after the Terror.[61] Too much should not be

[57] A.D., Gironde, 12L 19, undated list of about 400 members. Because there is no complete list of members, the figures presented here can only be considered approximations.

[58] Forrest, *Revolutionary Bordeaux*, pp. 63–66.

[59] Beyssi, "Le Parti jacobin," p. 46.

[60] There is no single list of Jacobin Club members in Toulouse. Jean Beyssi based his analysis of the "Jacobin party" on political allegiance during the Directory regime rather than on documented club membership (ibid.). The list of Jacobins used here is based on all the names mentioned in the minutes of the Club. Such a procedure is fruitful (and probably more accurate than Beyssi's method), yet not entirely satisfactory, because the minutes of the Club only extend to 24 August 1793 (A.D., Haute-Garonne, L 4542–4544). The other registers for the Club cover the same time period (6 May 1790–24 August 1793), but they include few names.

[61] A.M., Amiens, 2I 46, Registre de présence des membres de la société populaire, du 10 pluviôse an II au 7 frimaire an III. The register covers both the zenith of

made of the differences between the cities, however, because the available membership lists come from different years. There are also some important similarities. In all three cities, merchants, artisans, and shopkeepers gained most from Jacobin Club membership. In Amiens 30 percent of the Jacobin councillors were merchants, and 30 percent were artisans or shopkeepers.[62] In Bordeaux 42 percent were merchants, and 13 percent were artisans or shopkeepers (a large number of occupations were not listed); in Toulouse 28 percent were merchants, and 23 percent were artisans or shopkeepers. Lawyers came in far behind everywhere. The Jacobin clubs were the testing ground for a coalition between the merchants and manufacturers, on the one hand, and the artisans and shopkeepers, on the other. The Jacobins never controlled all of the seats on the city councils, yet, even after the clubs had been closed down in 1794–95, former members continued to be elected to city office (at least one-quarter of the Directory officials in each of the three cities had been Jacobins). This was not necessarily a testimony to continuing radical influence in city affairs, but rather a sign of the broad appeal of the Jacobin clubs and the strength gained from belonging to an overtly political organization.

In a sense, the Jacobin clubs took up where the Freemason lodges left off. Freemasonry drew men interested in philanthropy, fellowship, and, to some extent, new ideas. In contrast to other Old Regime political institutions and cultural organizations, the lodges were open to greater social mixing. The clubs pursued some of the same philanthropic goals and provided some of the same

---

the Terror and a few months of the reaction (29 January 1794–27 November 1794). Yet it probably leaves out men who joined in the early years and then left, and thus most likely exaggerates the proportion of artisans and shopkeepers, many of whom joined after 10 August 1792. The proportion of Jacobins on the city councils in Aix-en-Provence was remarkably stable: it ranged from 51 percent under the Thermidorian reaction to 69 percent in November 1790 (at all other times it was between 51 and 58 percent) (Derobert-Ratel, *Institutions et vie municipale*, p. 602). In Aix, the correlation between general city politics and the local Jacobin Club position was extremely close. In this regard, Aix resembled Toulouse, but for different reasons: both were middle-of-the-road in Aix, while both were generally on the left in Toulouse.

[62] Only the percentages of those with known occupations are given here because the proportion of unknowns varied considerably from city to city. In Toulouse, for example, there were 11 percent unknown occupations (among Jacobins on the councils). Of the known occupations, 16 percent were lawyers and 11 percent came from the other liberal professions.

kinds of fellowship, but they added a new, organized, political dimension. Freemasonry had been a loosely knit network; the Jacobins thrived on communication between clubs in a region and between the provinces and Paris. The Jacobin clubs were the critical links in the republican movement. There was much room within them for disagreement, and they were often pressured by even more popular organizations from below. Nevertheless republicanism was inconceivable without them. Even in federalist Bordeaux, the Club made a substantial contribution to the republican cause. The merchant Pierre Balguerie, a Directorial official, had been an early member along with three other men in his family. Under the Directory he tried to revive the Club as a "constitutional circle" along with another former Club member, Soulignac, who then joined him in the Central Municipal Bureau, which coordinated Bordeaux government. Both publicly praised the Directorial coup against the royalists in the Councils in September 1797 and directed local efforts to keep royalism in check.[63] Even where they were outnumbered, the Jacobins were able to keep the faith, thanks to their previous experience of organization.

The new political class may have been, as Morris claimed, "new in Power, wild in Theory, raw in Practise,"[64] but its members did not come out of a metaphysical vacuum. They had family networks, neighborhood ties, and organizational connections behind them. Being outsiders, they also had a built-in affinity for the Enlightenment ideals of religious tolerance, secularization, and widened political participation. They were neither power-mad (witness how quickly most of them gave it up) nor much interested in becoming party bureaucrats. One last example suggests their conviction. In 1799 after a decade of turmoil Bordeaux was again racked by anticonscription riots and resurgent royalist activity. Nevertheless, one of the city's administrators dared to face down a crowd with these words: "We are republicans, because we believe that it is the government which best suits men; everyone is called to serve, according to their talents, to unite in the formation and execution

[63]Gaston Ducaunnès-Duval, *Ville de Bordeaux: Inventaire-Sommaire des Archives municipales: Période révolutionnaire (1789–an VIII)*, 4 vols. (Bordeaux, 1896–1929) 3: 66 and 76–77 (A.M., Bordeaux, D 156, 1 messidor an V and 28 frimaire an VI).

[64]Beatrix Cary Davenport, ed., *A Diary of the French Revolution by Gouverneur Morris (1752–1816), Minister to France during the Terror* (Boston, 1939), p. 68, 22 November 1790.

of the laws."[65] Even in right-wing Bordeaux and in the last months before Bonaparte's coup, there were many who continued to believe in the promise of the Revolution.

Every merchant and lawyer, artisan and shopkeeper, village schoolmaster and innkeeper did not become a member of the new political class. Yet merchants and lawyers, artisans and shopkeepers, village schoolmasters and innkeepers were more likely to become politically involved than peasants, judges, nobles, rural landlords, or city workers. If they lived in certain places or occupied particular sociocultural positions, their chances of engagement were all the greater. Most of the politically committed lived on the margins of the modern world or occupied the spaces on the periphery of the former elite. They were not the "outs" as opposed to the "ins" so much as the nearly "in" who felt excluded. They were relative outsiders, not social pariahs.

The social profile of the class, the critical role played by intermediaries and culture brokers, and the rationalizing and nationalizing values espoused through the new political networks all point to the influence of urban culture within the revolutionary movement. In its social origins, the new political class was heavily urban; the culture brokers brought urban influences into the countryside; and secularism, rationalism, and universalism had all been associated with the supposedly corrosive effects of city life. This pattern would seem to support a modernization interpretation of the Revolution. In such a view, the revolutionaries were modernizers carrying forward the rationalistic and cosmopolitan values of a society increasingly influenced by urbanization, literacy, and differentiation of functions. Should we, then, replace the Marxist interpretation with a modernization interpretation in the mold of Tocqueville, Durkheim, or Weber?

Much recent research suggests some version of a modernization interpretation. In her study of the revolutionary festivals, Mona Ozouf emphasized the common cultural conceptualization underlying the many, different political aims of the organizers; they all worked for the "homogenization of humanity."[66] The preference for large, open spaces, for circular arrangements, and for huge

[65] Ducaunnès-Duval, *Ville de Bordeaux* 3: 99–104 (A.M., Bordeaux, D 159, 20 thermidor an VII).
[66] Mona Ozouf, *La Fête révolutionnaire, 1789–1799* (Paris, 1976), p. 337.

monuments all bespoke the desire to submerge individuality and particularity in the new collectivity. When categories and divisions were required in the festival processions, they almost always turned out to be functional: by age, by sex, and by occupation or position in the new order. Old Regime corporate and castelike distinctions were effaced, and troublesome social and economic disparities were overlooked in the rush to celebrate a new community of equal citizens. As presented by Ozouf, therefore, the festivals exemplify the leveling, standardizing, and rationalizing process that in Toqueville's opinion served the further extension of absolute state power.[67]

Viewed from the perspective of its opponents, the Revolution seemed to embody a struggle between traditional society and Jacobin innovation. As Colin Lucas argues in his study of Thermidorian violence in the southeast: "The terrorists broke the tacitly admitted equilibrium; they introduced an exterior power and values which were foreign to the community in order to become in some sense abnormally powerful."[68] The terrorists innovated "brutally," and the Thermidorian youth gangs (of the post-1794 period) reacted by punishing them in traditional ways with the traditional aim of restoring vertical relations of community control. The youth gangs were not composed of rowdy peasant boys, however, but of the sons of landowners, lawyers, and merchants who still felt attached to the old ways and values. Hence Thermidorian violence did not set countryside against town but rather cut across the small town communities where it took place.

As described by Lucas and others, the revolutionary battle between "tradition" and "modernity" resembled the recurrent struggles over innovation that accompanied the growth of monarchical power in France.[69] The introduction of the *intendants* in the mid-seventeenth century, the periodic efforts to reform judicial institutions and eliminate venality of office, even the efforts of the church

---

[67] Ibid., pp. 149–87. On the link between festivals and urban life, see Michel Vovelle's quantitative study, *Les Métamorphoses de la fête en Provence de 1750 à 1820* (Paris, 1976), esp. pp. 151–56.

[68] "Violence thermidorienne et société traditionelle: L'Exemple du Forez," *Cahiers d'histoire* 24 (1979): 3–43, quote on p. 28.

[69] T. J. A. Le Goff and D. M. G. Sutherland, "The Revolution and the Rural Community in Eighteenth-Century Brittany," *Past and Present*, no. 62 (1974): 96–119.

to restrict saints' days and the more raucous religious festivals—all ran up against the protests of traditional communities, whether of magistrates or of villagers. How different was the attitude of modernizers after 1789? In 1790 the newly elected village council of Lourmarin complained that the cause of poverty was "the debauchery and irreligion which is caused entirely by the *cabarets*; the impiety and disorder occasioned by *fête* days which are too numerous."[70] The solution was to control the cabarets more closely and to suppress several festival days, that is, to increase the power of government to ensure discipline in daily life.

Under the Republic the same kinds of conflicts centered on the celebration of the *décadi* of the new revolutionary calendar. One of hundreds of such incidents occurred in a village in the Ain department in 1799. On his afternoon walk, the local agent of the Directory happened on a group of people playing a drum and dancing in the central square (a Sunday by the old calendar, which was no longer supposed to be a rest day). After summoning the nearest gendarme, the agent found himself set upon in the street by the revellers. The leader grabbed him by the throat, shoved him up against the wall, protested in a loud voice his attempt to prevent dancing on Sundays, and threatened to kill him. Despite the assistance of several onlookers, and even though the commissioner knew the fellow by name, he got away or so the agent reported.[71] In many ways, this incident varies little from the attempts of locals under the Old Regime to maintain their favorite saints' days and festivals.

However, the Revolution did more than just continue the modernizing efforts of Old Regime monarchs and notables. Although government administrators continued to face local resistance to their demands for money, men, and ideological support, and though in some villages the notables continued to represent the outside world encroaching on the village, the identity of the parties had changed. In place of the priest, the seigneur, and his minions came the innkeeper, the schoolmaster, and their patrons at the departmental capital. Now many priests and Old Regime officials were in

[70] Thomas F. Sheppard, *Lourmarin in the Eighteenth Century: A Study of a French Village* (Baltimore, 1971), p. 192.
[71] Eugène Dubois, *Histoire de la Révolution dans l'Ain*, 6 vols. (Bourg, 1931–35) 6 (*Le Directoire*): 203–5. The incident occurred in Seyssel on 13 January 1799.

the opposition. The change in identity accompanied a transformation in the foundations of the state's legitimacy. In the name of liberty and equality, the agents of the Republic actively promoted change; they wanted to maintain order, to be sure, but they also wanted to mobilize the population in support of the Republic, both on the military and ideological fronts. They were not simply asking for money and collecting information on an ever-grander scale; they were also going around stirring people up, planning new festivals, organizing banquets, giving speeches, naming committees, in short, screwing up the pitch of political awareness. Roquette's activities as a revolutionary official in Saint-Amans were very different from those he undertook as a seigneurial judge.

Still, if it is granted that the modernization efforts of the revolutionaries were more thoroughgoing than those of the reforming monarchy and based on new principles of sovereignty, does not the process nevertheless remain one of modernization? Much depends, obviously, on how modernization is defined. Unfortunately, modernization is one of the loosest terms in the vocabulary of the social sciences. Unlike Marxism, modernization theory does not have a canonical text. Most of the great social theorists of the nineteenth and twentieth centuries took modernization of some kind to be the salient characteristic of contemporary social life: for example, Max Weber emphasized rationalization and bureaucratization, while Emile Durkheim focused on the alternation between social breakdown and rebuilding solidarity.[72] In most modernization theories, moreover, the French Revolution often occupies a pivotal position; just as Marx defined the Revolution as the characteristic bourgeois revolution, so too many theorists of modernization define the Revolution as the characteristic modernizing movement. As a consequence, in both kinds of accounts the Revolution is explained tautologically. The Revolution is bourgeois or modernizing by definition.

Perhaps the most influential example of a modernization account using the French Revolution as a touchstone is Samuel P. Huntington's *Political Order in Changing Societies*. Huntington defines political modernization as a three-part development: the ra-

---

[72]Some useful comments on the literature can be found in Reinhard Bendix, "Tradition and Modernity Reconsidered," *Comparative Studies in Society and History* 9 (1967): 292–346.

tionalizing of authority; the differentiation of new political functions and the development of specialized structures to perform
those functions; and the increased participation in politics by social
groups throughout society. In his view revolution is an aspect of
modernization, which "is most likely to occur in societies which
have experienced some social and economic development and
where the processes of political modernization and political development have lagged behind the processes of social and economic change."[73] As might be expected, this account rings true; the
French Revolution did promote the rationalizing of authority, the
development of new political institutions, and the increased participation of the people through an expanded electoral process.

The influence of the political modernization model can be seen
in Theda Skocpol's recent analysis of the French Revolution. Modern social revolutions, in her view, "occurred in countries caught
behind more economically developed competitor nations," and in
these revolutions, "the exigencies of revolutionary consolidation in
a world of competing states helped ensure that leaderships willing
and able to build up centralized coercive and administrative organizations would come to the fore during the Revolutions, and that
their handiwork would create a permanent base of power for state
cadres."[74] Although she gives priority to international competition
over internal disparities between economic growth and political
adaptations, the working of the model is apparent: a gap between
economic demands and political development precipitates revolution, which in turn fills the gap. In this view, Jacobinism facilitated
the building of a modern state by giving its adherents cohesion as a
leadership group and by mobilizing the masses.[75] As in Huntington and Tocqueville, democracy as an ideology only increased
the powers of the central state.

Like the Marxist interpretation, the modernization account has
its own lockstep quality. Everything that happens refers back to the
original set of definitions. Modernization disrupts a preexisting
equilibrium of forces in traditional society, and the ensuing break-

[73] (New Haven, 1968), quote p. 265. In this sense, revolution is a particular form
of violence and instability.
[74] *States and Social Revolutions: A Comparative Analysis of France, Russia, and China*
(Cambridge, 1979), p. 286.
[75] Ibid., p. 170.

down ends only when some kind of harmony is restored. In this way one outcome of the Revolution (political modernization) becomes the teleological focus; institutionalization, rationalization, democracy, and political mobilization are all equally subordinated to the outcome of the growth of state power. Just as Marxist accounts interpret every particular struggle within the Revolution as necessary to the outcome of capitalist development, so too the modernization interpretations make every particular political innovation necessary to the outcome of increased centralization. In the former, democracy, authoritarianism, universalism, and rationalism all work for the development of capitalism (economic modernization); in the latter, they all work for state power (political modernization).

Like the Marxist interpretation, the modernization interpretation is not so much wrong as it is lacking in analytical precision. Almost everyone in France's political elite favored modernization, including the king, the Old Regime courts, the liberal nobles, the constitutional monarchists of 1790, the Girondins, the Jacobins, and the Directorials. Once the Revolution began, however, divisions within the broad consensus for change became increasingly acute. It is impossible to attribute these divisions to differences over modernization in general; rather they were differences over democracy in particular. Although the revolutionary elite shared values that set them apart from traditional society, the most radical of them were often the least modern; the village innkeepers, the local itinerant textile merchant in Foncines, and the saddler who sat on the council in Meximieux, for instance, were all less modern than the confident manufacturers of Amiens and merchant-shippers of Bordeaux who found radical republicanism unattractive. Moreover the most modern departments were often right-wing in politics.

The same observation applies to the role of urban culture within the revolutionary movement. Urban places and urban people were in the forefront of revolutionary mobilization, but the cities were also the site of greatest political division. Radical revolution was most often the work of small and medium-sized places and of people who were new to urban affairs or who had experience in the big cities but made their careers in smaller locales. Roquette in Saint-Amans and Taillard in Pacy are two examples of the latter phenomenon. Just as counterrevolution did not occur in the most backward areas, but rather in regions that had begun to experience the process of what Charles Tilly called urbanization, so too revolution appealed not to those who were the most urban or most modern, but to those who were experiencing firsthand the conflicts between two kinds of culture.[76] On the boundary between urban and rural, modern and backward, in the places of confrontation, and in the positions occupied by outsiders and intermediaries—there the new gospel of participation and innovation was most warmly received.

The belief in democratic participation initiated an "apprenticeship" of republicanism in France, and the new political culture was absorbed deeply enough to form the foundations of a revolutionary, republican tradition.[77] This outcome of the Revolution is overlooked in the modernization interpretations, from Tocqueville to Skocpol, because they focus instead on state power. Bonaparte learned the value of popular mobilization from the Jacobin experience, but he did not foster it in the same fashion; he eliminated all meaningful political participation. Voting and political clubs gave way to massive state propaganda; active participation was replaced by passive spectatorship. Thus, the political outcome of the Revolution was not "fully consolidated" under Bonaparte, because he picked up only the modernization half while supressing the rest. Democracy was never efficient; it was usually unpredictable and always potentially dangerous. As a consequence, the modernizers, those who valued rationalization and standardization *above all else*, flocked to the Napoleonic banner instead. It was possible to be modern without believing in democratic republicanism.

The most ardent republicans introduced new bases of political rule and even social relations. Deference gave way to persuasion, tradition to innovation, "fanaticism" to rational republicanism and patrimonial offices to elections and political mobilization. Republicans did not espouse these ideals because they found them useful

---

[76] *The Vendée* (Cambridge, Mass., 1964), p. 11.

[77] In this apprenticeship during the 1848 revolution, Maurice Agulhon distinguishes between "une republique à conception morale et à contenu maximum" and a more conservative "republique à conception purement constitutionelle, et à contenu minimum." This distinction characterizes the difference between republican leaders in Toulouse (the maximum program) and Amiens (the minimum) (*1848 ou l'apprentissage de la République, 1848–1852* [Paris, 1973], p. 230).

for political modernization or because they were desperately trying to avoid being "crowded off the historical stage."[78] In the 1790's they were just climbing onto the historical stage. Looked at in the long term of the nineteenth and twentieth centuries, republicans were the party of movement, the men of the future. They were the forerunners of the Second and Third Republics, not of the First and Second Empires. Their ideas were compelling, not because they appealed to either the winners or the losers in the process of modernization or capitalist development, but because they offered hope for a new social and political order. They held out an ancient ideal of political participation and dignity in a new guise of democratic elections, broad-based responsibility, and organized political activity. That they failed in the short term is not nearly so remarkable as their long-term success.

[78] I am arguing here against the modernization view expressed by Barrington Moore, Jr. (*Social Origins of Dictatorship and Democracy: Lord and Peasant in the Making of the Modern World* [Boston, 1967], esp. n. 112, p. 84).

Conclusion:
Revolution
in Political Culture

THE REVOLUTION was, in a special sense, fundamentally "political." The creation of a new political rhetoric and the development of new symbolic forms of political practice transformed contemporary notions about politics. Politics became an instrument for refashioning society. French people believed that they could establish a new national community based on reason and nature without reference to the customs of the past. Such lofty ambitions required new political practices for their realization. The techniques of mass propaganda, the political mobilization of the lower classes, and the politicization of everyday life were all invented in order to regenerate the nation. They soon became the defining elements of the revolutionary experience.

Although the new language and symbols were collective, anonymous, and in large measure unself-consciously developed, they did not change in a vacuum. The rhetoric was spoken and the symbols were taken up and constantly modified by those who felt some commitment to the revolutionary process. Revolutionary politics were neither the instrument of a social class in Marxist terms nor the tool of a modernizing elite. They came into being along with a new republican political class, and both the politics and the class were shaped by the ongoing interaction between widely shared rhetorical assumptions and collective political practices.

Even though revolutionary political culture was by definition always in the process of change and development, it did have sources of coherence and unity. Revolutionaries shared a set of expectations that followed from their reliance on reason and nature as the bases for the new social and political order. They held that careers ought to be based on talent, rather than birth; that there should be no special privileges for castes, corporations, or particular places; and that participation through elections and officeholding should be open to a broadly based citizenry. In short, they believed that the new order should be rational in basis and national in scope. These self-conscious political principles were drawn from the writings of Enlightenment thinkers, and they were common to many educated French people. The revolutionaries were distinguished from the rest of the educated classes by their implicit rhetorical assumptions. They acted on the conviction that the regenerated Nation was a new community without precedent in history, and this community was based on an ideal of transparent social and political relations. They consequently saw no need for distinctions of office or even dress and, at their most extreme, saw no need for any kind of representation. The new community needed no politicians and no parties; deputies and officials were to act temporarily and at the people's pleasure.

If the revolutionaries shared these assumptions about the way the political world ought to work, they also had in common the sobering experience of the practical limits to this political vision. In practice, they had to search for an adequate system of representation both in institutions and in symbols. The people could not always be in action, and the people could not always be trusted to recognize the requirements of the general will. The Revolution had challenged the patriarchal model of power, but even the radicals were eager to maintain some kind of legitimate (and in their eyes, masculine) authority. As republicans encountered ever more difficult obstacles in their political path, they placed more and more emphasis on their didactic functions. If the French people could not be refashioned right away, then at least an instructive example would be left for posterity. This was the legacy of republicanism.

The rhetoric of innovation and the symbolic forms of revolution got their motive force from the new political class. Their newness to political affairs, their relative youth, and their position as relative outsiders had the effect of accelerating the development of the rhetoric and symbols of revolution. Transparency and didacticism, rupture and regeneration, spoke directly to the concerns of those called "vile Innovators." Because they were new to power and had been previously excluded, they were especially susceptible to the uncertainties and anxieties of revolutionary innovation. They were uncertain about the authority of their text of revolution; they could not predict the denouement in the social and political drama in which they were the central characters. No doubt their newness to the corridors of power also predisposed them as a group to believe in the reality of the threat of conspiracy. The recent immigrants, the religious minorities, the new schoolmasters, the lawyers who had only practiced in lower courts, the merchants and tradesmen who had never spoken to political gatherings before 1789—all of them had as many reasons to worry about the directions of political affairs as they had reasons to seize the opportunity to take over the reins. Although some of them had belonged to Masonic lodges before 1789, the great majority of the new politicians had had no experience of democratic sociability.[1] The Jacobin clubs were their first schools of political education; public office was their practical training ground.

The political culture of revolution thus had both symbolic and social sources of coherence. Revolutionaries spoke the same language and sought the same qualities in their symbols and images of authority. Hercules and Marianne stood for all alike. The diversity of their social backgrounds and economic interests made the appeal of rational, national, and universal figures all the greater. Because the new political class in France had no precise social boundaries, revolutionaries found themselves devoting an enormous amount of time and energy to the search for suitable representations of themselves and their actions. The concern with words, festivals, seals, and measures of time, space, and distance was not a diversion from some more real or important political issue; it was essential to the definition of the revolutionary process and to the identity of the new political class. Ironically, therefore, the lack of social definition of the new political class made the experience of revolution all the more dramatic in its challenge to custom and tradition. The search for a new national identity led to a rejection of all previous models and standards of authority.

If political, social, and cultural boundaries were uncertain during the decade of revolution, then it is hardly surprising that men who occupied boundary positions became especially important.

[1] For the classic argument on the origins of democratic sociability, see Augustin Cochin, *L'Esprit du Jacobinisme: Une interprétation sociologique de la Révolution française* (Paris, 1979), esp. pp. 128–36.

The recent arrivals, young notables who had gone away to school, merchants who traveled around the countryside, lawyers with connections in the departmental capital or Paris, innkeepers who met all the visitors, and tradesmen who occupied the social space between a town's workers and its upper classes—such men were likely to become builders of political networks, carriers of new ideas, and agents of outside political authority. Their professions and social standing were often different, but their roles as brokers of culture and power were fundamentally similar.

The new men and the new political culture came into being together. In this case, it is fruitless to try to determine which came first. In 1789 no one knew that revolutionary politics would attract such men, and no one imagined how important a ribbon, a name, or a style of dress would become. The new men and the new politics reinforced each other. In the early days of the Revolution, when some kind of reconciliation with the Old Regime still seemed possible, the political leadership included many nobles, many royal officials, many men experienced in local politics, and a fair number of men from the older generation (mayors, for example, were often senior notables). Participants still hoped for a painless resolution to the revolutionary drama, and there was little thought that a complete break with the past was required. As the rhetoric of revolution became more radical and more insistent on the rupture with all existing customs and traditions, the character of the political class also changed. Replacing the rich merchants, lawyers, nobles, royal officials, and former political leaders were modest merchants and tradesmen, teachers and functionaries, and men with little or no experience in office. Supplanting the sympathetic insiders of the Old Regime were first those who were closest to them on the social and political scale and then those who were increasingly marginal to the former centers of power.

The new political class was not therefore one fixed, stable category. Although I have emphasized the sources of its unity, it was also marked by political, social, and cultural lines of division. As the emplotment of revolutionary history changed from comedy to romance to tragedy between 1789 and 1794, the cast of characters also changed. The political class included more and more representatives of the lower orders (though rarely workers or poor peasants) and fewer and fewer upper-class figures. Over time, political and social distinctions began to merge. "Sans-culottes" and "aristocrats" had both social and political meanings. The people were those on the side of the radical republic, while the aristocrats, "moderates," and royalists were lumped together as its enemies. A similar process took place in the cultural dimension. Those who were closely tied to the Old Regime by family or social connection were pushed aside first by the "nearly in" and then progressively by men further and further from the previous centers of power. By early 1794 very young men (Lacombe in Bordeaux was only 29 in 1789, the same age as Roquette in Saint-Amans) and men with no ties at all to previous elites (even those of 1790–91) emerged in positions of leadership. During the most radical period of the Revolution (1793–94, the Year II), political leadership was exercised by the newest and most marginal of men. The radicalism of the period was essentially produced by that newness and marginality. In 1793–94 the presence of such men made the break with the past concrete and palpable. The rhetoric and symbols of revolution had an enormous impact on subsequent history, because they had mobilized and been mobilized by this new political leadership.

Divisions within the new political class had a spatial as well as a temporal dimension. In 1789 people almost everywhere in France were enthusiastic about the prospect of constitutional renewal. As the potential for conflict became clearer and more threatening, some places began to demonstrate their reluctance and even resistance to the revolutionary process. By the middle of 1793 the west was in open rebellion, and several cities along the coast and along the major rivers (most notably Lyon) had announced their secession from the revolutionary movement. Spatially as well as temporally, there were multiple lines of division. In many regions, the Revolution in a sense withdrew to the towns and cities. Within the big cities, the radicals often based themselves in certain neighborhoods. Within the country as a whole, the revolutionary movement found most determined support near the frontiers and in the left-wing regions of the center and southwest. Along both the dimensions of time and space, the process of radicalization was structurally similar: as the Revolution became more radical, it also became more peripheral. Yet, at the same time, the rhetoric and symbols of Revolution retained and even enhanced their universalistic, nationalistic, and rationalistic qualities.

"Peripheral," "marginal," and "outsiders" are words heavily loaded with invidious connotations in the vocabulary of the social sciences. They seem to imply isolation, strangeness, extremes, and they are particularly associated with psychological interpretations of political behavior. Marginal people do not act normally; they do not act like those at or near the center. They are structurally and behaviorally deviant. Theories of revolution that employ these terms tend to assume that revolutions are abnormal events and that the people who are active in them are themselves abnormal in some way. In what Chalmers Johnson calls "actor-oriented theories," the revolutionaries are portrayed as responding to social pathology (deviants who have become rebels under the right circumstances), to a crisis of identity, or to some kind of personal frustration.[2] They are men with a propensity to violence.[3] I hope that it is clear that I do not hold this view. In my view, the new political class was not a collection of violence-prone extremists united only by their shared frustrations, agressiveness, or deviance. They were motivated rather by a shared commitment to fashion a new community. They found themselves able to act on this engagement with the future because they were free of most ties to old institutions and in a position—for reasons of age, mobility, religion, social status, or family ties—to break with the political customs and commonplaces of the past. At the same time, they were not rootless or entirely marginal. Networks of family, neighborhood, profession, and social and political association enabled them to act collectively. Marginal, peripheral, and outsider describe relationships; they are not absolute categories filled with automatic psychological consequences.

Debates about revolution are often cast in dichotomous terms. Some authors emphasize anonymous, structural forces; others call attention to personal, "voluntarist" choices and characteristics.[4] The distinction between a focus on origins and outcomes and a focus on process or experience seems to fit into the same dichotomy between structure and individual actions. Structural accounts

[2] *Revolutionary Change*, 2nd ed. (Stanford, 1982), pp. 169–94.

[3] A variation on this argument can be found in E. Victor Wolfenstein, *The Revolutionary Personality: Lenin, Trotsky, Gandhi* (Princeton, 1967).

[4] A discussion of the two types that emphasizes the virtues of the structural can be found in Theda Skocpol, *States and Social Revolutions* (Cambridge, 1979).

concentrate on the origins of revolution in structural problems (e.g., in the economy, the class structure, or the balance of international forces) and the structural determinants of outcomes. Actor-oriented accounts and process theories point to the role of individual leaders, organized parties, ideologies, or, more generally, the ineluctable movement from one stage to the next within the political process.[5] My account has focused on the process of revolution in so far as it emphasizes the ways in which rhetoric, symbols, and the participation of certain groups and places shaped the ongoing experience of revolutionary change. Rather than looking for structural origins or outcomes, I have concentrated on determining the sources of unity and diversity in the political process. These sources are not to be found in the role of individual leaders, a totalitarian party, a single ideology, or some inevitable political "life-cycle," however. The individual leaders, the role of parties and ideologies, and the movement from one "stage" to another were themselves made possible by underlying patterns in the "poetics" and sociology of politics. Rhetorical assumptions and symbolic practices limited the possibilities in the political field; they worked against the emergence of identifiable "founding fathers," and made liberal politics (the Anglo-American model) difficult to establish. At the same time, they opened up other previously unknown options: daily life was politicized, and the Revolution moved from one stage to another as revolutionaries sought answers to the problems and anxieties of conspiracy. Revolutionary poetics were not fixed, however; their process of development was decisively influenced by the changing patterns of political leadership, that is, by the evolving sociology of politics. In other words, there were structures or patterns implicit in the revolutionary process, but those structures were in turn shaped and transformed by the interaction between unself-consciously held political assumptions and self-consciously acting, socially embedded, political actors.

In this sense, my account is both structural and process-oriented. But, unlike most other structural explanations, my focus is on the unfolding of the revolutionary event(s), rather than on its long-term determinants. And, unlike most process theories, my focus is on general patterns of thought and action rather than on person-

[5]Johnson, *Revolutionary Change*, pp. 169–94.

alities, parties, or defined ideologies. Ultimately, however, one of
the advantages of such a method is the new light it is able to shed
on the issue of origins and outcomes. Once the character of the experience is determined, then the analysis of origins and outcomes
takes on new meaning.

Hierarchical models of explanation have proved long-lived because they offer elegantly simple explanations for change over
time. Marx explained the movement of history and revolution in
particular by the appearance of new modes of production: a new
mode of production grows up in the interstices of the old one and
ultimately causes social and political conflicts that tear apart the
foundation for the old and build another from its remnants. Modernization theorists usually avoid the phrase "mode of production," but they too attribute change either to the disruption of
economic growth or to the demands of economic competition. In
both, social change has its origin in some prior or underlying level
of existence (instead of economy, it might be demography or even
climate).

Revolution brings the general problem of historical change into
particularly sharp relief, because an accelerated pace of change is
a defining characteristic of revolution. It has consequently been
the focus of most hierarchical models of historical explanation. In
Marxism, revolution plays a pivotal role; it is the means by which
postfeudal societies lurch forward. In the French Revolution, the
bourgeoisie came to power; in a future revolution, the proletariat
will come to power. In modernization theories, revolution is cast
more often as a particularly telling example of more general processes of development. In Samuel P. Huntington's analysis, for
instance, revolution is a dramatic example of the violence and
instability caused by disparities between economic growth and political modernization.[6] Barrington Moore, Jr. turns this formulation
on its head and argues that "sick societies are ones in which revolutions are impossible."[7] Revolutions, in his view, were essential to
the establishment of capitalist democracy, whereas failed revolutions or revolutions from above led to fascism. Yet, despite their
differences, all of these models incorporate revolution into more

[6] *Political Order in Changing Societies* (New Haven, 1968).
[7] *Social Origins of Dictatorship and Democracy: Lord and Peasant in the Making of the
Modern World* (Boston, 1966), pp. 457–58.

general causal explanations of historical development in which economic and social structures have priority.

In my view the social and economic changes brought about by the Revolution were not revolutionary. Nobles were able to return to their titles and to much of their land. Although considerable amounts of land changed hands during the Revolution, the structure of landholding remained much the same; the rich got richer, and the small peasants consolidated their hold, thanks to the abolition of feudal dues. Industrial capitalism still grew at a snail's pace.[8] In the realm of politics, in contrast, almost everything changed. Thousands of men and even many women gained firsthand experience in the political arena: they talked, read, and listened in new ways; they voted; they joined new organizations; and they marched for their political goals. Revolution became a tradition, and republicanism an enduring option. Afterward, kings could not rule without assemblies, and noble domination of public affairs only provoked more revolution. As a result, France in the nineteenth century had the most bourgeois polity in Europe, even though France was never the leading industrial power. What requires explanation, then, is not the appearance of a new mode of production or economic modernization, but rather the emergence of the political culture of revolution.

The invention of a new political culture required an opening, a space for maneuvering. An alternative government was not taking shape before 1789; there was no secret revolutionary party, no mass political organization. The ideas of republicanism, virtue, transparency, and even democracy were in circulation, thanks to the *philosophes* and the American independence movement. But no one acted on them until the monarchy began to collapse.[9] Here the political modernization model, and in particular Skocpol's analysis, is appealing.[10] The French monarchy disintegrated because it could not foot the bill for competition with England. The American war was costly, and the crown ran up huge debts. Most important,

---

[8] For an excellent review of social and economic trends, see Louis Bergeron, *France under Napoleon*, trans. by R. R. Palmer (Princeton, 1981), pp. 119–90. Bergeron summarizes an enormous literature and provides excellent bibliographical suggestions.

[9] For a comprehensive review of the literature on origins, see William Doyle, *Origins of the French Revolution* (Oxford, 1980).

[10] *States and Social Revolutions.*

however, its creditors then demanded expanded political participation for the upper classes. The result was the convocation of the Estates General. This original opening was not in the last instance economic, however. The debts themselves were not insurmountable; the English state managed to borrow even more heavily. The opening was created rather by a breakdown in the Old Regime political culture; ennobled financiers, court magistrates, and army officers demanded fundamental changes in the organization of the polity, and their "political" demands set in motion an escalating spiral of events.

The collapse of the monarchy in the face of "aristocratic revolution" was only the first act. What distinguished the French Revolution from the American War of Independence and the English Civil War of the 1640s was the intensity of competition within the Old Regime elite. In both prior events, the breakdown of government opened up the possibility of political, social, and cultural conflict, but that opening was never institutionalized. The political elite in England and America quickly recognized the dangers of democracy and popular mobilization, and they closed ranks to defend the rule of property owners (and, in the case of America, slaveowners). Tocqueville recognized the importance of the democratic impulse in France, and he attributed its power to a combination of political, social, and psychological factors. In reaction to the crown's success at depriving the nobles of all political responsibility, nobles insisted on defending their social privileges to the last, and, as they became more caste-like, the bourgeoisie too became more preoccupied with maintaining the barriers against the lower classes.[11] As a consequence, the desire for social leveling was particularly intense; almost every group had some reason to resent other groups in French society.

For all its subtleties, Tocqueville's account nonetheless underplays two essential elements in the French situation. Although nobles had lost their "aristocratic" functions of social paternalism and political responsibility, they were still strong enough and tenaciously determined to block Third Estate control of the fateful Estates General. Their resistance as an order, rather than their weakness, directly engendered the Third Estate's constitutional

[11] Alexis de Tocqueville, *The Old Regime and the French Revolution*, trans. by Stuart Gilbert (New York, 1955), esp. pp. 81–107.

breakthrough—the invention of the National Assembly as a body of individual citizens rather than "orders" or estates. Faced with the armies of the crown, which had been placed in the service of the nobility's resistance, the Third Estate found support in the mobilized lower classes of town and countryside. Thus the nobles were stronger and more cohesive, and the Third was more willing to cross social barriers than Tocqueville imagined.

Just as competition between the crown and the nobility and then between the nobles and the Third Estate opened up political space in 1789, competition within the Third kept accelerating the tempo of political mobilization from 1789 to 1794. The space for popular politics grew apace, and popular political organizations (sectional committees, popular clubs, even reorganized guard and army units) became an important force in the political arena. Although many bourgeois leaders were primarily concerned with establishing a legal and political framework for individual rights (including property rights), many others gave priority to the requirements of a new national community.[12] They espoused the rhetoric of innovation, regeneration, and virtue. The competition between the two sides—between Feuillants and Jacobins, Girondins and Jacobins, and even later between Directorials and Jacobins—kept open the possibility of popular mobilization and organized, collective political action. The years of experiment with popular political organization, in which food riots were replaced by more-or-less organized political demonstrations, pushed the French beyond the "early modern" confines of political activity. The experiment continued as long as the political elite was divided. To be sure, Jacobin clubs and popular societies also existed in England and America at the time, but they were never officially encouraged, and most of them were officially repressed. Their opening was very narrow, because they did not have the explicit support of any segment of the ruling elite.

Tocqueville saw more clearly than anyone else the need to seek the origins of the Revolution in the peculiarities of French political culture before 1789. He examined the connections among ideas, social relations, social psychology, and politics in order to explain

[12] The tension between these two "bourgeois" conceptions (individualism and universalism) is developed at length in Patrice Higonnet, *Class, Ideology, and the Rights of Nobles during the French Revolution* (Oxford, 1981).

how the Revolution could have been "so inevitable yet so completely unforeseen." [13] At every critical point, Tocqueville emphasized neither social structure nor politics in themselves, but rather the interactions among political designs, social relations, intellectual ambitions, and even popular psychology. His account is less successful, however, as an explanation of why the Revolution developed as it did, once it had begun. Democratic republicanism, terror, and socialism, for example, did not follow inexorably from the strains apparent in French political culture *before 1789*. The structural weaknesses of Old Regime political culture fostered the kinds of division within the elite that allowed new political forms and principles to develop more freely than elsewhere. Yet, once underway, those forms and principles were shaped by their inclusion in a new political culture, that is, by the rhetoric, the symbols, and practices of the new political class. Terror and socialism were no more inevitable than conservatism and authoritarianism.

Historians have always argued about the true beginnings and endings of the revolutionary experience; this was already true in the 1790s. Viewed in the perspective of the long term, there were three strands in French political culture that were in formation during the Revolution: democratic republicanism, socialism, and authoritarianism. All three of them departed from the traditional royalist model in significant ways. I have emphasized the first strand, in part because democratic republicanism has been underemphasized in general interpretations of the Revolution. Marxists usually highlight the progression from democracy to terror to socialism, while modernization theorists, including Tocqueville, focus on the progression from democracy to terror to authoritarianism. Both of these outcomes were indisputably present, but so was the continuing strength of democratic republicanism. In many respects, moreover, democratic republicanism was the most important outcome of the Revolution, both in terms of its immediate impact and its long-term influence.

All three outcomes can be derived in some fashion from the principles of revolutionary rhetoric and the tensions implicit in revolutionary political practice. Democracy, terror, socialism, and au-

[13] *The Old Regime and the French Revolution*, p. 1.

thoritarianism were all made possible by the expansion of political space and the organized participation of the popular classes. The Terror was unthinkable without the previous experience of democracy; it was the disciplinarian side of the democratic community, invoked in time of emergency and justified by the needs of virtue and the nation's defense. The government used the Terror to get control of the popular movement, but without the popular movement there would have been no demand for terror in the first place.

Revolutionary socialism, in its origins, was one possible lesson learned from the failures of the Terror and of democratic republicanism. In the view of Babeuf and his followers in 1796, true democracy and equality could only be accomplished through yet another insurrection, this one *secretly* organized by a "Conspiracy of the Equals."[14] Their doctrine of primitive, agrarian communism was derived from Enlightenment sources, but they added to it a novel dimension of insurrection and popular dictatorship, which had considerable influence in the nineteenth century. Authoritarianism was another sort of lesson learned from the institutionalization of popular mobilization; Bonaparte replaced elections with plebiscites, outlawed clubs, and expanded service in the army. He maintained the principle of popular sovereignty but made himself the only real political actor, thus removing the dangerous unpredictability of organized popular mobilization.

Although it is interesting and important that the Revolution fostered the emergence of the first socialist and even proto-Leninist ideas of revolutionary action, it cannot be argued that socialism played an important organizational or ideological role in the Revolution itself. Babeuf had only a few followers, and most of them did not advocate communism of any sort; they were more interested in the insurrectionary half of the "Conspiracy." As soon as the plotters were betrayed, the Directorial government quickly rounded up the leaders. The subsequent trial gave Babeuf more publicity than he could have hoped for. As one historian concluded, "The government's attempts to conjure up a 'red peril' looked pathetic when applied to this handful of incompetent dreamers."[15]

[14]For a detailed, but one-sided account, see J. L. Talmon, *The Origins of Totalitarian Democracy* (New York, 1960), pp. 167–247.
[15]Martyn Lyons, *France under the Directory* (Cambridge, 1975), p. 35.

The authoritarian outcome, on the other hand, was far from chimerical, and it requires some explanation. Given the strengths and persistence of democratic republicanism, how was the elevation of Bonaparte possible? Was authoritarian government just a further development of democratic republicanism (it did follow chronologically, after all), or was it a different phenomenon altogether? More generally, what accounts for the weakness of the liberal parliamentary tradition in France? Bonaparte's regime has elicited almost as many different interpretations as the decade of revolution preceding his access to power, but this is not the place for a review of that history. Yet, Napoleon's seizure of power must be included in any account of the revolutionary decade, because it illuminates the failures of democratic republicanism in the short term.

In some respects, Bonaparte's coup in 1799 did not mark a sharp break. The Directory regime had witnessed two, perhaps three, coups already, depending on one's definition, and one of them (in 1797, against the right) had been carried out under the auspices of a friendly general.[16] The new regime was called a republic, and Napoleon emphasized his loyalty to revolutionary principles. In his first proclamation, he declared: "I refused to be a man of party spirit." He assured the French nation that "conservative, tutelary, liberal ideas have regained their rights by the dispersion of the factious who were oppressing the Councils."[17] In the first months and even years of the new regime, ambiguity about its intentions (conservative, tutelary, and liberal all at once) was deliberately cultivated in order to appeal to as many different groups as possible.

Given the turmoil of the preceding decade, Bonaparte's accession to the newly formed Consulate can seem almost expected. The main lines of the story are well known. After 1796 the Directorial government pursued a *politique de bascule* (see-saw politics); whenever elections failed to return a center majority, the five-man executive body organized legislative purges against either the right or the left in the councils. Instability in the legislature, high voter abstentions, an inflexible constitution, and continuing agitation in the provinces over the status of the Catholic Church, inflation, and

[16] Albert Meynier, *Les Coups d'état du Directoire*, 3 vols. (Paris, 1928).
[17] *Proclamation de général Bonaparte, le 19 brumaire, 11 heures du soir.*

conscription were offset most dramatically by the success of French armies in Italy and the German states. The generals, and especially Napoleon Bonaparte, parlayed the uncertainties of the domestic situation into virtual autonomy for themselves in the field. As the representative system declined in prestige, that of the generals rose, thus setting the stage for Bonaparte's participation in the famous coup of 18 Brumaire, Year VIII (see plate 18).

Viewed in this way, the continuing competition within the Third Estate proved fatal to the prospects of liberal, representative government. Thus the very condition that permitted the flowering of popular organizations also undermined the liberal republic. Fundamental divisions within the political class did not facilitate government stabilization. Yet this argument is not entirely satisfactory, because it neglects an important consideration: during the coup itself, Bonaparte came close to failure, thanks to his own impetuosity.[18] If his brother Lucien, who was president of the Council of Five Hundred, had not intervened and convinced the soldiers surrounding the meeting hall to act, the gamble might have been lost. Even then, the coup might have failed if the deputies had been able or willing to organize resistance. After seven years of a representative republic, which survived despite divisions within the political class and despite alterations in the constitution, republicanism crumbled from within. The few cries in Saint Cloud of "Down with the dictator" went unanswered.

Ultimately the success of the authoritarian solution in 1799 was made possible by weaknesses in revolutionary political culture. Food and conscription riots, battles over religion, and purges of the legislature had all taken place before, but the Republic had endured. The crisis of 1793 was in almost every respect more critical than the crisis of 1799: the war had just spread to several fronts, the armies of the Republic were untested, popular mobilization was at its zenith, de-Christianization was alienating much of the population, the king had just been killed, and the government was run on a day-to-day basis. It was not the circumstances of crisis that brought down the Republic in 1799.

Some of the weaknesses of revolutionary political culture had

---

[18] The classic account is Albert Vandal, *L'Avènement de Bonaparte*, 5th ed. (Paris, 1908) 1: *La Genèse du Consulat, Brumaire, la Constitution de l'an VIII.*

18. BONAPARTE IN THE COUNCIL OF FIVE HUNDRED ON 18 BRUMAIRE

This engraving represents the presumed attempt to assassinate General Bonaparte in the council chambers at Saint Cloud on 9 November 1799. Several deputies are trying to have him declared an outlaw. Eventually, Napoleon's brother Lucien saved the day, and the coup was successful despite Napoleon's bungled entry.

been present from an early date. Primary among them was the rhetorical refusal of party politics. Directorial politicians retained the principle of representative government; national elections were held *every year*, and the suffrage was widely defined. However, the government failed to organize a center party, and it refused to countenance the development of any organized opposition.[19] As the Director La Revellière-Lépeaux claimed, "it was better to die with honor defending the Republic and its established government than to perish or even to live in the muck of parties and the playthings of the factious."[20] Liberal politics, politics as the representation of interests, could not develop within this rhetorical framework. The center could only maintain its hold by artificially tampering with the legislative balance, that is, by purging its opponents once they had been elected. Bonaparte capitalized on the subsequent disrepute of legislative politics and justified his own accession on the same principles of revolutionary rhetoric; he stood above party and factions and promised to rid the nation of such unseemly political machinations. Liberal politics was thus stymied from the start; Napoleon took the process a step further and virtually eliminated electoral politics.

Bonaparte made similar use of the revolutionary symbolics of politics. He appreciated the power of symbols as much as anyone, and, for the first months and even years of his rule, he continued to use the symbols most sacred to republicans. He was the protector of Marianne. As his seal declared (plate 19), he spoke for the French people (*au nom du peuple français*). He guaranteed the Republic (plate 20), even while marking her with his own image. Eventually he replaced Marianne altogether (plate 21) and became himself the personification of the French nation; his profile adorned the currency and the seal of the Empire, just as the kings of old had adorned those of the monarchy.[21] The tensions built into revolutionary imagery made Napoleon's task that much easier; the people were no longer directly represented in images under the Directory, and Marianne had become a more distant and less active symbol.

[19] This argument is developed at length in Lynn Hunt, David Lansky, and Paul Hanson, "The Failure of the Liberal Republic in France, 1795–1799: The Road to Brumaire," *Journal of Modern History* 51 (1979): 734–59.

[20] *Mémoires de La Revellière-Lépeaux*, 2 vols. (Paris, 1895) 1: 379.

[21] P. Ciani, *Les Monnaies françaises de la Révolution à la fin du premier empire, 1789 à 1815* (Paris, 1931).

19. NAPOLEON'S SEAL AS CONSUL
(Photo courtesy of the Archives nationales)

20. FIVE-CENTIME COIN FROM THE YEAR XIII
As reproduced in P. Ciani, Les Monnaies françaises de la Révolution à la fin
du premier empire, 1789 à 1815 *(Paris, 1931), p. 143*
(Photo by Library Photographic Services, University of California, Berkeley)

Napoleon was able to retain her figure, the name of Republic, and
give the people a voice again, his voice. The revolutionary impulse
to symbolize politics and to work out politics via symbols also
served Bonaparte well; it was almost possible to overlook the emp-
tying out of political content. Protests against the revival of oligarchy and the end of mass participation were difficult to mount

21. NAPOLEON'S SEAL AS EMPEROR
(Photo courtesy of the Archives nationales)

when the symbols of revolution had been taken over by the new "moral and constitutional movement." [22]

The appeal of authoritarianism was not simply rhetorical and symbolic, however. Bonaparte succeeded not so much because he had a massive constituency (witness his rapid fall in 1814 and again in 1815), but because the constituencies of his potential opposition were so limited. The rhetoric and imagery of radical revolution did not have universal appeal, despite their nationalizing, rationalizing, and universalistic content. The experience of 1792–99 showed that democratic republicanism was far from solidly entrenched; the apprenticeship was just beginning. A movement that was most successful on the periphery, in poor, illiterate, and rural regions far from the capital, would have trouble maintaining its hold nationally. Once the militants of Paris and the leading Jacobin deputies had been arrested and executed or harried into silence, democratic re-

---

[22] *Opinion de Boulay (de la Meurthe), sur la situation de la République, et sur le projet présenté par la commission chargée d'examiner la cause de ses maux, et d'indiquer les moyens de les faire cesser* (séance de la nuit du 19 brumaire an VIII, à Saint Cloud).

publicanism everywhere went on the defensive. Most of the cities and the most modern regions of the country had already moved to the right by 1799; Bonaparte had only to generalize the development. A movement that had appealed to the outsiders, to minorities, to immigrants, and to intermediaries had difficulty overcoming the resistance of insiders, their clients, and all those who felt threatened by the coming of a new order. Bonaparte promised an amalgam of old and new and thus for a time reassured all but the most convinced partisans of democratic republicanism.

At the same time Bonaparte's success showed the weakness of royalism in France. Republicanism had won enough converts to make a return to the status quo ante impossible in 1799. Monarchy on the absolutist model was unacceptable. And it was only after many more years of war, final defeat, the revival of aristocracy under a new name, and the pressure of foreign intervention that monarchy of any sort was possible in France. Even then, its tenure was brief. The revolutionary political class—those thousands of merchants, lawyers, doctors, artisans, and shopkeepers, who had experienced the frustrations and opportunities of office and membership—were unwilling to turn the clock back. They had entered a new era, and there were too many of them to ignore.

Above all else, however, Bonaparte benefited from the dissolution of the political center in France. By 1799 Jacobinism had been restricted to the periphery, both within the nation and within the legislature.[23] Royalism, despite a brief resurgence in 1797, continuing agitation in the west, and periodic demonstrations in the cities, had also been contained. Every royalist-inspired invasion failed miserably. The major change after 1797 took place within the majority in the legislature. As a result of the principled resistance to party formation (even of a government party) and the consequent purges of the legislature, the Directorial councils were left with a lethal combination of new men with half-hearted republican convictions and parliamentary veterans who were obsessed with preventing a leftward drift of the Republic. By the Year VII (1799), only 12 percent of the deputies had been members of the Convention, and only 5 percent had been regicides. Only 16 percent had ever

[23]The information in this paragraph is taken from Hunt, Lansky, and Hanson, "The Failure of the Liberal Republic in France."

served in the legislature before 1795; over one-half of the deputies chosen in 1799 were elected for the first time in that year. With no experience of national politics, these men were particularly susceptible to the views of Sieyès and other "revisionists." There were few deputies prepared to risk their lives to defend the Republic.

The importance of the center can be clearly seen in the composition of the "Brumairian elite." In a study of 498 high officials of the Consulate government (holding office in the Year VIII right after Napoleon's coup), Werner Giesselmann found that 77 percent of them had been deputies under the Directory (83 percent had been deputies at one time or another since 1789).[24] A large number of them were elected for the first time in either 1798 (15 percent of the entire group) or 1799 (16 percent). Thus the trend toward newcomers reflected in the Directorial councils as a whole had a direct impact on the political situation: the newcomers did not simply fail to resist the change in regime; they actively participated in running the new one. There was considerable continuity with the Directorial regime, therefore, but continuity in particular with the right and center: as Giesselmann concludes, the coup "eliminated the left-leaning, Jacobin minority of the outgoing Directorial elite." Any further experiment with democracy was foreclosed in the interests of "bourgeois authority."[25] The core of the Napoleonic elite was made up of disenchanted republicans who preferred a stabilizing modernization to the upheavals and uncertainties of widespread political participation.

The same conclusion can be drawn from examination of the small group of deputies who sat on the commission that prepared the actual transition to the Consulate government (see Appendix A, under PROBON). In contrast to the 59 presumed Jacobins who were arrested at the time (Appendix A, under ANTBON), the Bonapartists came from urbanized departments ($r = .41$), with high literacy ($r = .30$), and great wealth (land tax $r = .31$; other tax $r = .52$). Interestingly, they also tended to come from departments where either or both the right and left had been strong previously; the presence of commission members in a department's delegation

---

[24] *Die brumairianische Elite: Kontinuität und Wandel der französischen Führungsschicht zwischen Ancien Régime und Julimonarchie* (Stuttgart, 1977), pp. 111–12.

[25] Ibid., p. 430.

was positively correlated with success of the right in 1797 ($r = .35$) and with success of the left in 1798 ($r = .24$).[26] In other words, the Bonapartists came from departments where elections had been previously annulled; they were the products of the Directorial *politique de bascule*. The Jacobin opposition showed none of these characteristics.

Giesselmann's analysis of the Napoleonic elite shows that the coup did mark a new departure. Although many of the leaders of the new regime had been revolutionaries and republicans of one stripe or another, their reconstitution as the elite of a new order had far-reaching consequences. They excluded the left from the political class, they dropped democracy out of republicanism, and, through a system of cooptation, they helped pave the way for the reintegration of the old nobility into an oligarchy of notables.[27] The rule of notables that "revisionist" historians saw in the making before 1789 was only accomplished under the auspices of authoritarianism. In this sense, the true heirs of the modernizing monarchy were Napoleon Bonaparte and his followers. They had links with the republicanism of the decade of revolution, but they only represented one type of devolution from the original ideal.

Capitalism, socialism, the rule of notables, a strong central state, democratic republicanism—these were all in some sense outcomes of the French Revolution, because they all followed it in some fashion. At the core of the revolutionary experience was the last of these, despite its unforeseen novelty and despite its failures and weaknesses. Democratic republicanism was not caused directly by a clash in modes of production, a crisis in social mobility, or the spread of Enlightenment ideals. These economic, social, and intellectual strains and conflicts had been present since the mid-eighteenth century. The origins of democratic and revolutionary republicanism must be sought in political culture, where all the

[26] However, the discriminant analysis showed that the elections of 1798 were not consistent with the results of 1795 and 1797; right and left departments did not separate in the same way, and therefore the results of 1798 were statistically excluded. See Lynn Hunt, "The Political Geography of Revolutionary France," *Journal of Interdisciplinary History* 14 (1984): 535–59.

[27] *Die brumairianische Elite*. Giesselmann provides detailed discussions of social background, ideology, and political careers. Unfortunately, he does little with departmental provenance.

strands of the polity came together. Democratic republicanism was made possible by contradictions in Old Regime political culture, but it only took definitive shape in the midst of revolution, when it was given voice and form by a new political class, which itself was molded by its responses to new ideas and new symbols. Democratic and revolutionary republicanism in France did not lead directly to capitalism, socialism, the rule of notables, or a strong central state. Monarchies and empires fostered capitalism, the rule of notables, and strong central states in the nineteenth century, and radical republicanism competed with socialism for votes and loyalties well into the twentieth. Democratic republicanism had its own, often quite separate, legacies and traditions.

The fact that democratic republicanism appeared first and most forcefully in the context of revolution in France had important consequences for French political development in the nineteenth and twentieth century. Republicanism was associated in the minds of its proponents and opponents alike with revolutionary action. As a consequence, the "transition" to republican government was always abrupt and difficult. It was not just another political option among many. It signalled profound upheaval and triggered memories of deep conflict and division. The Revolution, in this sense, made the achievement of republican and representative government more difficult. It also gave republicanism lasting affiliations with socialist and communist movements, even as those movements denounced its failures. Republicanism too had been revolutionary; republicans had learned the art of revolution first. The transition to republicanism was not finally successful in France until the cities and more modern agricultural regions were won over to the ideals that had first appealed to the less modern periphery. Yet to this day, the democractic left is often most successful in the same kinds of regions, if not the same places, as it was in the 1790s. French socialism under the Fifth Republic still has deep connections to the republicanism of the First.

Although the French Revolution had indisputable importance as the model for revolutionary politics, its origins, outcomes, and nature of experience were distinctly French. Ironically, much of its originality derived from the conviction of revolutionaries that they were breaking through the bounds of past European experience. Their rejection of religious referents and historical compacts was

very much a product of the particularities of French political culture, which distinguished French revolutionaries from radicals
in England and America. Yet those same particularities impelled
them to think in universal terms and thus to have, as Tocqueville
recognized, a messianic impact.[28] The Anglo-American belief in
common law, precedent, and perhaps even Puritanism made
Anglo-American radicalism less generalizable.

The Revolution intrigues us still today because it gave birth to so
many essential characteristics of modern politics. It was not just an
example of the violence and instability caused by modernization,
or an essential step on the road to capitalism, or a link in the birth
of totalitarianism, though it can be considered as contributing to all
of these. More centrally, it was the moment in which politics was
discovered as an enormously potent activity, as an agent for conscious change, as the mold for character, culture, and social relations. Different conclusions could be drawn from this discovery,
and many different ones were. Despite his horror at the "dark and
sinister" sides of that experience, Tocqueville nonetheless concluded: "Thus the French are at once the most brilliant and the
most dangerous of all European nations, and the best qualified to
become, in the eyes of other peoples, an object of admiration, of
hatred, of compassion, or alarm—never of indifference."[29]

[28] "It created an atmosphere of missionary fervor and, indeed, assumed all the
aspects of a religious revival" (*The Old Regime and the French Revolution*, p. 13).
[29] Ibid., pp. 210–11.

Appendix A:
Correlation Matrix of Selected Political, Economic, and Demographic Variables

Correlation Matrix of Selected Political,

	URB1806	TOTLIT	TERPER	EMIPER	ANTI93	DEATH	GIRONDE
URB1806	1.000	0.007	0.263	0.267	-0.218	0.188	0.151
TOTLIT	0.007	1.000	-0.179	-0.010	-0.112	-0.210	0.107
TERPER	0.263	-0.179	1.000	0.039	-0.048	0.091	0.067
EMIPER	0.267	-0.010	0.039	1.000	-0.136	0.154	-0.075
ANTI93	-0.218	-0.112	-0.048	-0.136	1.000	-0.257	0.213
DEATH	0.188	-0.210	0.091	0.154	-0.257	1.000	-0.351
GIRONDE	0.151	0.107	0.067	-0.075	0.213	-0.351	1.000
FRUCTI	0.641	0.023	0.263	-0.033	-0.088	0.143	0.229
FLOR	0.411	-0.096	0.158	-0.075	-0.035	0.218	0.055
ANTBON	0.172	-0.075	0.213	0.177	-0.058	0.128	0.121
PROBON	0.414	0.299	0.073	-0.164	-0.167	-0.142	0.127
PCFONC	0.279	0.301	-0.007	-0.097	-0.214	0.106	0.074
PCOTHR	0.653	0.131	0.257	-0.078	-0.156	0.158	0.123
AGPROD	-0.102	-0.052	0.050	-0.187	-0.093	0.049	0.218
OATH	0.009	0.064	-0.227	-0.263	-0.033	-0.044	-0.041
POP98	0.355	0.149	0.262	-0.061	-0.127	0.086	0.360
DENSITY	0.661	0.248	0.291	-0.020	-0.095	0.173	0.012
PROTPOP	0.105	0.014	-0.027	-0.131	0.218	-0.217	-0.022
MASONIC	0.463	0.053	0.153	0.183	-0.067	0.037	0.410
ACADEMY	0.326	0.218	0.042	-0.082	-0.175	-0.004	0.308
MARINERS	0.194	-0.176	0.288	0.096	0.096	-0.110	0.356
PCTACTIFS	0.113	-0.066	-0.132	0.076	0.071	0.201	-0.142
DISTPAR	-0.042	-0.395	-0.085	0.169	0.298	-0.091	-0.033
AGYIELD	0.585	0.367	0.160	0.075	-0.254	0.132	0.282

Sources: URB1806 = Percentage of department's population in towns over 2,000 inhabitants in 1806 as reported in response to a ministerial request of 1809 (the most reliable, complete data available for the revolutionary epoch). René Le Mée, "Population agglomérée, population éparse au début du dix-neuvième siècle," *Annales de démographie historique*, 1971, pp. 455–510. Le Mée's figures are quite highly correlated (r = .81) with those reported for 1798 in Marcel Reinhard, *Etude de la population pendant la Révolution et l'Empire* (Gap, 1961), pp. 48–49.

TOTLIT = Mean of literacy for men and women combined, from 1786–90. Michel Fleury and Pierre Valmary, "Le Progrès de l'instruction élémentaire de Louis XIV à Napoléon III, d'après l'enquête de Louis Maggiolo (1877–1879)," *Population* 12 (1957): 71–92.

TERPER = Rate of death sentences during the Terror per 100,000 inhabitants. Data for death sentences from Donald Greer, *The Incidence of the Terror during the French Revolution* (Cambridge, Mass., 1935), pp. 145–47. Data for departmental population, see POP98 below.

Economic, and Demographic Variables

FRUCTI	FLOR	ANTBON	PROBON	PCFONC	PCOTHR	AGPROD	OATH
0.641	0.411	0.172	0.414	0.279	0.653	−0.102	0.009
0.023	−0.096	−0.075	0.299	0.301	0.131	−0.052	0.064
0.263	0.158	0.213	0.073	−0.007	0.257	0.050	−0.227
−0.033	−0.075	0.177	−0.164	−0.097	−0.078	−0.187	−0.263
−0.088	−0.035	−0.058	−0.167	−0.214	−0.156	−0.093	−0.033
0.143	0.218	0.128	−0.142	0.106	0.158	0.049	−0.044
0.229	0.055	0.121	0.127	0.074	0.123	0.218	−0.041
1.000	0.459	0.028	0.350	0.320	0.645	−0.187	0.085
0.459	1.000	−0.131	0.243	0.167	0.433	−0.057	0.033
0.028	−0.131	1.000	−0.136	−0.157	−0.088	0.171	−0.234
0.350	0.243	−0.136	1.000	0.301	0.518	0.182	0.132
0.320	0.167	−0.157	0.301	1.000	0.741	0.273	0.338
0.645	0.433	−0.088	0.518	0.741	1.000	−0.007	0.213
−0.187	−0.057	0.171	0.182	0.273	−0.007	1.000	−0.092
0.085	0.033	−0.234	0.132	0.338	0.213	−0.092	1.000
0.331	0.328	0.237	0.369	0.127	0.320	0.381	−0.325
0.643	0.487	−0.044	0.483	0.304	0.812	−0.236	0.013
0.088	−0.036	−0.102	0.131	−0.036	−0.016	−0.067	−0.033
0.226	0.158	0.370	0.198	0.173	0.130	0.404	−0.165
0.193	0.070	0.149	0.290	0.187	0.217	0.265	−0.088
0.057	−0.140	0.302	0.116	−0.272	−0.045	0.214	−0.250
0.007	−0.018	0.038	−0.098	0.219	0.077	−0.147	0.372
−0.210	−0.101	0.206	−0.221	−0.569	−0.393	−0.155	−0.164
0.457	0.352	0.170	0.503	0.461	0.644	0.199	−0.120

EMIPER = Rate of emigration per 100,000 population. Numbers of émigrés from Donald Greer, *The Incidence of the Emigration during the French Revolution* (Gloucester, Mass., 1966), pp. 109–11. Departmental population from POP98 below.

ANTI93 = Sum of No and Conditional Yes votes divided by total votes in balloting for the Constitution of 1793. Vote totals from René Baticle, "Le Plébiscite sur la constitution de 1793," *La Révolution française* 58 (1910): 5–30, 117–55, 193–237, 385–410.

DEATH = Compound variable based on Alison Patrick, *The Men of the First French Republic* (Baltimore, 1972), pp. 317–39. Death votes equal the proportion of "radical" votes cast to the number of deputies eligible to vote in three decisive votes: against the *appel au peuple*, for the death sentence, and against a reprieve.

GIRONDE = Number of Girondin deputies from M. J. Sydenham, *The Girondins* (London, 1961), pp. 222–26.

(continued on next page)

FRUCTI = Proportion of departmental delegation sentenced to deportation in coup of 19 Fructidor, Year V. List taken from *Réimpression de l'Ancien Moniteur* 28: 1419 (24 Fructidor, Year V). Counted in the tally were 53 deputies to the Councils and the Director Carnot, an ex-deputy.

FLOR = Proportion of departmental delegation excluded as presumed Jacobins in the coup of 22 Floréal, Year VI. Counted in the tally were 84 men listed as Jacobins in Jean-René Suratteau, *Les Elections de l'an VI et le "coup d'état du 22 floréal" [11 mai 1798]* (Paris, 1971), pp. 370–82.

ANTBON = Proportion of departmental delegation excluded from the Council of Five Hundred as presumed Jacobins after the coup of 18 Brumaire, Year VIII. Fifty-nine deputies were listed as excluded in *Réimpression de l'Ancien Moniteur* 31: 200 (21 Brumaire, Year VIII).

PROBON = Proportion of departmental delegation chosen for the "Intermediate Commission," which prepared the constitution for the Consulate. The 50 deputies chosen were listed in ibid.

PCFONC = Per capita *contribution foncière* for 1791 from P. E. Herbin de Halle, ed., *Statistique générale et particulière de la France et de ses colonies* (Paris, 1803) 2: 390–97. Data divided by POP98 below. The *foncière* tax was levied on net revenue from property. The departmental totals were determined by the National Assembly on the basis of taxes assessed in the last years of the Old Regime; consequently, they have only an approximate value.

PCOTHR = Per capita *contribution personnelle et mobilière* for 1791–92 from Maurice Minoret, *La Contribution personnelle et mobilière pendant la Révolution* (Paris, 1900), pp. 709–10. Divided by POP98 below. This tax was assessed on the basis of external indicators of wealth: domestics, horses and mules, carriages, and rents paid for property. Departmental totals were assessed by the National Assembly in the same manner as PCFONC above.

AGPROD = A compound variable based on grain, wine, meat, and wool acreage for 1812, which measures the acreage of land devoted to agriculture from Thomas D. Beck, *French Legislators, 1800–1834: A Study in Quantitative History* (Berkeley, 1974), pp. 154–57.

OATH = Percentage of clergy swearing the oath in 1791. Figures provided by Timothy Tackett. His data are highly correlated (.82) with the results reported by Michel Vovelle in *Religion et Révolution: La Déchristianisation de l'an II* (Paris, 1976), p. 63.

POP98 = Departmental population in 1798 from Reinhard, *Etude*, pp. 48–49.

DENSITY = POP98 divided by surface area as reported in ibid.

PROTPOP = Number of Protestants divided by POP98 from Emile G. Léonard, *Le Protestant français* (Paris, 1955), p. 21. Provincial figures for ca. 1760 converted into departmental rates by dividing by number of departments in province.

MASONIC = Number of masonic lodges from Alain Le Bihan, *Loges et chapitres de la Grande Loge et du Grand Orient de France* (Paris, 1967).

ACADEMY = Dummy variable distinguishing between those departments that had a provincial academy and those that did not from Daniel Roche, "Milieux académiques provinciaux et société des lumières," in G. Bollème et al., *Livre et société dans la France du XVIIIe siècle* (Paris, 1965) 1: 95.

MARINERS = Maritime population divided by POP98 from Jacques Peuchet, *Statistique élémentaire de la France* (Paris, 1805), pp. 253–55 (data for 1803).

PCTACTIFS = Citizens eligible to vote in 1791 divided by POP98 from Reinhard, *Etude*, pp. 26–28.

DISTPAR = Distance in *lieus* of capital city from Paris from Peuchet, *Statistique.*

AGYIELD = Agricultural yield per hectacre in 1812 from Beck, *French Legislators*, pp. 154–57.

Note: Given in the correlation matrix are the correlation coefficients. The results for tests of significance are not reported, but all correlations over .2 were significant at the .05 level. With the exception of TOTLIT (where $N = 76$), all variables range in number of cases from 81–83.

Appendix B:
Occupational Analysis
of City Councillors
in Amiens, Bordeaux,
Nancy, and Toulouse

Many authors have argued that occupational designations were vague and variable during the revolutionary decade; magistrates called themselves "men of the law," merchants claimed artisanal status when that seemed advantageous, and peddlers could puff themselves up into merchants. (See Alfred Cobban, *The Social Interpretation of the French Revolution* [Cambridge, 1964], pp. 56–57, and Martyn Lyons, *Revolution in Toulouse: An Essay on Provincial Terrorism* [Berne, 1978], pp. 168–69.) Fortunately, however, most of the men elected to the city councils in these four big cities were too well known to escape correct classification, and their designations could be verified in several sources in order to come up with the most accurate classification.

Some of the lines of demarcation remain fuzzy, nevertheless. The most noteworthy case is the division between commerce and manufacturing, on the one hand, and artisans and shopkeepers, on the other. Included in the first category are wholesale merchants, bankers, manufacturers, shippers, and clothiers (*fabricants*). Only a few men identified themselves as *fabricants*, and, though the range of wealth within this group could be great, those few who were elected paid high taxes. There are cases in which the difference between manufacturers and artisans or between wholesale merchants and retail shopkeepers is difficult to establish; hence, the numbers in these two categories must be considered approximations.

The example of the *épiciers* (grocers) in Amiens shows the ambiguities involved in classification by profession. The tax records for two of them indicate that they were probably wholesale dry goods merchants, but a third grocer paid only a moderate tax, and the fourth was not listed on the rolls (see below for reference). Because tax data are incomplete and often unreliable, classification has been made solely on the basis of occupation. Most grocers were shop-keepers of only moderate wealth. In Toulouse, for example, the average marriage contract of a wholesale merchant was evaluated at nearly three times that of an *épicier* (Jean Sentou, *Fortunes et groupes sociaux à Toulouse sous la Révolution [1789–1799]: Essai d'histoire statistique* [Toulouse, 1969], pp. 153, 294). Despite the difficulties of classification, revolutionary social identification was precise enough to make such distinctions plausible.

In tables 4 to 8, only the mayors, *procureurs*, and *officiers municipaux* were counted. In the early years of the Revolution, each municipality also had a number of *notables*, but these were less important than the "officers," whose numbers were quite large. Information about elections was often incomplete and sometimes inconsistent from source to source. Where possible, consequently, results were compared in different sources. The best sources were: A. Janvier, *Livre d'or de la municipalité amiénoise* (Paris, 1893); Gaston Ducannès-Duval, *Ville de Bordeaux: Inventaire-Sommaire des Archives municipales: Période révolutionnaire (1789–an VIII)*, 4 vols. (Bordeaux, 1896–1929); Christian Pfister, *Les Assemblées électorales dans le département de la Meurthe, le district, les cantons et la ville de Nancy: Procès-verbaux originaux* (Paris, 1912); and J. Mandoul, "Les Municipalités de Toulouse pendant la Révolution," *Recueil de législation de Toulouse*, 2nd ser., 2 (1906): 348–409.

Information about occupation, age, address, wealth, and political careers was checked in a number of different sources, which varied from city to city depending on availability. The most essential sources were as follows.

Amiens

A.D., Somme, 2C 703–710, Tables alphabétiques des contrats de mariage, 1749–1792.

A.M., Amiens, 1G 2.11, Contribution foncière, Table alphabétique des noms, 1791.

Bordeaux

A.D., Gironde, 4L 117, Emprunt forcé, an II.

A.D., Gironde, 12L 19, Société des Amis de la Constitution.

Nancy

A.D., Meurthe, 3M 1, Consulat: Listes de notabilités communales, an IX–an XII.

Charles Bernardin, *Notes pour servir à l'histoire de la Franc-maçonnerie à Nancy jusqu'en 1805*, 2 vols. (Nancy, 1910).

Toulouse

Almanach historique du département de la Haute-Garonne, 1791–1793.

A.M., Toulouse, 1G 38–53, Contribution foncière, 1791.

Index

References to Illustrations are printed in boldface type.